D1491184

Governing Out of Order

Governing Out of Order

Space, Law and the
Politics of Belonging

Davina Cooper

Rivers Oram Press
London and New York

First published in 1998 by
Rivers Oram Press
144 Hemingford Road, London N1 1DE

Distributed in the USA by
New York University Press
Elmer Holmes Bobst Library
70 Washington Square South
New York NY10012-1091

Set in Perpetua by NJ Design Associates, Romsey, Hants
and printed in Great Britain by TJ International Ltd, Padstow, Cornwall

British Library Cataloguing in Publication Data
A catalogue record for this book is available from the British Library

ISBN 1 85489 102 2 (cloth)
ISBN 1 85489 103 0 (paperback)

Dedication

For Emma and Frania Cooper

Contents

Acknowledgments

This book could not have been written without the help of a great many people. I would like to begin by thanking all those who agreed to be interviewed, thereby sharing their experiences of the events explored in this book. Several of the essays concern conflicts involving a great deal of emotion. I am therefore particularly grateful that participants were willing to discuss what happened and to explore the feelings such recollections generated. Because several interviewees have asked to remain anonymous, I have not identified any in this book. I would, however, like to express my particular thanks to those participants who not only agreed to be interviewed, but also gave their time and assistance to provide me with useful materials and documents, set up other interviews, and took me to the places of my study. In this respect, I would particularly like to thank Edward Black, United Synagogue Eruv Committee; Christopher Kellerman of the Hampstead Garden Suburb Trust; Mal Treharne who took me out on a hunt; Denys White; and the officers and councillors of Somerset Council, including Tony Bull who, amongst other things, went well beyond his duty in forgoing a lunch break to drive me up into the Quantock Hills.

In carrying out my field studies, I am particularly indebted to the research assistance of Madeleine Wahlberg, Beth Widdowson and Wendy Ball. Steven Goodman also helped carry out useful library research in the final stages of completion. Thanks also to Nihid Iqbal, Samira Lycett and Maria Tompkins for their transcription of interview tapes.

Much of the research for this book was made possible by the generous funding of the Economic and Social Research Council. This book primarily draws on the field research carried out under the project, 'Community, Democracy and the Governance of Difference: Intra-State Conflict and the Regulation of Local Power', award no. R000221591.

However, the chapter on religious education is based on research carried out for an earlier project, 'The Power of Law in Municipal Politics', award no. R000232035 (organised with Ann Stewart). Undertaking the work for these projects was assisted considerably by the support of Warwick University Law School. Research leave in the autumn of 1996 enabled me to make substantial progress on the manuscript. My work has also been helped by the administrative support of Lesley Morris, and by the general help and kindness of Valerie Innes and Carol Hughes. I also want to thank Katherine Bright-Holmes and Liz Fidlon at Rivers Oram Press for their ongoing encouragement, suggestions and work in publishing this manuscript.

Governing Out of Order has benefited from the advice, suggestions and support of a number of people. They include Wendy Ball, Lee Bridges, Doris Buss, Charles Cooper, Kitty Cooper, Sue Elworthy, Debbie Epstein, Katherine O'Donovan, Hillel Furstenberg, Ken Foster, Marie Fox, Michael Freeman, Lisa Herman, Jane Holder, Bernard Jackson, Robert Jackson, Judith Masson, Mike McConville, John McEldowney, Alan Norrie, Peter Oliver, and Shauna Van Praagh. My work has also been enriched by the ideas raised in ongoing discussions with Joel Bakan, Robert Fine, Marlee Kline, Daniel Monk, Michael Thomson, and Deborah Steinberg. In addition, I would like to give particular thanks to Carl Stychin for his thoughtful reading of many of the chapters.

This book has also benefited enormously from the comments and questions generated by presentation of the studies as seminar and conference papers at University of British Columbia Law School (1994); Simon Fraser University's Department of Criminology (1994); Socio-Legal Studies Conference (1995, 1997); British Sociological Association Conference (1995); American Law and Society Association (1995, 1996); UCL Faculty of Laws (1995, 1997); Queen Mary and Westfield College Law School (1995); Critical Legal Studies Conference (1996); Keele University Law Department (1996); Birmingham University Department of Cultural Studies (1996); Osgoode Hall Law School (1996); Institute for Advanced Legal Studies (1997).

Finally, my deep-felt appreciation goes to Didi Herman, not only for her careful reading, extensive comments and search for clarity in my densest writing, but also for her capacity constantly to invent new forms of distraction and fun.

Journal Acknowledgments

Chapter 2 is a revised version of a paper, co-authored with Didi Herman, which appeared as 'Anarchic Armadas, Brussels Bureaucrats and the Valiant Maple Leaf: Sexuality, Governance and the Construction of British Nationhood through the Canada-Spain Fish War', *Legal Studies*, 1997. Chapter 5 is a revised version of 'Governing Troubles: Authority, Sexuality, and Space', *British Journal of Sociology of Education*, 1997. Chapter 6 extends the argument developed in an earlier paper, 'Talmudic Territory? Space, Law and Modernist Discourse', *Journal of Law and Society*, 1996. Chapter 7 is a revised and extended version of, '"For the Sake of the Deer": Land, Local Government and the Hunt', *Sociological Review*, 1997.

Preface

Material for this book comes primarily from two field research projects conducted between 1993–6. From 1993–4, a colleague and I examined law's impact on power relations within local governance. Our aim was to focus on the contradictions and unexpected effects within the local political arena of legal change. One issue of particular interest was the religious provisions of the Education Reform Act 1988 which attempted to re-establish Britain as a Christian country. Drawing on documentary research and approximately 20 interviews with teachers, governors, officers and councillors, I explored the impact of these reforms in the face of intense, localised opposition.[1] This project led on to further research, begun in 1995, on community and governance conflict. Targeted at the boundaries of legitimate governance, and focusing on the political management of cultural difference, this project provides the core field research for chapters five to seven. Again, my field research consisted of semi-structured, detailed interviews—approximately 45 were conducted—supplemented by official documents, correspondence, committee reports minutes, and media coverage. I was fortunate that participants in these conflicts were generous with their files, making it possible for me to acquire a detailed picture of events and interactions that otherwise might have become hazy.

Governing Out of Order draws on several methodological perspectives. The main influences are Foucauldian political analysis, discourse theory, socio-legal studies and cultural geography. In the main, my essays are attempts to interpret conflict—to provide a reading of events that sheds light, not only on the specific episode examined, but also on other similar or related incidents. I have therefore focused on interpretations with a wider resonance—which do not reduce the conflict to the individuals involved—without implying this is the only way the conflicts can be meaningfully understood. For example, an alternative reading of the disputes could take a political economy perspective, focusing on the changing character of state regulation in a context of wider, international, economic shifts. Yet, this reading, like any other, would, inevitably, be selective, centring certain themes and marginalising others.

The perspective I have chosen highlights cultural and spatial issues of power, authority, legitimacy and consent. Given this interpretive focus, many of the chapters draw on textual analysis of parliamentary debates and legal decisions. However, not all my discussion is textual. While I do use discourse analysis to explore more mobile 'texts' such as governing techniques, my methodology is not limited to deconstructing arguments, concepts and perspectives. Drawing on social and political theory, I have adopted an approach which highlights the fluid, constantly evolving character of political conflict, and which explores the implications of using particular discourses, and the bases for institutional actors' choices. Why, for instance, was public land ownership used as a means of fighting hunting? And why did a local education authority construct hypersexualised representations to attack one of its primary schools?

Part One

Introduction

1 Governing Through Space and Belonging

Excessive Governance

Claims of a crisis in Western governance have become ubiquitous: welfare provision can no longer be sustained; political authority and legitimacy are in decline; the state as we know it is in jeopardy. Yet, a narrative which argues that old forms of state practice have weakened, and which pits private market against public rule is too simple. While governing practices and structures may be changing, the nation-state remains implicated in global economic developments. In addition, questions of political authority, legitimacy and ideological transformation remain live issues.

Governing Out of Order is an exploration of political authority and its boundaries at the end of the twentieth century. Against a backdrop of changing governance forms and relations, the book examines what one might call *conventional* attempts to restrain, exceed, and restructure institutional power. At the same time, to say such attempts are conventional may be to mislead. The conflicts I discuss are, in many ways, unusual, embedded in the politics of the late 1980s and 1990s. However, at the level of institutional practice, they are not novel, forming part of a historical narrative involving state and civil authority. My focus is conflict rather than political crisis, but this does not mean an absence of the latter. Rather, instead of treating crisis as the defining quality of modern political relations, I examine the way discourses of disaster, emergency and panic have themselves been mobilised in struggles both to reproduce and to reorganise existing forms of political hegemony.

Governing Out of Order consists of a series of essays, each dealing with a situated, flash-point issue: hunting, the arts, religious orthodoxy, sexuality, international politics, public space and secondary education. While the common ground may appear obscure, together these issues offer a mosaic of modern, liberal governance. One example is deer hunting. In the early 1990s, after more than a century of protest, local councils followed the lead of private individuals and animal welfare organisations across Britain, and introduced hunt bans. The bans were partly motivated by environmental concerns, but also because of the growing public perception that hunting was cruel. Local governments' entry on to the terrain of animal rights generated, however, tremendous consternation amongst local hunters who saw the bans as explicit condemnation of their sport and identity. In 1993 they sought judicial review, targeting Somerset County Council in south-west England which had just banned deer hunting across land it owned in the Quantock Hills. The hunt argued that the council had overstepped its remit by making land use decisions on moral grounds. The court agreed, and declared the ban *ultra vires*—beyond local government's power.[1] Despite Somerset being owners of the land and of its sporting rights, the argument that hunting was cruel took the decision outside its statutory authority. Somerset County Council was forced to reinstate hunting. The lifting of the ban was followed by many other councils across Britain who had taken similar decisions.

This issue of governmental excess—institutions exceeding the boundaries of their role, remit and authority—forms a key theme of *Governing Out of Order*. It is also a standard topic of political discourse: is the state going too far? Should it be rolled back? Where does the boundary between public and private lie? Governmental excess has been traditionally associated with authoritarian regimes. Communist, fascist and military states are regularly identified in this way. However, high levels of regulation and control also exist in liberal and neo-liberal states. For instance, despite the Thatcherite rhetoric of a minimal state, critics such as Stuart Hall described British Conservative rule during the 1980s as a form of authoritarian populism, where, under the guise of popular support, state powers were extended.[2] In North America, the Right identified excessive governance during the early 1990s with the other end of the political spectrum in the form of 'political correctness' (PC). While PC was linked to extending state control over commercial affairs, such as corporate hiring and firing policies, the primary criticism was directed at policies perceived as reducing 'legitimate' professional discretion within public institutions, such as universities.[3]

To see governmental excess as characteristic of particular regimes, whether right or left, ignores its pervasiveness. While what is deemed excessive will be territorially specific, the techniques for constituting, challenging, and resisting transgressive activity are more general. My example of the hunt points to two different ways in which bodies may go beyond the boundaries of what is deemed acceptable: the hunt by hunting; the council by banning. It also implicitly raises the question: acceptable to whom? In exploring excessive governance, I do not wish to trivialise the reality of highly autocratic, disciplinary regimes with the facile suggestion that all regimes are authoritarian. However, the subject matter of this book is the way governmental excess permeates western democracies and liberal forms of rule. My focus is therefore on what might be defined as micro-excesses-'everyday' institutional actions within, as well as beyond, traditional left-right divisions, that generate opposition and conflict. While some of these concern the traditional political terrain of resource allocation, others concern issues whose very articulation to governance is controversial: sexuality, religion and animal welfare. These latter issues highlight the contradictory character of modern governance.[4] On the one hand, their lack of 'fit' defines them as inherently inappropriate subjects for government practice. On the other, their ability to represent wider alignments, to stand in symbolically for a host of other issues, makes them 'sexy'. As has been particularly apparent in the USA, issues at the margins of governmental concern, such as abortion, school prayer and homosexuality have been able to dominate political debate.[5]

The approach to excessive governance in *Governing Out of Order* differs from a conventional, common sense understanding in three main ways. First, my examination of excess goes beyond the traditional culprits of central and local government, the police, and military. I consider not only the practices of review bodies such as the courts— usually seen as *containing* excess—but also institutions within civil society, usually seen as victims.[6] When government goes too far, it is claimed, the latter's freedoms are placed in jeopardy. However, as I discuss below, civil bodies such as religious institutions and the hunt can also be seen as governance structures. There are parallels here with private governance.[7] The development of neo-liberal public policies has led to private companies increasingly being brought into the web of government activity, through contracting to provide public services, and through jointly funded projects.[8] There is a difference though, in that such forms of private governance tend to be articulated to the state's agenda. In other words, the private sector participates in, and to some degree facilitates, state governance. In contrast, in the conflicts explored in this book, civil governance has its own objectives. Not only are these not necessarily articulated to state agendas but they may be directly at odds with it. Consequently, civil bodies, such as the hunt, can be perceived by state institutions as excessive, and subject to containment strategies as a result.

The second aspect of my analysis rejects the idea of excessive governance as an objectively identified, political condition. While some bodies may be more prone at particular times to being designated excessive, the designation is relational. In other words, it concerns the relationship between two or more institutions at a particular juncture. The notion that an institution is behaving excessively is constituted within the context of political struggle or conflict. Thus, it becomes a means of invalidating or delegitimising the targeted policy or institution.[9] As I discuss in chapter three, conflicts are not simply over what practices become defined as excessive, but also about how the role, function or remit of the institution is reconstituted within the process. In the case of religious education, discourses of nationhood, spiritual health and parents' rights, deployed to legitimate British government's promotion of Christianity, became reaffirmed, more generally, as valid government objectives.

The construction of excess is a relational one; it does, nevertheless, take place within a political context in which dominant views about governing behaviour exist. While these are not rigidly fixed, they do determine which actions and policies are likely to be vulnerable to charges of transgression. A third aspect of my argument, therefore, concerns how conceptions of appropriate governance are structured according to a liberal political and economic logic. Despite the wider political changes mentioned earlier, this logic has a historical continuity constituted according to a range of foundational principles that include amongst others: the central importance of the nation-state and its cultural heritage; an institutional division of power; the legitimacy of governing according to managerial and commercial norms; public heterosexuality; and anthropocentrism. These principles help determine the boundaries of *legitimate* governance practices. At the same time, despite being politically dominant, they are not uncontested. Challenges come from institutions and wider social forces.

If institutions are declared excessive within a context of political conflict and prevailing liberal norms, we need to question the designation of institutional transgressions as a priori wrong. I am not dealing with societies run according to a fully informed consensus where any act of institutional excess or insubordination is a clear, unequivocal derogation of legitimacy. The validity of institutional practices and policies in the contexts discussed here are far more complex and contested. The third aspect of my argument, then, is an openness to the progressive possibilities of institutional excess. Clearly, not all institutional failures to conform come within this category. The validity of transgressing the boundaries of institutional role, rights and responsibilities depends on the motivating norms and values—in particular, I argue, whether institutional border-crossing occurs in pursuit of social and economic justice.

This normative position is set out more fully in the final chapter. The rest of the book, however, aims to explore the ways in which activities and policies, generated by a diverse range of governing institutions, are constructed, and contested, as excessive. In so doing, I address four issues. What conditions produce accusations of institutional excess? What techniques are used to reassert institutional boundaries and hierarchies? What strategies do institutions adopt in an attempt to protect controversial initiatives and decisions? Finally, in what ways are images of space and belonging mobilised within these conflicts? As I go on to discuss below, while not emerging directly from a Foucauldian problematic, these questions, nevertheless, draw on and reverberate Foucauldian issues of governmentality: the how of governing.[10] Thus they are 'as much about critique, problematisations, invention and imagination, about the changing shape of the thinkable, as...about the actually existing'.[11]

Mapping the Terrain[12]

Governance and the fractured state

The subject-matter of this book is bodies that govern. The plural identification of 'bodies' gives a clue to my approach. My interest is not in drawing a line between the state and civil society, but to explore the ways in which bodies on both sides of the line, and on the boundaries, govern. The notion that the boundary between state and civil society has become more permeable in recent years has become a defining norm of much political analysis, based on the idea that a crisis in the legitimacy and capacity of the welfare state has caused new forms of governance to emerge.[13] These include, as I mentioned above, state collaboration with the private sector in the provision and funding of public services. They also involve the creation of new governmental forms that cannot be unequivocally identified as state or non-state. Yet, this debate raises a prior conceptual question: what do we mean by the state?

Arguments have raged for generations about the nature and character of the state. Theorists have variously identified the state by its form, function, institutional framework, practices and by the power relations that it condenses.[14] While most approaches argue that the state encompasses more than one of these elements, they are articulated together in different ways, with usually one element or other perceived as paramount. In my first book, *Sexing the City*,[15] I focused on the state as a set of interlinked institutions that condensed dominant power relations in uneven ways. This allowed me to explore the extent to which radical forces can enter and take control of 'vulnerable' state institutions, such as local government, in order to contest dominant ideologies and other state practices.[16] *Power in Struggle* took the contradictory and contingent character of the state further, influenced by the work of feminist and poststructuralist theorists.[17] There, I considered the state as a contingently articulated set of identities, with no fixed form, essence or core.[18] Different identities, for example, as coercive, democratic, institutional, or relational, come to the fore—or are read as predominating—at different historical junctures; but these identities remain intricately connected to, and densely informed by others. For instance, the state that participates in international relations is expected to appear as a coherent actor, not as a matrix of institutions reflecting inconsistent or contradictory norms. However, this identity as a coherent political actor is articulated to other identities: deployer of (legitimate) force; representative of economic, racial or gender interests. (In considering who the state 'represents', the contested character of the state's identities, and of the relationship between identities, becomes immediately apparent.)

At the same time, my approach towards the state does not mean that the state is indeterminate. Rather, we need to recognise that it is first and foremost a concept for identifying a particular social phenomenon. While such a concept could have been initially attached to an arbitrary range of 'signifieds', today conceptions of the state are shaped by past understandings as well as by other aspects of modern political theory, practice and ideology. Thus, while conceptualisations of the state will differ, most will be recognisable as relating to a common phenomenon. An interpretation of the state that was completely unrecognisable, for example, the state as a field of mushrooms, would probably be of little value, unless at least the wider explanation had some point of connection (even if a critical one) with other paradigms. My conception of the state as a set of articulated identities shares with other approaches a conceptual emphasis on the interrelationship of force, political and regulatory power, dominant social relations, and institutional structure. These characteristics are what I would call definitional characteristics. They tell me I am looking at a state. However, *how* a state functions, in particular, how the western, liberal state actually functions at the end of twentieth century—its relationship to accountability, legitimacy, and authority, for instance—is more contested.

Four major implications emerge from my approach to the state. First, given the state's multiple identities and lack of essence, restricting analysis to conventionally identified institutions is limited since it omits those bodies whose location is more equivocal. In most contexts a hunt would not seem to be part of the state, and indeed I do not discuss it as such. However, in those instances where the state appears foremost as a purveyor of ideology, hunts might seem an integral state structure since they help to reproduce dominant social norms and relationships.[19] Second, the changing relationship of different bodies to the state becomes a site of interrogation and analysis: for instance, I explore the contested status of schools as institutions that British local government in the 1980s and 1990s tried both to domesticate and to distance; I also examine how bodies such as hunts and eruvin, conventionally seen as beyond the state,[20] attempted to mobilise the power of review held by state institutions such as the courts and public inquiries in order to defeat other governmental bodies.

Third, recognition of the state's diverse identities leads me to focus on one particular identity: institutional structure. Recent poststructuralist theory, drawing on Foucault, has criticised the analytical privileging of institutions.[21] Instead, Foucauldians have centred relations and techniques of governance, treating institutions as an effect of such processes and practices rather than their origin.[22] Though institutions are not the source of techniques of power, such techniques often have an institutional base, and are deployed by particular governing bodies. I have chosen to focus on institutions as agents of conflict because I want to explore the capacity of institutions to engage in and provoke imaginative, innovative political practice. I therefore treat them, from an 'external' perspective as relatively coherent entities, rather than focusing on their internal divisions and contradictions as in my earlier work.[23] Nevertheless, it is important to remember that institutions incorporate differences and tensions. Talk about institutions is also largely figurative, since they are as much about processes, practices, norms and relations as they are about physical space and structures.

Identifying institutions corporately in contrast to certain strands of organisational theory,[24] I use institution interchangeably with 'body' and, to a lesser extent, 'organisation'.[25] I also use institution to encompass structures whose differences seem far greater than their similarities—the hunt and European Union, for example. However, my focus is on bodies that govern beyond their own corporeal boundaries. Thus, despite the enormous differences between the European Union and a hunt, the emphasis is on what they share, in particular how they, and bodies at all levels, deal with issues of governmentality that include the reproduction of authority and legitimacy, strategy, resources, obstructions and techniques. At the same time, institutional common concerns are cut across by differences. Practices of state and civil bodies, for instance, are likely to reflect differences of political location. I explore this most directly in chapters six and seven, where I consider, respectively, the role of the state in relation to minority religious structures, and the way in which state and civil bodies are differentially positioned in relation to land-use decisions and animal culling. In doing so, I draw—more implicitly than explicitly—on some of the civil society/state debates.[26] My aim is not to arrive at a broad, overarching meta-narrative of the relationship between state and civil society, rather to demonstrate some of its complexities and contradictions, in particular, how differently positioned actors (such as community groups, local government, the courts) *understand* the state—civil society relationship and how they attempt to *mobilise* it.

But difference of perception is not only between civil society and the state; within the state, different institutions also express disparate and, at times, contradictory interests, values and identities. The assumption of tension and conflict between state bodies is at the core of my analysis. At the same time, this does not mean different state bodies are unconnected.[27] One of the aims of this book is to explore the ways in which links between institutions are mobilised in conflicts, for instance, senior state bodies attempting to redomesticate uppity subordinates. In this way, the power to review and discipline is used to counter the limited dispersal of political resources which enables institutions to resist or evade the pull of political hierarchy.

Governing techniques

How do institutions govern in and through situations involving conflict? Three forms of governing provide a matrix for my subsequent discussion: governing direct, mid-way and at a distance. These governing forms identify some of the ways in which institutional and other bodies interrelate. Because *Governing Out of Order* focuses on situations of conflict, I do not explore more consensual forms of governance.

Considerable work, for instance, exists on the role of lateral relations and networks between institutions (within and beyond the state).[28] However, while this work identifies important political developments in governance practices, my analysis offers an antidote to taking this perspective too far. In other words, the focus is on the ways in which institutional hierarchy and rule remain powerful forces as do hegemonic cultural and social norms.

The framework of governance I am using draws on the work of Nikolas Rose.[29] Influenced by Foucault's work on governmentality, Rose explores the way in which modern forms of liberal rule function through governing at a distance rather than through more direct techniques. 'Political forces seek to give effect to their strategies, not only through the utilisation of laws, bureaucracies, funding regimes and authoritative State agencies and agents, but through utilising and instrumentalising forms of authority other than those of "the State" in order to govern—spatially and constitutionally—"at a distance".'[30] Governance at a distance operates by guiding the actions of subjects through the production of expertise and normative inculcation so that they govern themselves.[31] In my work here, I explore how governing functions through the establishment of rules of conduct, as well as by triggering or motivating action in the targeted field.[32] Subjects, including state institutions and bodies within civil society, internalise these rules in the sense that they 'know' their powers, duties, functions, responsibilities, and what is appropriate or inappropriate behaviour (see chapter five).

A key quality of governing at a distance is that it appears impersonal and anonymous. The rules established are both general in character and do not appear to originate anywhere in particular. We might see this kind of rule as analogous to the relationship between the originators of a card- or board-game and the players. The latter's strategies, choices and identity are structured by the rules, but the rules are not seen as personally targeted nor are their origins perceived as relevant. The rules just 'are'. However, a key difference between the rules of a game and governing at a distance is that while the former are clearly apparent—players read the rules before commencing play,[33] the codes of conduct that constitute governing at a distance tend to be naturalised so their own existence is rarely apparent.

Direct governing, in contrast, identifies a direct relationship of rule in which the parties to the relationship are clearly visible. The demands of governance are equally visible since these are established as commands or prohibitions rather than necessarily being internalised by the governed subject. While governing at a distance works through the subject's agency or exercise of discretion, direct governance tends to restrict such discretion. However, this may not be through saying 'no'. Direct governing can also be productive, in the sense of demanding new policies or initiatives, as I discuss in relation to religious education law reform. I also use direct governance to refer to the provision of services and resources to individuals and institutions. In many ways, resource provision might seem more compatible with governing at a distance since it enables and works through discretion, rather than constraining it. However, I include it within direct governance because it highlights the *relational* character of direct governing. In other words, the provision of services and resources, such as welfare benefits or grants, draws the subject body's attention to an external institution that acts in relation to them. This is different from the concept of governing at a distance which emphasises the internalisation of norms, and the anonymous construction of rules.

The third form of governing is mid-way governing which lies between the other two. Here, the governing body attempts to structure the actions of its governed subject; however in comparison to governing at a distance, governing occurs in a way that is more personal and visible—the governed subject sees the rules being established as ploys or tactics rather than internalising them as conduct. Mid-way governing is also more reactive to the actions and agenda of the governed subject or institution. It tends to operate within situations of overt or latent conflict rather than, as in the case of governing at a distance, to prevent conflicts from occurring. In contrast to direct governing, mid-way governing often reflects a breakdown in a formal, hierarchical relationship (see chapter five). The governing body, unable effectively to deploy mandates, instructions, prohibitions and resources, is forced to use more indirect, strategic techniques to generate the outcomes it requires.[34]

Before leaving this discussion of governance, I want to raise briefly four further points. First, I do not assume a general shift from direct to more indirect governing forms. While this has occurred in some of the contexts I address, for instance, in relation to local government's fiduciary duty (chapter four), the opposite, if anything, is apparent in others, such as religious education law reform (chapter three). Second, governing bodies draw on a complex combination of forms, even in relation to one particular object (see chapter five). Direct, mid-way and distance governing are not as easy to disentangle in practice as their conceptualisation might suggest. Third, it is important to keep in mind the complex web of relations between different institutions within the governing process. Although my analysis focuses on specific bodies as utilising governing techniques, their actions are intertwined with the techniques and agendas of other bodies.[35] For instance, direct governing by a local authority may draw or depend upon the steering mechanisms established by central government. Finally, governing may not be effective. My discussion of different governing forms does not assume success (see chapter three). Different theorists have analysed some of the reasons for regulatory and implementation failure.[36] My aim is not to provide a sociological perspective on why governing breaks down, rather to explore the discourses through which governing is constituted as excessive or 'out of order', and to consider the techniques bodies deploy in an attempt to reinvent authority and achieve success.

Symbolic space

The second key theme running through this book is that of space.[37] Interest in space has grown considerably in recent years amongst academics outside geography's traditional disciplinary boundaries.[38] Some of this work has drawn on cultural geography to deconstruct the discourses through which particular spaces are constituted,[39] and to raise 'questions concerning the role of geography in the creation, maintenance, and transformation of meaning'.[40] Other research, more influenced by human and political geography, explores the interrelationship between space and economics,[41] and the place-specificity of regulatory and cultural norms,[42] looking, for instance, at how different locales produce (and are constituted by) specific forms of regulation or governance.[43] I draw on both of these trajectories, as well as a third, largely anthropological in background, which considers the symbolic meanings both space in general and particular spaces possess.[44]

I explore the concept of space at a number of levels. First, all the studies are located in particular places and, with one partial exception (chapter four), location is central to understanding the reasons for the confrontation, as well as the particular form events and their outcomes took. Second, I explore space's functioning as a discursive technique. For instance, opponents of the establishment of a London eruv—a symbolic structure allowing orthodox Jews to carry on the sabbath—portrayed orthodox Jews as territorial: intent on seizing public space for their own community ends (chapter six). Their depiction as 'out of place' parallels the treatment afforded to lesbian-feminists perceived as taking over an inner-city school (chapter five). In both cases, the construction of excess was articulated to a particular group's non-belonging, and the perceived threat posed to existing spatial relations. Expressed through a naturalised, historical narrative, what 'was' functioned as a powerful basis for what 'should be'.[45] Yet, as a political technique, space also functions through its absence.[46] In other words, portraying institutions as despatialised—dislocated from place—is a way of undermining the legitimacy that emanates from representing local needs and interests.

Finally, I explore how space operates as a political technique beyond the level of representation, for the symbolic effects of space are produced by material as well as discursive practices. The interrelationship between political authority and space in the form of land, as I discuss in chapter seven, means the seizure or withdrawal of the latter can threaten institutional legitimacy and control. This is well recognised at an international level, where the loss of territory can jeopardise a nation's standing and authority. However, the symbolic impact of a loss of territory or spatial control at the level of local government has received less attention.

Belonging

The third theme, belonging, has had a rocky history within political theory. Given weight in communitarian, nationalist and locality studies,[47] it has been attacked by poststructuralist and other critics who see belonging or membership as inextricably tied to practices of exclusion.[48] In the chapters that follow, I explore how the terms of belonging are mobilised by institutions in their struggles over acceptable political practice. Yet, as becomes quickly apparent, belonging is a conceptually ambiguous term. It can identify community membership and national identification, but it can also signify property ownership, political accountability, a relationship to place,[49] and a behaviour or identity that 'fits', or is at home. Contests over belonging therefore work at a number of levels. For instance, because belonging as ownership *enables* political action, conflicts occur over the identity, as well as the character, of ownership. In chapter four I explore how courts created and exploited ambivalence over the question of who taxes belonged to in order to restrict municipal action. By suggesting taxes remained, on some level, the property of those who paid them, local government's capacity to pursue its own expenditure policies became restricted by its fiduciary duty to taxpayers.

The different meanings accorded to belonging, identified above, are not discrete, considerable slippage and overlap of meaning takes place. For instance, in chapter five, I explore the situation of a school subjected to different paradigms of belonging: one based on community, the other based on property. The chapter concerns a controversy that arose over sexual orientation policies between a school and its local education authority. In its attempt to engineer the school's submission, the council articulated a proprietary relationship which depicted the school as a subordinate body subject to local authority policy and decisions. Their ownership was contested, however, by local school supporters. They argued the school belonged to those who 'made it work'. In focusing on the staff and parents who had made the school successful, supporters linked belonging, not to hierarchy and formal accountability, but to kinship metaphors of home and family.

Governing techniques can also be utilised to (re)produce relations of belonging. This invokes three issues: which members belong, what do they belong to, and the terms of belonging.[50] In chapter three, I explore the British government's legislative attempt to reassert Christianity as the basis for a nation-state community. While religion is *a priori* an illegitimate basis for belonging in disestablished nations such as the USA and Canada, in countries such as Britain, where an established church exists, this is not the case. Yet, even here, as chapter three reveals, centring Christianity in the regeneration of national community and identity was not unequivocally accepted. The increasingly multicultural ethos of Britain was seen by many as undermining both religion's capacity, as well as its right, to function as a primary mechanism of belonging.

Law structuring conflict

Conflicts over the right to govern, control and name local space raise fundamental issues regarding boundaries: spatial, but also jurisdictional. Exploring these boundaries requires us to examine the role played by law. For instance, in chapter two I analyse the construction of national identity in the Spain—Canada fish war of 1994. This conflict was largely precipitated by questions of jurisdiction—could Canada pass domestic law to regulate international, maritime space? The confrontation that emerged is a useful point to examine the relationship between boundaries of space, law, and identity.[51] For instance, how does legal compliance, brinkmanship and transgression impact on the construction of national identity? The relationship between legality and national identity is not straightforward. Spain was criticised by British parliamentarians for its legal formalism—exploiting legal technicalities when it suited them, at the expense of wider issues of justice. In contrast, Canada was praised for its converse approach—prioritising environmental and social concerns above formal international conventions.

A second theme is law's engagement in 'meta-governance'—the governance of governance. Meta-governance can operate through constraint, such as the judicial imposition of additional criteria to restrict and skew political discretion, for instance, the outlawing of hunt bans on grounds of animal cruelty. It can also work by redefining the identity of subordinate governance bodies, such as local government or schools. In other contexts, law structures power relations between governing bodies, and the way debates are held—organising certain issues in, whilst others are organised out. Conflicts do not need to generate litigation for the law to have this latter effect. In chapter six, I explore the confrontations that occurred over the establishment of a London eruv. In this conflict, the presiding legal framework—development control—shaped the way supporters and opponents argued over the issues, an impact not only apparent within formal planning arenas, but also in wider fora. Conducting interviews, several people told me that their *main* concern was not ethnic or cultural, but the visual blight caused by the installation of eighty more poles attached by wire in their neighbourhood.

Yet, as the eruv example demonstrates, law cannot always fully exclude the issues it perceives as insignificant.[52] While development control did marginalise symbolic and cultural concerns, generating a hierarchy of relevance, the planning process also provided an opportunity for these other issues to be raised. This largely occurred at informal gatherings, but a number of objectors raised cultural issues as well at the planning enquiry. In the main, these were ruled by the inspector to be irrelevant. This can be interpreted as a failed attempt by objectors to extend the boundaries of legal relevance; indeed several objectors described to me their sense of grievance at the narrow parameters of legitimate debate. At the same time, the planning permission process offered them an institutional focus for their grievances as well as a range of public spaces within which such concerns as demographic balance, territorialism, and the undermining of modern secularism could be expressed (see chapter six).

The story of the eruv provides one example of legal resistance, the opposition to legislation promoting Christianity in schools is another. However, in the main, the conflicts explored in this book do not target law as the problem. This may seem surprising given the politicised law reform agenda of the period under review. Nevertheless, my approach is to focus on conflicts where the law plays a structuring rather than a clearly antagonistic role, and to explore how all sides used law during their confrontations. This comes across, perhaps, clearest in my analysis of educational conflict in chapter five. As a result of the education reforms of the 1980s, legal power in Britain was perceived to have shifted from local education authorities (LEAS) to schools;[53] it was not surprising therefore that in a conflict between a school governing body and its LEA, the former would draw on their new legal authority.

However, what is more interesting is the way in which LEAs also drew on law. In chapter five, I explore how one authority used law as a nego-tiating framework; a means of estrangement; and as a way of keeping the school chained to their authority.

The public/private divide

The public/private divide surfaces within this book in ways that both reflect the term's usage within popular and political debate, as well as within feminist, geographic and socio-legal analysis. Subject to extensive debate and critique, work in recent years has focused on the gendered character of the divide, the norms attributed to each sphere, and the place of men and women within it.[54] My use of the term is not intended to confirm the existence of a divide, rather to reflect its importance as a discursive structuring device. In this respect, my main focus is on the relationship between the public/private divide and the governance of social space: how some activities are constituted as legitimate within the visible spaces of parks, schools and public streets, while others are required to remain within the private domain.[55]

In discussing the public/private divide, I want to separate five different aspects which are often fused together. These are: state regu-lation; visibility; articulation or nexus to affective criteria; geographic location of the activity; and institutional identification.[56] Disentangling these elements is important as they raise quite different issues. For instance 'publicisation' might refer to government regulation of domestic or marital relations, the spatial process of relocating an activ-ity, such as childcare, sex or drug-taking, into the public domain, extending public accountability over a decision-making process, or deciding to give a practice, community, or set of social relations visi-bility.

While issues of regulation, visibility and location focus on current binary practices, the concept of affective criteria draws attention to a more normative approach—the bases on which we would wish for some degree of autonomy for our choices. Weeks uses a similar, affec-tive conception of private life when he describes it as 'the things that matter most to us as social beings: home, family, friends, sex and love...the rhythms of leisure and relaxation, comfort, sadness and happiness'.[57] Jeffrey Weeks relates the private here not only to affective criteria, but also to particular spaces and activities. However, the important point is the way in which, conventionally, only certain domains and activities are seen as appropriate locations for the expression of affective criteria. Thus, governing bodies may be perceived as excessive when they apply seemingly affective criteria to areas where it is not deemed appropriate. For instance, in the case of Somerset's hunting ban, the court perceived the ban as motivated not only by opposition to hunting, but also by an antipathy towards hunters. While a private landowner could legitimately restrict access on this basis, local government as a public body could not. Bodies like local government are expected to reach decisions on grounds deemed 'rational' rather than arbitrary (affective equals arbitrary in this context). If a decision is perceived as, or can be constructed as, affective—based on likes and dislikes rather than more acceptable criteria—it may move outside of statutory discretion. More fundamentally, it can become defined as antithetical to public authority and power. I explore the ideologies underlying the identification of decisions as arbitrary or affective, and the implications that follow from the way rationality is defined.

The complex identification as public or private relates not only to activities and spaces but to institutions themselves. My approach to the state, outlined above, means many governing bodies cannot be unequivocally defined as public or private. This conceptual multi-location is also apparent within political discourse, and is strategically mobilised by different forces. Local government, for instance, is normally considered a public body as a result of its electoral accountability, administrative links to central government, political objectives/functions, and public service ethic.[58] However, while the courts have constituted local government as a public body where to be public is to have less freedom to act,[59] they have depicted it as a private body in other circumstances. And it is not just the courts that have adopted contradictory identifications. Local government has also represented itself in competing ways; drawing on private landlord power in certain contexts, while, in others asserting its state or governmental identity.

In the final section of this chapter I outline the rest of the book. Before doing so, I think it is worth summarising the main elements of my approach. As I stated at the beginning of this chapter, this book is about governmentality. It is also about conflict. Thus, my analysis looks two ways. First, it explores the issues over which conflicts emerged: sexuality, religion, animal rights, national identity; and the constituencies who mobilised: Eurosceptics, the Christian Right, teachers, taxpayers, lesbian-feminists, hunters, orthodox and liberal Jews. In interpreting these episodes, I focus on the discursive and contested role of symbols, territory and belonging within the disputes. Second, I engage with questions of governance: who governs, what is governed, how does governing take place? Within this broad approach, the book focuses on the problematic of institutional excess summarised by my title, *Governing Out of Order*. This has three parts. The first is the idea that governance has broken down or is generally failing to work properly. I explore this in relation to the perceived crisis of identity of the nation-state, both domestically and within the international arena. The second theme is a lack of *proper* order: councils trying to introduce socialism; schools attempting to challenge heterosexual dominance; religious bodies appropriating public space. These are instances of institutions who have 'forgotten' their place, either by appropriating other institutions' remit or by exceeding the boundaries of 'legitimate' governmental activity altogether. The final reading of my title treats 'out of order' as meaning 'from a position of order'—social, cultural, religious or economic. Normative order is intended to bestow authority and credibility on the governing body; however, as I explore, the values that might appear to one body to confer legitimacy may appear to opponents as a fundamentally inappropriate exercise of authority.

Governing Antagonisms

Let me now turn to the rest of the book. Chapters two and three examine different aspects of the 'emasculation' thesis, as applied to central government and the nation-state. Both chapters explore the construction of British national governance as ineffectual and in

crisis, and the remedial strategies posed: strong, normative government that places English essence at its centre. Chapter two explores
these issues in the context of the Canada—Spain fish war. Drawing
on British parliamentary debates, the chapter analyses how a conflict
over international jurisdiction, territorial control and fishing in the
North West Atlantic provided the terrain for a political struggle
between Eurosceptics and Euroadvocates over the role and nature of
the British nation-state *vis à vis* wider, international loyalties and
community affiliations. Contrasting narratives of Canadian and
Spanish statehood were mobilised by Eurosceptics in which Canada
functioned as the aspirational metaphor for a renewed, virile Britain,
while Spain represented the anarchic, self-interested, excesses of
European federation. Eurosceptics argued that Britain was acting like
a timid 'old woman', placing its loyalty to the European Union over
its loyalty to the Commonwealth. In response, the British government
articulated a countervailing paradigm of its own national identity. This
highlighted Britain's contribution, through a long history of states-
manship, to the maintenance of international law, order and collective
responsibility.

Chapter three continues this discussion of British identity within the
context of domestic relations. The chapter explores the role of
Christianity in hegemonising a particular image of Britain, and as an
attempt to re-create a traditional, conservative nation-state. The law
reforms of the 1980s and 1990s recentred Christianity within British
education. The chapter explores some of the ideologies underlying the
pressure for law reform, together with how the relationship between
the Christian subject and other faiths was conceived. I also ask how the
British government was able to represent its policy as acceptable.
While the existence of an Established church allowed government to
become entangled in religious promotion, government intervention
was also justified through appeals to national security, parents' rights
and spiritual welfare, raising wider questions as to the boundaries of
legitimate state action.

Chapters four and five move away from the initial focus on the institutional deficiencies of national government to relations between local
government and other bodies. Discussion centres on the problematic
of subordinate bodies deemed to have exceeded their mandate, and the

techniques adopted to bring them back under control. Chapter four examines judicial review of local government decisions on *ultra vires* grounds—outside local government's power and authority, in particular, the courts' use of one, specific, legal technique: fiduciary duty. The term fiduciary duty is more familiar within commercial contexts; however, it is increasingly being used to regulate public-sector practice, and state relations with indigenous people in Canada and the USA. In Britain, fiduciary duty has been a way of judicially managing local government by requiring councils to give special consideration to taxpayers' interests. The conception and application of fiduciary duty not only undermines progressive, redistributive policies but also helps restructure local government's identity along neo-liberal lines acting on behalf of a self-interested, atomised community of property interests.

Judicial attempts to subordinate local government have interesting parallels with the techniques used by a London borough council to subordinate one of its primary schools (discussed in chapter five). This chapter focuses on a high-profile struggle, generated by a head-teacher's refusal to purchase tickets to a ballet of *Romeo and Juliet* on the grounds (amongst others) that it was a tale of exclusive heterosexual love. Her action precipitated severe censure from the local education authority. It also led to her 'outing', intense media surveillance, and, more positively, the mobilisation of support from parents, gay staff and lesbian-feminist activists. My reading of the conflict focuses on the governing techniques deployed by the council as they attempted simultaneously to alienate and domesticate the school. In response, school supporters drew upon parents' rights, kinship metaphors, and techniques of fortification. Through these strategies and through the refusal to be intimidated, parents and lesbian and gay supporters posed an alternative, kinship paradigm of belonging to the council's proprietary model.

While the previous chapters raise spatial questions, chapters six and seven focus specifically on the symbolic role space plays within institutional conflicts. In doing so, they also put civil governance at the centre. My aim in these chapters is two-fold, first, to explore the struggles that can arise when spatial authority is threatened, and second, to examine the way governing from a position of normative order (by both civil and public bodies) can come under attack. Chapter six addresses the intense confrontation generated by British orthodox Jews' attempt to establish an eruv. Eruvin exist in a range of countries, including Australia, the USA, Canada and Israel. In trying to understand why the British eruv proved so controversial, I explore its meaning within what I call a 'cultural contract': an illusory framework through which the terms of national belonging and cultural expression are constituted. Perceived as an inappropriate (governance) structure, the eruv proposal was attacked on several grounds: for privatising public space; placing minority religious practices within public space; prioritising religious law (with its implicit assumption of legal pluralism); and for undermining the liberal concord that links the individual directly to the state.

Chapter seven moves from the intensely urban space of eruv territory to the soil of rural England where conflict occurred after a local authority banned deer hunting on its land. By exploring the ways in which notions of excessive and appropriate governance were constructed and disputed in relation to both the council and the hunt, my discussion focuses on the relationship between governance authority and land. Both the hunt and Somerset council gained status and legitimacy through their rights over land. Thus, the withdrawal of rights, first by the council from the hunt, and then by the court from the council, provided a means of undermining their respective authority. In exploring how rights were withdrawn, I also consider the way rural land was represented by the different institutional actors involved, and how the contingency of land-rights was articulated to good management. The final part of the chapter considers the implications this has for thinking about governance; in other words, by linking land-rights to a discourse of appropriate management practices the possibilities for governance contract.

The final chapter brings my discussion together at a more normative level. It aims to provide, somewhat tentatively, an intervention into a wider discussion about the politics of governance. My objective is to underscore three points: first, to argue that governing bodies should make visible their ideological motivations rather than offering misleadingly 'neutral' rationalisations. Second, I criticise the reliance on legal principles of *ultra vires* or insubordination as the basis for rejecting or penalising institutional activity and policies. Third, I argue for institutions to be seen as positive surrogates for the playing out of ideological differences, partly through debate, but also through their capacity to operationalise new practices at or beyond the boundaries of their conventional remit. Thus, this final chapter affirms institutional excess or governing 'out of order', not in the sense of institutional breakdown, but rather as support for governing that emanates from explicit normative frameworks (order), and that contests or transgresses divisions of authority in pursuit of its own conception of responsibility.

Part Two

Governing Identities
(Mythological) Crises and Cures
for the Nation-State

2 Our 'Kith and Kin'

Identity and Belonging in International Fish War Politics

In March 1995, amid ongoing Balkan conflict, international hostilities exploded from a seemingly unlikely quarter. Canada, angered by over-intensive European harvesting of Greenland halibut (turbot) in the North-West Atlantic, struck back, sending warships to a region of the high seas just outside of its 200-mile fishing zone. A vessel belonging to the main offender, Spain, was arrested by Canada who threatened further action if Spain did not withdraw from the area. Spain refused, arguing its fishing practices, unlike Canada's intervention, were internationally lawful. Conflict escalated, and political interest intensified on both sides of the Atlantic. The British government, facing increasing domestic support for Canada, attempted to steer a middle path and to use its 'unique position' as a member of both European Union (EU) and Commonwealth to negotiate a compromise. Its strategy won it few friends. The EU saw Britain as once again adopting an isolationist stance, withholding consent to an agreed European position. Canadian supporters, on the other hand, disparaged the government for its disloyalty to Commonwealth kith and kin.

The Canada-Spain fish war can be interpreted in several ways: as a conflict over international jurisdiction, or, from a political economy perspective, as the hardly surprising consequence of growing national tensions over scarce maritime resources.[1] In this chapter I adopt a different approach to focus on the conflict that ensued, not between nations, but amongst members of the British Parliament. How did a dispute over maritime authority and resources provide the symbolic terrain for a debate about national identity, governance norms, and community belonging? What kind of nation was flagged in the process?[2]

Questions of national identity and community belonging played themselves out in three ways within the dispute. First, parliamentarians constructed rhetorical and strategic models of Spain and Canada's national identity. Second, the community of Common *Wealth* was juxtaposed against that of Common *Market*. Third, the question of Britain's own identity was raised and problematised. These three elements were articulated together to form two primary alignments. On the one hand, Eurosceptics constructed a highly derogatory image of Spain and the EU alongside a complimentary portrayal of Canada and the Commonwealth. Their argument was that Britain had lost a sense of internal purpose and international identity; overwhelmed by EU politics, Britain had lost sight of its 'true' allies and community. On the other, Eurosupporters offered a more neutral vision of Spain, and a more ambivalent picture of Canada. Instead of constructing a hierarchy of belonging between EU and Commonwealth, Eurosupporters argued that Britain played a distinct role through its membership of both international communities.

The starting point for this chapter is a conflict over excessive governance. Yet, as the rest of the book explores, the very concept of who or what is excessive becomes highly contested. In this chapter several possible culprits emerge: over-fishing by Spain; 'unlawful' interventions by Canada; and the apparent 'nation-state' aspirations of the EU. These images of excessive governance were mobilised by parliamentarians and linked to a normative struggle over British nationhood. In addition, discourses of 'belonging' constituted governance bodies and their practices as acceptable or unacceptable. This worked in two primary ways. First, identifying a relationship of belonging strengthened the validity of governance practices. For instance, the legitimacy of Canada's actions were contingent on successfully demonstrating their rights to and responsibility for nearby fish stocks. Second, paradigms of belonging were accorded a differential value. They can be seen as functioning on a continuum; at the preferred end, a membership conception of belonging, at the other a proprietary model. Within this dispute, the Commonwealth was generally depicted as close to the membership pole, while the EU was portrayed, particularly by Eurosceptics, as closer towards the proprietary end of the spectrum.

To explore these issues further, I begin with representations of

Spain and Canada within parliamentary debate. My emphasis is two-fold: the construction of Spanish governance as excessive and illegitimate on the one hand, and the idealised portrayal of Canada as a role-model for British governance on the other. The second section explores representations of the EU and Commonwealth. While the EU slides, within debate, between two paradigms of practice, both of which are seen as threatening the nation-state, the Commonwealth poses a model of community which centres it (at least for Britain). The final section focuses more explicitly on British governance, by looking at its portrayal by different Parliamentary factions. In particular, I contrast Eurosceptics' representation of Britain as frail patriarch of a bygone age with the portrayal offered by government spokespeople of a matured statesman playing a distinguished role within the international community. Yet, despite the differing image, both depictions reveal a common, normative emphasis on the importance of a strong, masculinised, national identity.

The Fish War[3]

The background to the Canada-Spain fish war lies in two paths that converged in the Spring of 1995. The first concerns Spanish access to European fisheries following entry into the then European Community (EC) on 1 January 1986.[4] Fishing by EC members was regulated by the Common Fisheries Policy (CFP), a series of agreements setting out, amongst other things, who could fish where and when, and for what catch in EC waters.[5] At the time of Spanish accession, members expressed concerns about allowing Spain equal access since its fishing fleet amounted to 70 per cent of other EC members combined; in addition, Spain had a widespread reputation for immoderate fishing practices. As a result, an interim entry agreement limited Spanish access to European waters.[6] One effect of this was to shift the problem of over-intensive fishing on to other, Spanish fishing grounds such as the North-West Atlantic. Yet saturation fishing here collided with a second development: growing international concern to protect depleted fish-stocks from exhaustion.

Overfishing led many nations to seek ways of restricting foreign vessels from harvesting their surrounding waters. In the 1970s, several countries extended their exclusive coastal fishing zones to two hundred miles. Iceland's extension generated considerable opposition from Britain—leading to their own fish wars, although by 1977, Britain had shifted its approach from protecting domestic fishing interests in foreign waters to supporting the interests of the coastal state.[7] Indeed, Britain developed its own, unilateral, conservation measures to protect juvenile stocks off north-east Scotland.[8] Canada, one of the first countries to declare an extended fishing jurisdiction, found by the late 1980s, that this move was insufficient to protect stocks, particularly of those fish that straddled the 200-mile boundary. Having introduced restraints on domestic fishing off the coast of Newfoundland, Canada saw its measures undermined by foreign fishing just beyond its own 200-mile zone. In May 1994, the Canadian Parliament passed legislation allowing the government to take action in the high seas of the North-West Atlantic if a foreign fishing vessel contravened Canadian conservation and management measures in relation to 'straddling stocks'.[9] In early March 1995, Canada imposed a sixty-day fishing moratorium beyond the 200-mile zone and declared it would turn back EU ships from the area known as the Grand Banks.

On 9 March 1995, conflict erupted. Canadian gunships surrounded a Spanish vessel, the Estai, which had defied the moratorium; armed crews boarded and arrested the captain. Jean Chrétien, the Canadian Prime Minister, and Brian Tobin, the Canadian Fisheries Minister, declared the action legally and morally justifiable.[10] However, Canadian action was immediately condemned by the EU. In late March, the situation escalated further when Canadian fisheries officers attempted to board a further Spanish vessel in international waters.[11] Furious with Canadian behaviour, Spain sent its own naval boats into the area, and pushed for EU sanctions, a proposal that Britain opposed.[12] Britain also objected to a warning being sent to Canada from the EU, arguing that the Commission should hold off while talks continued in an attempt to reach agreement about turbot quotas in the North-West Atlantic.[13] Earlier failure to reach agreement, and the EU's adoption of an autonomous quota had contributed to the souring of relations between the two sides. On 5 April, the Canadians cut further Spanish nets. Once more, a strongly worded condemnation was sent to Canada, with the British government, caught between its loyalties to the Commonwealth and to the EU, blocking the communiqué as coming from the European Commission as a whole.[14]

At a meeting of EU foreign ministers on 10 April, participants concluded there was little possibility of an early deal unless Spain moderated its position.[15] Jacques Santer, President of the Commission, also declared that although it was necessary to safeguard solidarity within the EU, it was also important to protect the interests of allies and friends in Canada.[16] Finally, on 16 April 1995, an agreement was reached.[17] This offered a compromise on the question of quotas for turbot, while also agreeing to the stricter enforcement and surveillance measures Canada wanted in order to protect stocks. Yet, despite formal acceptance of the settlement, Spain remained angry.[18] Dissatisfaction was targeted not only at Canada, but also at Britain and Ireland for supporting Canada throughout the dispute.

Images of Nationhood

Spanish excess

During the conflict one of the most striking qualities of the parliamentary debate was the degree of hostility expressed towards Spain. True, their Armada had sailed towards Britain 400 years earlier, but could this still be the cause of such animosity? From the fish war debates this might appear to be the case. Parliamentary speeches were replete with images of armadas and plundering Spaniards, recalling not only the threatened invasion but also a narrative of wealth and lives seized on the high seas. As one peer declared,

> We must also have great sympathy with the Canadians...whose livelihoods are put at peril by the *piratical pillaging* of their fish stocks by the *marauding* Spanish fishing fleet.[19]

Speakers drew on stock, historic representations of Spain; their motives, however, were somewhat more current. Partly they reflected ongoing antagonisms between Britain and Spain over the latter's access to the waters surrounding the British Isles.[20] The denigration of Spain also performed two further functions. First, Spanish dishonour was rhetorically deployed to highlight the contrasting bravery and courage shown by Canada. Second, Spain was demonised to reveal the dangers of a powerful European Union. A discourse of excess constituted Spain as transgressing the boundaries of appropriate nation-state action, in some instances deliberately, in some instances unconsciously, and in some instances without the capacity to stop.

Deliberate transgression can be seen in the notion of inappropriate taking. Spain was portrayed as both voracious and parasitic on the husbandry and hard work of others; Spain r(e)aped what more diligent nations sowed. Parliamentary speakers highlighted Spain's practice of fishing beyond its territorial seas, in a manner that respected neither the needs of the coastal nation's fishing industry nor the international imperative to conserve stocks. 'Spain's policy is geared towards taking everything that it can get, even when that means piratically depredating fish stocks around our shores and everywhere it can in the world—while giving nothing in return'.[21]

The illegitimate and excessive character of Spanish taking was accentuated by articulating it to violence, especially in relation to the fish. Halibut were seen as the immediate subjects of Spanish aggression, particularly the young fish which critics accused Spain of 'plundering'.[22] One peer rhetorically asked whether fish knew they would be safer in Canadian waters than in the high seas where they were subject to Spanish aggression.[23] While other nations 'take', the essential unacceptability of Spanish appropriation is apparent through the deployment of a *homo*sexualised imaginary that is not only sexual but more specifically homosexual.[24] Spain, like the gay men in anti-gay discourse,[25] is fundamentally predatory; it seeks out the most vulnerable, under-age catch it can find.[26] Spanish vessels scoop up tiny turbot as they lie, hoping for safety, on the sea-bed.[27] Within dominant discourse, homosexuality signifies an essential non-belonging: two subjects whose linkage can only be deviant. While fish may be naturalised as resources for harvesting by a masculinised nation-state, here they function as anthropomorphised subjects whose objectification as 'catch' by Spain testifies to the inappropriateness of its desires.

Spanish excess was also articulated to a discourse of disgrace, a demonstrable lack of the civilising influence evidenced by honourable political manners.[28] This was apparent in Spain's refusal to conform to accepted governmental norms. Paradoxically, one demonstration of this was Spain's 'hailing' of formal, international law. Spain's charge that Canada was acting unlawfully in attempting to apply domestic law beyond its national boundaries was decried by Eurosceptics. They criticised Spain for, first, placing procedural norms above substantive justice, and second, for being hypocritical, since Spain broke the law when it suited them. Spain might attempt to enforce certain legal provisions, but this was an entirely cynical action. Spain played with rules, but not according to the rules.[29] Fundamentally, Spanish international practice did not reflect the internalisation of legal norms. In other words, practice was determined by self-interest rather than prevailing normative codes. Despite—indeed because of—the pragmatic call to the law to aid them, Spain was characterised, as essentially, and corporeally unlawful. One peer declared: '[t]he hands of the Dons are some of the dirtiest around'.[30] Unwilling, if not unable, to comply with international good practice,[31] parliamentary criticism questioned Spain's capacity to act as a nation-state on the world stage. Not playing 'according to the rules'[32] endangered more than fish stocks. It also undermined the possibility of a healthy international community. If nations were articulated as one (as in the EU), and that one was Spain, the international community too was in danger of contamination and being brought into disrepute.[33]

Spain's lack of poise within the international arena, however, was portrayed as reflecting more than external self-interest and poor, international manners. It also spoke of an internal disorder and incoherence. Speakers identified such disarray in Spain's inability to contain the demands of nation-aspiring regions. British parliament's dismissal of localised concerns in the context of Spanish Galicia (home of the Spanish North Atlantic trawlers), can be contrasted with the legitimacy granted to other regional interests—the Newfoundlanders in Canada and Cornish fishers in Britain. In contrast to Galician demands which spoke to the internal chaos of Spain, its lack of effective, domestic governance, in Britain and Canada, it was the *willingness* to respect local interests that functioned as a sign of proper rule.

Parliamentary debate drew on a metaphorical language of race and gender, as well as sexuality, to denigrate Spain.[34] A similar language was also used in relation to Canada. However, here, such metaphors assisted in its glorification. In the case of Spain, excess was linked to out of control southern temperament and desires, far from the rational moderation of nations 'coloured white'.[35] Spain's lack of political manners, its inability to govern its territory effectively and its grasping of others' resources, identified a nation racially and sexually 'other'. This portrayal functioned most explicitly in the metonymic portrayal of Emma Bonino, the European Fisheries Commissioner. Despite being Italian, Bonino's sympathies caused her to 'stand in' for Spain within anti-Spanish discourse. Labour MP, Peter Shore, described her language as 'hostile' and 'bellicose';[36] Bill Rogers, Liberal Democrat MP, declared it 'thuggish';[37] while Lord Carter stated, in the House or Lords, 'the process is not helped by the intemperate comments of the European Commissioner whose Latin temperament seems to be more suited to the corrida than the corridors of power'.[38] This characterisation as 'intemperate' was used by several speakers, highlighting the way in which racial and gender stereotypes are condensed together.[39] It is women who are hotheaded, lacking the rationality and detachment needed for public affairs, and, in particular, statecraft.[40] While 'intemperate' tends not to be applied to women from northern Europe, they may be coloured 'southern' in certain conditions, for instance, where they are engaged in (political) expressions perceived as unbecomingly passionate.

A Canadian role model

Spanish excess contrasted sharply with the portrayal of Canadian good sense. Representations of Canada clustered around three key images: loyalty, bravery and resource management. Each counterpoints representations of Spain as, respectively, dishonourable, thuggish and immature. Despite the fact Canada rather than Spain had formally breached international law—sending warships to threaten and arrest boats on the high seas—Canada was not generally portrayed as engaged in illegitimate or excessive governance. Contained within many parliamentary contributions was the belief that the waters and fish belonged (at least morally) to Canada, despite Spain's historic fishing claims and the considerable distance of the high sea from Canadian soil. Why was Canada the recipient of such adulation?

On the one hand, support for Canada was linked to Euroscepticism. Canada, in this sense, functioned as a rhetorical device for denying European claims; it provided an alternative object of loyalty and allegiance to detach Britain from its EU alliances. On the other, Canada functioned, like the Falkland Islands during the early 1980s,[41] as a role model for Britain itself. In this way, Canadian brinkmanship in defence of its fish stocks provided a standard to which Britain should (and could) aspire. Canada offered a role model that, while aspirational, was rooted in an idealised vision of Britain's own past: a time of pride, courage and action. The urgent need to rediscover a historic, national valiance can be seen in the declaration of Lord Morris, that Canada's action had made Canadians the heroes of Cornish fishers such that the latter now fly the Maple Leaf rather than the Union Jack.[42] In its praise of Canada's courage, Morris's comment inverts conventional nationalist discourse in which the hopes of others rest upon 'us'.[43] The intense, nationalist significance of flags transforms it instead into a tale of British dishonour and shame: why does the Cornish fishing community not fly 'our' flag? Can we imagine the disappointment that would generate such drastic action?

The first image of Canada—loyalty to Britain—functioned as a primary 'nation-placing' device. Canada understood what ties of history, culture and family really meant.[44] A country that had 'never failed to come to our rescue',[45] Canadian loyalty was juxtaposed against British ambivalence and Spanish treachery. One speaker, contrasting Canada's support in the fight against oppression with Spain's endorsement of fascism, declared,

> People were aghast that, in the year of the 50th anniversary of the end of the last war, the British Government should side with Spain against a Commonwealth country, remembering that many Canadians died in defence of freedom throughout the world while the Spanish were in fact giving moral, if not tangible, support to Hitler and the Nazis.[46]

'It seems very odd', noted another, 'that people who stood by us from

Paardeberg to Vimy and from Dieppe to Normandy should be treated in that shabby way'.[47] The praise lavished on Canada contrasted with Parliament's inventory of Spanish betrayal: lack of support for Britain's conflict with Iceland over cod;[48] hesitancy during the 1992 Gulf War;[49] and support for Hitler during World War Two.

Alongside its loyalty, and historic courage fighting fascism, Canada, in the 1990s, was portrayed as fearless and valiant in its willingness to confront any opponent undermining its conservation strategy.[50] One interesting aspect of parliamentary discourse in this context is the relative erasure of Canada's use of domestic law to justify its intervention. Peter Fitzpatrick and others have argued that law functions as an assertion and condensation of national identity.[51] In this instance, Canada might be seen as projecting an augmented national identity in its deployment of domestic legislation to regulate fishing in international waters. Yet, British parliamentarians for the most part ignored Canada's exercise of law. Instead, members, such as the left-wing Dennis Skinner, praised Canada for its show of 'guts',[52] while others applauded Canadian brinkmanship. Eurosceptics endorsed Canada's demonstration of physical action and strength; law, in contrast, was portrayed as weak and petty. In this sense, legality was both differentiated from, and juxtaposed against, justice. While the latter was identified as crucial, it was linked to policy objectives, such as conservation, rather than to legal form (see also chapter eight).

Eurosceptics equated legal rules and procedures with pejorative, feminised attributes: pettiness, feebleness, and lack of proportionality. In contrast, both justice and Canada were masculinised.[53] Canada's maleness, within the fish war debate, was constituted as young and virile, while also firm and controlled—disciplined by its desire to achieve coherent, rational objectives. The sublimation of Canada's sensuality into a leadership of society and nation[54] is evident in the third, and probably most pervasive, image of Canada: its fish stock management. While some government spokespeople infantalised Canada as reckless rather than brave, for the majority, Canada's action demonstrated an enviable commitment to good husbandry.[55] Despite the suggestion that Canada too was responsible for fish stock decimation in the North-West Atlantic,[56] and despite the international character of conferences, conventions, codes and agreements concerning conservation measures for straddling stocks,[57] the general portrayal of Canada was of an almost exceptional nation desperately trying to conserve marine resources. In the international press, Canadian Prime Minister, Jean Chrétien and Fisheries Minister, Brian Tobin, exemplified a single agenda: environmental protection. In Britain, this representation was almost entirely persuasive.[58] As Roger Knapman MP put it, upon conclusion of the final settlement, 'game, set and match, as they say, to the Canadians, the conservationists, and common sense'.[59]

In contrast to Spain's short-term, self-interested, 'out of control' harvesting, supporters depicted Canada as an advanced nation-state engaged in complex, forward planning. This was articulated to both a modern and postfordist national portrayal.[60] While the governance of stock draws on modernist discourses of science[61] and management (see chapter seven), Canadian demands for strengthened protection configured into a postfordist agenda of differentiated, flexible control.[62] Canada did not dismiss the value of borders; rather, the crude binarism of boundaries, however constructed and located, were inadequate to conserve a transgressive fish stock, unable to heed national frontiers. Borders required supplementing with more sensitised forms of internal and external control: surveillance, monitoring and 'satellite tracking'. Parliament's discussion of extra-border control focused on the harvesting of fish; however, within the speeches, we can see echoed and condensed other migratory concerns. Thus, the regulation of fishing offers a discursive terrain through which more flexible mechanisms for controlling the movement of peoples can be considered.[63]

International Belonging

Community as kinship

While Eurosceptics portrayed the EU as conditional on ties that were self-interested and cynical, the Commonwealth posed an alternative model of community. In a quintessential example of 'collective forgetting',[64] the Commonwealth was depicted as solidaristic: a community of nations bound together by loyalty and the common good. The Commonwealth formed a network of kinship in which the traditional linkage between families and nation was inverted.[65] The supranational status of the Anglo-Commonwealth 'family' was identified by several parliamentary members. According to one MP, 'many of us were very unhappy about our entry into the European Community because we felt that we were betraying the Commonwealth, our history and, in many cases, family and friends'.[66] Repeatedly, Canadians were described as 'friends' or 'cousins'.[67] Secretary of State, William Waldegrave, Minister for Agriculture, Fisheries and Food, even declared, 'Newfoundland was discovered from my constituency'.[68] Others emphasised Canada's 'long and important links' with Britain,[69] and its place as 'part of the British ethos, culture and traditions'.[70] As Roger Knapman MP, stated: 'If we are given the choice between supporting our kith and kin in Canada or our so-called fellow Euro-citizens, should not we choose the former every time?'[71]

Knapman was not alone in prioritising friendship and familial relations as the basis for according Canada support.[72] While many Eurosceptics stressed Canada's pursuit of justice, others privileged the claims of loyalty, implying that to deny the obligations arising out of allegiance and fidelity would be to demean and debase Britain's place and standing in the international community, with its 'old boys club' norms. The Commonwealth was also *more than* a space of reciprocal loyalty; it represented, within parliamentary debate, a community in which Britain could feel itself to be the cultural and historical originary moment. The Commonwealth re-claimed Britain as more than a small European nation. While the EU diminished Britain's significance, the Commonwealth produced an expansive reading in which British lands and culture enveloped and 'ruled the waves'.

Yet, the anatomy and role played by the Commonwealth needs complicating in two ways. First, despite competition between European states in their colonial pursuit for economic and political power, colonialism, according to Delanty, involved exporting a European rather than specifically British or Anglo-culture.[73] In other words, the extent to which the Commonwealth represents the promotion of an exclusively English identity should not be overstated. At the same time, although Britain may have operated, and even perceived itself, during its colonial period as, to some degree, a *European* nation, post-World War Two, the Commonwealth played a different role within, the British imaginary. Identification with, and participation within, the Commonwealth offered Britain an identity and power-base independent of both the USA and Europe.[74] Churchill's doctrine of 'three circles': the British Commonwealth, English-speaking world and a United Europe, placed Britain in a special position as the only nation spanning all three.[75]

Second, the echoes of colonialism and imperialism complicate a discourse of the Commonwealth as kith and kin. Yet, Parliament's reading of the Commonwealth has to be seen in the context of a debate about Canada. It seems unlikely the language of kith and kin would have been used if the nation in question had been located in the ex-colonial Caribbean or South Asia. Nor is it likely that references to a shared history, culture and traditions would have been as pervasive.[76] Yet, the two images of family and colonised lands are not incompatible. Rather, they combine into a racially hierarchical and patriarchal community: illustrated in the comments of speakers such as the Labour Eurosceptic MP, Peter Shore, who emphasised Canada's status as a *senior* Commonwealth member.[77]

The European Union—nationhood threatened

Despite the (implicit) centring of Anglo-culture and ancestry, Eurosceptics portrayed the Commonwealth as an affiliation of nations bound together through common loyalty, history and shared interest. In contrast, the EU was depicted as a bureaucratic hierarchy of disparate nations linked by individualistic ties of self-interest. Images of the EU in the fish war debates took two different forms: meta-state and meta-governance. These share similarities with the two models identified by Gary Marks et al., of, respectively, multi-level and state-centric governance.[78]

The multi-level model shares with the meta-state image the perception that states have lost autonomy. However, the model of Marks et al., unlike the meta-state, does not see power as having been transferred to an alternative state structure. Rather, multi-level governance suggests a dispersal of power between different bodies at subnational, national and international levels. The second, state-centric model shares with the image of meta-governance the notion that authority remains with nation-states. However, it differs in suggesting that EU decisions reflect the lowest common denominator. Eurosceptics' portrayal of meta-governance, in contrast, implied that the EU reflected the asymmetrical balance of political and economic power existing within the European community.

The depiction of the EU as a meta-state[79]—a state comprised of states—relocates member-states as quasi-institutional citizens. Portrayal as a state suggests the EU has its own identity and corporate interests, symbolised by its flag, anthem and Parliament.[80] As a state, the EU makes possible a specifically European way of knowing and acting.[81] 'Integration means building a cultural identity in terms of a shared view of what Europeans have in common...It implies the construction of a European world view.'[82] Within this representation, the relationship between Britain and the EU—homologous nation-states—is zero-sum:[83] Europe's gains correlate with Britain's losses. While the taking of British nationhood may not have been by force, this does not negate the aggressive character of the seizure. Sceptics charged the EU with appropriating British soil, authority and identity, illustrated by the erasure of British naming. Cornish fishers would no longer be hailed as British, only as EU fishermen. Changing interpellation announced a coerced, changing allegiance. Thus, the once 'British' navy could be forced to attack its countrymen,[84] those Cornish fishers attempting to hold back the 'Spanish invading armada'.[85]

Alongside this meta-state representation of the EU was the second image of meta-governance. This identified the EU as a cold, bureaucratic machine, structuring relations between nations rather than aspiring to nationhood itself. As a machinery engaged in meta-governance—the governance of governance—the EU's only response to crisis was to generate more systems and procedures. In the House of Lords, Viscount Mountgarret, for instance, criticised Brussels bureaucrats for issuing directives like confetti, and for responding to problems with yet more rules.[86]

The meta-governance image, in contrast to that of the meta-state, denied the EU agency or authority as a political actor in its own right. While the EU hailed itself as a primary party in the dispute with Canada, British sceptics re-presented the EU as condensing powerful European interests. Federation, thus, slides into empire. 'A state which stands in a relationship of periphery to some other state or power ... is not a 'nation-state', but a province of an empire.'[87] Britain is no longer a member-citizen of a larger, federated EU, but a nation governed by others. The EU—with its illusion of common, supranational government—provides the mechanism whereby one nation can control political and economic conditions across Europe.[88] So far, it would seem, this has not occurred thanks to the relative dispersal of European political power. However, each instance of transnational control signifies the coming of a new European empire.

In the case of the fish war, British sceptics depicted the EU as a structure for advancing a Spanish agenda under the guise of promoting EU interests as a whole. This portrayal was reinforced by Spain and Canada's actions. Ironically, Spain's attempts to force the EU to act as the primary protagonist facilitated Canada's reductive depiction in which EU opposition functioned as a front for Spain. In other words, EU action illustrated the power of Spanish interests. According to Tobin, the Canadian Fisheries Minister, EU foreign policy was being made by a Spanish fishing captain off Newfoundland.[89]

Before going to on to explore sceptics' discourse of British emasculation, I wish to highlight a tension between the portrayal of Europe discussed so far and the Europe discussed in the following chapter. This tension illustrates a contradiction in Britain's cultural relationship to the Continent. The corporatised, negative portrayal of Europe—now so pervasive and naturalised in the metonymic figure of Brussels— contrasts with a cultural imaginary in which Europe functions as the home of high art. In this latter image, elite, cultural traditions are juxtaposed against a less developed, albeit Commonwealth, South. The technocratic Europe represented by the EU is thus far removed from the continent of Plato, Socrates and Descartes. To the extent that these two competing images of Europe co-existed, they were largely achieved through a double movement. First, modernist Europe was denigrated in order to romanticise its past; second, Britain was linked to that past. While, Conservative Eurosceptics, in particular, claimed Britain had little in common with a current Europe constituted according to (illusory) transEuropean norms, Britain (or rather England) nevertheless managed to remain an integral part of classical European tradition (see chapter three).

A Vision of Britain

Emasculation

Both meta-state and meta-governance depict the EU as 'emasculating' Britain—'taking' from it the masculine qualities expressed more than a decade earlier in the Falklands' spirit, and now demonstrated by Canada. Yet Britain was also implicated in the EU's imperialistic move. Acting like an 'old woman'—the gendered connotations of the critique are not hidden—Britain had failed to make use of its full powers and capabilities, thereby leaving a governmental space the EU could fill (see chapter one). Lord Beloff encapsulated sceptics' frustration when he declared:

> Canada should be asked to lend us its Minister of Fisheries to take part in our own Cabinet, so that we would have someone in Brussels who would stand up for British fishermen as powerfully as the Canadian Minister has stood up for the interests of Canadian fishermen.[90]

Thus, the British government's weakness in not coming to Canada's aid was replayed in its inability to defend Britain's own fishing communities. Britain's entry into the Common Market, its agreement to the Common Fisheries Policy, were seen by Eurosceptics as damning Britain's domestic fishing interests—even threatening their right to be known as *British* fishermen.[91] Moreover, according to sceptics, if British fishers have been let down, we have all been let down. They may live at the rugged boundary of our nation-state but they are as much part of Britain as Westminster itself, indeed, perhaps more so, since they represent our front-line: geographically, economically and ideologically. Only a government dominated by the EU, where belonging is not evenly distributed, could ignore its topographical periphery.

More than a geographical fringe, fishing communities also symbolise Britain's national essence. One of the last remaining forms of acceptable, commercial hunting within Britain, fishermen represent a traditional, masculinised ideal (see chapter seven). This identity contrasts with, and is underscored by, the 'unethical' hunting practices and norms of the Spanish. British fishermen are also not just any hunters. In many ways, it is unsurprising that a fishing dispute generated an exploration of British identity, for Britain's identity (and that of Europe more generally) has been constructed historically through its relationship to, and mastery of, the seas.[92] For Britain, an imaginary self-identity was forged through exploration and expansion. Thus, the willingness of English fishing men to venture forth 'into the unknown' persisted as a potent symbol of the adventurous, courageous spirit Eurosceptics lauded.

In decrying Britain's emasculation, therefore, sceptics adopted a narrow target. They distinguished between ordinary people and government, and kept their shaming for the latter. British people, and in particular the fishing communities, were portrayed as fully supportive of Canadian action and outraged by the government's spineless behaviour.[93] Once more, a masculinised chain of associations was constructed between the hardy fishermen and the Canadian nation. Yet the existence of populist support for Canada did more than highlight the impotence of the British government, it also offered a remedy. Britain might be aging badly, but the nation as expressed through its people, and as epitomised in its rural communities, stayed constant. By sustaining the myth of an essential people, unsullied by urban norms and racial mixing (see chapter three), hope remained that the nation would one day achieve its normative potential. However, what this might be, beyond an heroic narrative of fishing people, remained opaque within parliamentary debate.

Statecraft and international order

In response to Eurosceptics' condemnation of governmental weakness, government spokespeople mobilised a counter-discourse of statecraft. Government was not 'out of order'. On the contrary, Britain's identity was expressed and strengthened through its expertise and continuing influence in the governance of international relations. In this sense, the British government commandeered the EU's position of umpire or negotiator between member-states, an appropriation which challenged Eurosceptics' claims that the government was thoroughly subordinated to EU agendas. Repeatedly, ministers depicted Britain as a negotiator bringing both sides to a compromise solution. Earl Howe declared,

'[W]e are actively working with all parties to reduce tension, to avoid further confrontation and to encourage sensible negotiation.'[94] Britain's 'unique position' as a member of both communities evacuated the notion of belonging as monogamous.[95] According to William Waldegrave,

> Britain's membership of the Commonwealth ... and our long-standing connections of friendship and trust with the Canadians ... enabled us, not for the first time, to fulfil a valuable transatlantic role in the relationship between the European Union and the North American continent.[96]

In acting as a mediator, the government rejected the 'either/or' approach which demanded a singular choice of loyalty.[97] Community membership was not exclusive but overlapping; Britain's loyalty to both Europe and Canada meant that it would work hard to resolve the dispute.

Portraying Britain as an active mediator allowed the government to present itself as lacking any interest in the dispute other than seeing the conflict effectively resolved. In denying self-interest, the government portrayed its priority as the protection of a system of management, and framework of negotiation, not the particular interests of either itself or one of the other parties.[98] Yet aside from the economic disingenuity of this posture, there are two interesting points of incongruity. First, the emphasis on 'common management'[99] and strengthened rules[100]—a single order—contrasts with the stress on two international communities. Does this mean that a single international community is not imagined, but rather that different communities—including the EU and Commonwealth—co-exist in one international, legal order? For an 'order' has connotations that community lacks; while the latter emphasises shared interests and concerns, order suggests an external disciplinary structure within which disparate states pursue their interests.

Second, the British government's emphasis on a common regulatory framework clashes with a conservative, positivist view of national sovereignty in which states function as autonomous entities.[101] Against this, it is ironic that several of the voices clamouring for national, autonomous action, praising Canada's brinkmanship, came from left-wing MPs. The irony of this was not missed by Waldegrave, who stated in one debate that the Labour Party's support of brinkmanship would be recalled when the government had to take tough action overseas and the opposition was demanding that everything be referred to the UN and its committees.[102] The government's support for an international, regulatory structure also appears incongruous given their established market outlook. A strong system of international regulation or law seems to undermine the notion of a 'free' international market, as well as undermining state autonomy. But through most of its reign, the Conservative government of 1979–97 did not advocate neo-liberalism in isolation. Rather, advocacy tended to be welded to neo-conservative norms of hierarchy and appropriate conduct (see chapter three). In the fish war, the government emphasised the importance of norms of international behaviour. As Foreign Secretary Douglas Hurd declared, the parties should not act as if they were engaged in a football match. '[T]his is not some sort of adversarial contest in which we simply have to decide which side to whoop on.'[103]

Moreover, even within a neo-liberal framework, states may decide that international regulation and collective decision-making accords with their self-interests, particularly in the context of communal or common property (the notion of an unregulated market is clearly a misnomer).[104] Thus, the question is not whether regulation exists, but the form a 'proper regime' takes.[105] In the case of international law, this has tended, not surprisingly, to be constituted according to a Western, legal imaginary. As Peter Fitzpatrick argues, '[International law] is one of the means of legalizing the world—an imperial extraversion of Western nationalism as the carrier of universal norms'.[106] Thus, championing regulation through international law becomes a way of promoting domestic interests as well as familiar, supportive, cultural forms.

Conclusion

This chapter has focused on two of the book's main themes: excess and belonging. Claims that national and supranational bodies were exceeding the legitimate boundaries of governance primarily targeted Spain

and the EU. In the case of Spain, its excesses were portrayed as physiological—its bodily constitution demonstrated an incapacity to
behave with dignity, honour and esteem. EU excesses, on the other
hand, were articulated to two different processes. On the one hand,
they resulted from the logic of emergent state-building. In other
words, as a body with national aspirations, the EU was inevitably going
to push forward the boundaries of its role and remit, thereby undermining the relative autonomy of others, particularly weak others. At
the same time, as a bureaucratic machinery, structuring relations
between member-states, the EU facilitated and strengthened already
powerful nations to impose their interests.

While Spain and the EU were portrayed by Eurosceptics as threatening the healthy survival of European nation-states, government
members hinted that Canada's actions were also hazardous.[107]
Ministers stressed their support for Canada's conservation objectives,
but argued the means being deployed exceeded the bounds of appropriate behaviour. Canada's rash use of domestic law to restrict
international activity might not directly threaten the nation-state, but
it placed crucial regimes of international regulatory order at risk.

The second theme introduced in this chapter is that of belonging.
My argument in this book is that discourses of (non)belonging are
mobilised by political institutions in order to designate their own
behaviour as appropriate, and that of opponents as excessive. This
requires presenting belonging as already determined—an *a priori* fact
on which other relations and boundaries can be based. However, as the
fish war conflict revealed, belonging is as contested and contingent as
the question of excess. For instance, Eurosceptics portrayed Canada as
having a special claim to the fish as a result of geographical proxim-
ity—using this special claim to constitute Spanish action as an
illegitimate 'taking'. However, such pre-existing rights functioned as
a rhetorical and political claim within the dispute. Indeed, the dispute
was largely about the basis on which nations could make special claims
to a common property, such as high-seas fish.

Questions of belonging did not only focus on ownership of
resources, they also focused on community membership. Did Britain
owe a primary loyalty to the Commonwealth or to the EU?[108] These
communities were portrayed in radically different ways—in one,

belonging was constituted according to norms of solidarity and the common good, in the other, belonging was proprietary, at best a matter of individual, national self-interest. Identifying Britain's primary allegiance functioned as a way of determining appropriate behaviour on the part of both the international community and of Britain. EU 'plans' to convert the British navy into an EU defence force was, Eurosceptics argued, excessive because Britain did not, at any deep or normative level, belong to the EU, despite some people's attempts to achieve federation. In addition, for Eurosceptics, Britain's refusal to show Canada proper support was, if not excessive, then at the very least inappropriate behaviour because it ignored the obligations placed on Britain as a result of its primary membership within the Commonwealth community.

In the chapters that follow I develop these themes further. In this chapter, I have explored excessive governance and belonging in the context of a struggle over national identity. Internationally, the Canada—Spain fish war functioned as a dispute about maritime authority, access to resources and legality. However, within the British Parliament, it reformed itself into a largely narcissistic dispute about national identity and governance. Michael Billig argues that as a nation-state becomes established, the symbols it once consciously displayed become absorbed into a 'mindless' common-sense.[109] Yet these symbols frequently come to the fore in moments of crisis. While the fish war did not produce the crisis, it provided a discursive terrain through which fears and anxieties about Britain's identity could be raised. These largely revolved around the question of what kind of nation Britain was becoming, and whether its distinctiveness and relative autonomy could withstand EU governance aspirations. Alternatively, we can understand the crisis as one of hegemony: which forces have the power and authority not just to construct a narrative of past and future, but also to shape the sort of nation Britain is today? In this context, declarations of a crisis of national identity should not be accepted at face value, but rather seen as rhetorical tools mobilised by those who fear a new hegemony coming to pass.

3 'Selling Our Spiritual Birthright'

Religion, Nationhood and State Authority

> Somewhere a decision has to be made about precisely what values are to be given the authority of the classroom. That is the central difficulty, and it is an unresolved one.[1]

In the previous chapter, I explored the two themes of excessive governance and belonging at the international level. In particular, I considered the threat posed to the nation-state from supranational aspirations and undisciplined regimes. In this chapter, I continue this discussion by considering the construction of excess and belonging within the nation-state. Who belongs? What do they belong to? In addition, does the attempt to reconstruct a national community transgress the limits of appropriate state activity.

My focus in this discussion is religion in schools; in particular, the law reform attempts of the 1980s and early 1990s to revitalise the place of Christianity within the British polity and community.

The drive to include religious education provisions in the Education Reform Act 1988 came from Christian Right activists who claimed legislation was essential to counter the widespread disregard of the existing law. Baroness Cox, a leading proponent, declared secularism and multiculturalism had developed to such a degree many teachers felt unable even to mention Jesus Christ.[2] In exploring the Christian Right's agenda, my objectives are two-fold. First, I examine the role played by Christian education policies in reconstructing community and belonging according to a neo-conservative, cultural agenda. Second, I consider the way religion was reconstituted as an appropriate matter for government intervention so that promoting Christian norms and values did not constitute an excessive state act.

The religious aspects of the Education Reform Act (ERA) 1988 need to be seen in the context of wider changes (see also chapter five). Religious education was not the only policy mechanism to assert an Anglo-centric, national identity. Several writers have focused on the implications of a national curriculum oriented towards English history and culture;[3] however, the extension of market principles, 'open' admissions and 'parents' rights' can also be seen as undermining multi-cultural, liberal education by allowing white parents, in particular, an enhanced ability to choose the ethnic and religious composition of schools they prefer.

The politics of British religious education also need to be located within an international context. Here we can see both similarities and differences. On the one hand, opposition to multiculturalism was not peculiar to Britain. Parallels exist in other countries, such as France and Australia, where the Right similarly asserted the importance of protecting a monocultural, national identity.[4] At the same time, the British experience of the late 1980s and 1990s is distinctive. Unlike the USA, for example, where disestablishment has entailed ongoing judicial review to ensure state action does not contravene the Establishment Clause (the 'wall of separation' between church and state),[5] in Britain, the Church of England's constitutional status has enabled right-wing forces to assert the state's responsibility to promote Christianity. Yet, the formally more secular position of the USA obscures the considerable pressure at a local level to reintroduce or strengthen Christianity within American schools.[6] In many cases this has occurred through a complex circum-vention of judicial decisions, for instance, by students rather than teachers leading prayers, or through legislating a minute's silence at the start of the school day.[7] In comparison, the Christian Right in Britain proved far weaker at a local level. Its members were not particularly effective in shaping syllabi, securing explicitly Christian assemblies or getting books withdrawn through local political action. Thus, the 1988 reforms and subsequent national policy initiatives can be seen as an attempt to use influential, sympathetic actors at governmental level in order to impose a Christian agenda on recal-citrants at the local.

Wholly or Mainly Christian

Origins

Under the Education Act 1944, religious education and a daily act of collective worship were compulsory elements within the school day. However, the law did not demand that either privilege Christianity. This lack of closure, while affirmed by some as crucial to maintaining a consensus and to keeping the courts out of religious adjudication, was seen by others as problematic.[8] One high-profile example of the 1944 Act's limitations concerned the Dewsbury conflict.[9] In 1987, a group of parents in the northern English town of Dewsbury withdrew their children from school and taught them in a room above a pub to protest the fact that the school to which their children had been assigned was not predominantly Christian. Backed by the right-wing organisation PACE (Parental Alliance for Choice in Education), parents requested that the Secretary of State intervene. Their request foundered; the Minister declared that nothing in the Education Act 1944 required religious education to be entirely Christian.[10]

This failure to give the 1944 Act a Christian reading strengthened demands for legal reform that would not so much rewrite as enforce the earlier settlement. Opponents of a multifaith approach argued that the 1944 Act did not mention Christianity explicitly because it then seemed unnecessary. Law reformers at the time had simply assumed Christianity would form the basis for religious instruction and prayer.[11] As a contributor to the right-wing *Black Paper 1977* suggested,

> No one in 1944 ... could conceive that ... the leading theorists of religion would be interpreting 'religious instruction' as a licence to teach any moral values which happened to take the fancy of the high-minded. So no one felt it necessary to create a uniform system ... [12]

From the 1960s, growing recognition of the needs of Britain's minority ethnic communities, and of the changing identity of British society, led many local RE syllabuses to become multifaith in orientation. Others extended even further into non-theistic belief systems, reported by Baroness Cox as including 'humanism and the militant atheism of Marxism'.[13] In many schools, Christian worship was replaced with interfaith prayer, secular stories, and information-based assemblies. At the same time, it is important not to overstate the departure from Christian education, despite the rhetoric of many on the Christian Right. Some local authorities remained committed to a predominantly Christian approach. The 1983 Agreed Syllabus for West Sussex, for instance, was prefaced with the declaration, 'It gives a clear lead in the prime importance in our country of Christian belief, values and heritage, and for this I am profoundly grateful'.[14]

Religion, panic and crisis

Despite the continuing existence of predominantly Christian religious education, the Christian Right strove in the 1970s and 1980s to generate a cultural panic over the crisis facing Britain. Multiculturalism was 'taking over', jeopardising not only a sense of English culture and Christian identity, but moral values more generally. These claims came to the fore in parliamentary debates around the ERA 1988. Members described Britain as in danger of losing its national identity and direction (see chapter two). Postcolonial guilt, and the welcoming of immigrant communities, had been so excessive that Britain had marginalised its own, true nature in order to construct a syncretic identity based on the amalgamation of others.[15] Religious education provisions therefore were to function as a form of exhuming—responding to the crisis of national identity by uncovering the nation's true self. Britain had been too humble, too deferential. In pretending that identity could be reduced to demography, it had mislead its newcomers and served badly its own.

The second crisis mobilised by the right concerned education more specifically. Since the late 1960s, with the first collection of *Black Papers*, the Right had launched an insistent attack on progressive education. They argued that anti-traditional, anti-disciplinary perspectives pervaded the unions and state educational bureaucracies. Ordinary teachers were sidelined, those who opposed the progressive mandate ridiculed. The educational crisis apparently produced by liberal, 'relativist', child-centred techniques,[16] with their emphasis on environmental and social causation rather than human responsibility and sin, was deemed particularly pronounced in the area of religious and spiritual development. There, a multifaith, 'detached', phenomenological approach (concerned with understanding observable expressions of faith from the perspective of different believers) had replaced committed learning on the basic principles and 'truths' from a Christian standpoint.[17] Opponents targeted what they saw as a trans-religious essentialism which constructed a shared core between faiths (rather than emphasising the essence and purity of individual faiths); they also contested a relational approach which claimed religious meaning could best be uncovered through interfaith dialogue.[18]

Parliamentary members such as Baroness Cox drew attention to what they saw as bizarre and alarming teaching. They described syllabi covering ancestor worship, the Chinese New Year and Shamanism, as well as Hinduism, Islam and Judaism. Baroness Cox told the House of Lords:

> Parents in York report that a class used all its RE lessons for a whole term to learn about witchcraft ... A number of RE inspectors in ILEA [Inner London Education Authority] sent a letter to all schools warning against the traumatic psychological effects of teaching the occult in London's schools.[19]

The breakdown in schooling caused by the relativist 'crisis of values' amongst the nation's educators[20] produced in its wake a further crisis: ignorant, undisciplined young people without a spiritual, moral code: 'There is chaos in the area of personal values and morality'.[21] During debate prior to the passage of the 1988 legislation, members in both Houses produced countless examples of the effect on young people of a lack of proper spiritual development.

> A survey of 15-year-olds in Cleveland only 12 months ago showed that no less than two-thirds thought there was little or nothing wrong with acts of vandalism.[22]

Rhodes Boyson, MP, told of a 'nice' ten-year-old boy who tied a banger to a cat's tail and watched it running around with the banger fizzing.[23] The cat had to be put down. Even so, the boy 'who was a perfectly nice lad' had no comprehension of what he had done wrong.[24]

While the focus is on violence and lack of morality, a racialised subtext runs through such parliamentary discourse (see chapter two). '[T]here are young people who know no more of our faith than they knew in darkest Africa when we sent missionaries there'.[25] Christianity is articulated to civilisation; religious ignorance to savagery. Barbarism and the primitive are deeply embedded in the construction of religious-less youth by parliamentary spokespeople; unable to appreciate culture, young people will grow up incapable of conforming to or understanding society's disciplines.

Conservative Christians and the NCR

So far I have used the term Christian Right to refer to a broad movement of Christians intent on using the political system to achieve conservative Christian values.[26] However, we might distinguish between the New Christian Right, and another group, Conservative Christians. Their differences are important in understanding some of the tensions and contradictions condensed within the government's legislative agenda. For Conservative Christians, their main concern was that all young pupils receive access to Christian beliefs and values, and recognise Christianity's privileged place within British culture and heritage. While they recognised the need for some general acknowledgment and understanding of minority faiths, and for minorities to be able to follow their own religion, in general their position was an assimilationist one. Lord Swinfen, for example, declared:

> In order that those of other religions can be fully assimilated into this great nation of ours while they do not have to be made Christians, I feel that they should be taught the tenets of the Christian religion so that they can understand why this nation works as it does.[27]

Christianity, not only through its beliefs and values, but also through its practices cements together the different constituencies within school and nation: Jewish and Muslim children sitting down with Christians to say the Lord's Prayer. Speaking for the Government, the Earl of Arran claimed, 'We would not wish to see a situation where children in maintained schools are divided into separate acts of worship for different religious groups'.[28] That this division of children became subsequently encoded within the legislation was largely because of the influence of the second main group: the New Christian Right (NCR). While the NCR has been linked with proselytism and evangelism in other contexts,[29] here their primary goal was to achieve exclusively Christian education within the mainstream and the exit of other faiths. Thus, on the whole, the NCR did not demand that other faiths participate within Christian-based education; in fact they supported Muslim requests for separate schools, arguing all children would benefit from being educated with their 'own'.[30]

The law[31]

The religious provisions of the Education Reform Act (ERA) are a good example of the ongoing relevance of direct governing. In other words, governance has not shifted entirely to steering and the deployment of expertise. It still functions through legislation that mandates and requires particular activities. However, the prescriptive aspects of the provisions discussed here are intertwined with governing through entrenched facts and norms.

The ERA begins by restating the 1944 requirement that religious education form a required part of the basic curriculum for all students within state schools (S. 2(1) ERA 1988).[32] More importantly—emphasising the centrality of Christianity and the exclusion of non-theistic belief systems—syllabi drawn up by LEAs (local education authorities) must 'reflect the fact that the religious traditions in Great Britain are in the main Christian whilst taking account of the teaching and practices of the other principal religions represented in Great Britain' (S. 8(3) ERA 1988). Initially, these requirements were only to apply to new syllabi. While LEAs could convene a conference to review their local syllabus, they did not have to. This loophole, allowing LEAs to retain old syllabi which contravened the 1988 requirements, was closed in the later Education Act 1993. This Act compelled those authorities that had not already done so, to convene a syllabus conference in order to draw up a new syllabus by 1 April 1995.

Ongoing concerns that local authorities were applying an unduly liberal interpretation of the law brought forward other methods to structure local discretion.[33] In 1994, the School Curriculum and Assessment Authority produced national, model syllabi. Although these were not statutory documents, they set out a recommended structure for teaching religious education. The models included five 'key' religions but asserted the privileged position and significance of Christianity. Importantly, they approached religions as discrete, distinct phenomena, in direct opposition to the more thematic approach of progressive educators.

Alongside religious education, the other key religious element of the ERA was the school assembly. Restating the 1944 Act, the 1988 provisions required all pupils to take part in a daily act of collective worship (S. 6(1) ERA 1988). The responsibility for arranging this lay with the head teacher, who if she did not wish to lead the assembly herself, was required to arrange for someone else to conduct it. The new element introduced by the ERA was for worship to be of a 'broadly Christian' (non-denominational) character (S. 7 ERA 1988). While not every assembly had to be broadly Christian, the majority of acts should be over a term.

The legal requirement for 'Christian worship' not surprisingly generated definitional dilemmas and tactics. Indeed, it can be seen as leading towards the juridification of Christianity earlier law reformers feared. In the case of *R. v. The Secretary of State for Education ex parte Ruscoe and Dando*,[34] brought by parents against the Secretary of State for Education for dismissing their complaints that Manchester LEA and their children's school were failing to comply with the ERA, the question of what constituted worship came under scrutiny. Did it require veneration to be paid to the divine, or simply respect and admiration for an object of esteem? The hearing also raised the further question of what *Christian* worship required. Did it need explicit references to Christian concepts such as Christ, the Trinity, or the saints, or simply the inclusion of more general Christian sentiments?

In response to the 1988 provisions, many educators had attempted to give Christianity a wide definition so that any theme which applied to Christianity, such as forgiveness, light and joy, despite also applying to other faiths, could constitute Christian worship. This interpretation was broadly accepted in *ex parte Ruscoe and Dando*, where McCullough J. stated 'this [broadly Christian] character would not be lost by the inclusion of elements common to Christianity and to one or more other religions'. However, it failed to satisfy the NCR. In 1994, a government Circular supporting their position was published. In the face of considerable concern and disagreement from a range of educators and religious experts, the Circular stated that Christian collective worship must 'contain some elements which relate *specifically* to the traditions of Christian belief and which *accord a special status to the person of Jesus Christ*' (para 63).[35]

Despite the requirements for religious education and worship, none of the new provisions took away parents' right of individual withdrawal which dated back to the Elementary Education Act 1870.[36] This was re-established in the Education Act 1944 which also confirmed that children of other faiths could receive instruction and worship in their own religion.[37] Schools must respect any parent's request that his or her child be excused from attending or participating in collective worship or religious education. Parents are not obliged to give reasons for their request.

In addition to this individual right, the 1988 provisions also laid down a new collective exemption procedure. This applied to schools that had large numbers of pupils for whom Christian worship would be inappropriate. An exemption or 'determination' might either allow a school to run a common, multifaith assembly or else permit pupils to worship within monoreligious groupings. The decision whether or not to grant a determination belonged to the local Standing Advisory Council on Religious Education (SACRE). Now mandatory under the 1988 Act, SACREs fulfil a number of roles. As well as considering applications for determinations, they also monitor religious education, determine when the syllabus might need reviewing and, in many instances, participate within the complaints process.

School, Christianity, Nation

The Christian religion is part of our country, part of our heritage, with the Queen as head of the Church and the nation.[38]

The three crises of national identity, education and immoral youth coalesced in the Right's demand for committed, Christian religious education. Personal moral growth would coincide with a strengthening of the wider community, based on, and in turn reproducing, a national, Christian identity. Religion thus formed the linchpin linking pupils to the nation-state. The Christian Right's conception of belonging raises two questions. What kind of nation-state was at its core? How was the character of pupils' belonging portrayed? Addressing these questions highlights the fundamentally unequal, exclusionary and conditional character of belonging where an Established church exists.

A Christian country

A key refrain during passage of the ERA concerned Britain's status as a *Christian* country. Even leading Labour spokespeople affirmed its truth, deriving from it the normative assumption that such a national identity should be able to continue.[39] While the 1988 Act contained the more restrained phrase: '*in the main* Christian',[40] Britain's religious character was nevertheless legislated as a central, national fact. Laws, democratic institutions, art, literature and architecture, all were 'profoundly influenced by Christianity ... the spiritual tradition which has inspired our country for nearly 2,000 years'.[41]

Parliamentary discourse did not constitute Britain as *any* Christian nation-state. Rather, it was inscribed according to an elite, Anglo-Protestant identity. This texturising of British identity is particularly apparent in the constant parliamentary references to classical culture. Construed as interdependent, Christianity and the arts each validate the other: if one is central to British culture than so is its counterpart. Consequently, Christian education can be justified on comprehension grounds. British or, more accurately, English culture cannot fully be understood without an appreciation of Christianity's influence.[42]

This argument, with its emphasis on understanding rather than religious commitment, may seem a more liberal justification for Christian-based teaching. However, it contains several assumptions. First, its highly selective interpretation of English culture assumes a particular cultural judgment about what is of value.[43] The relevance of Christianity to other, more populist or non-Anglo, Christian texts is, for example, largely ignored, thereby marginalising the status of those texts within English culture. Second, validating Christian education as a necessary basis for understanding Britain's culture, history and political traditions tended to assume both a significant and a positive correlation (that Christianity played a beneficial role). However, Britain's Christian history or heritage could be written in very different terms—exploitation, mass killings and discrimination, at home and abroad, rather than as high art, democracy and tolerance. One aspect of Britain's Christian heritage is the treatment of its Jews leading up to their expulsion in the thirteenth century. Without question, medieval Anglo-Jewish history cannot be understood in isolation from Christian theology, politics and society of the time. However, that kind of education about Christianity—historically rather than purely theologically located—does not seem to be what law reformers had in mind when they stated that religious education should reflect Christianity's predominance. To value Christianity *because* it is our heritage is already to prejudge the question of which Christian history is to be told. It is to indulge in a shared romanticisation of Britain's past as a stratified, compliant, ethnically homogenous society. Peers in the House of Lords fondly narrated a golden era where family and servants started each day with a shared morning prayer. According to the Earl of Halsbury, 'The whole household met before breakfast, servants and all, and my grandfather read the prayers and the blessing at the end'.[44]

The third assumption pervading the epistemological legitimation of Christianity is the belief that English culture is ethnically unadulterated, and that the Christian influence on history, politics and the arts can be understood apart from knowledge of other faiths. Yet, Britain's history and culture have always functioned within an international context comprised of different nations, religions and peoples, and English culture is hardly ethnically pure. Moreover, the impact of Christianity, even within Britain, makes little sense within a mono-religious vacuum. For instance, teaching about the Jewish expulsion from England, while it would need to incorporate an understanding of Christian theology, would be meaningless if Christian beliefs were not related to the existence and practices of Judaism. Similarly, it is misguided to assume that texts such as Shakespeare's *Othello* and *The Merchant of Venice* can be understood with a knowledge *only* of the Christian faith.

Belonging

The portrayal of the nation-state as Anglo-Protestant not only identifies the state to which people belong, but as well something of the character of belonging. The Christian Right agenda places considerable stress on the centrality of the past to determining British identity. Britain is not a blank slate to be written according to the transient whims of present demography. Its identity is fixed by history. The past rules who can belong and in what ways. Membership criteria are not satisfied by formal, legal citizenship; at the very least they require immersion within Anglocentric culture, and the adoption of its traditions, religion and language. More essentially, for many in the NCR, it is doubtful whether belonging can ever be fully attained by those who do not have an 'English' complexion and bone structure. While physiognomy remains unexplicit or undisclosed within representations of national identity, it is certainly evident in the classical tradition taken as sheltering England's essence.

Belonging in Britain is clearly not equal. To explore this further, I consider the position first of the outsider and, then, of the insider. The poststructuralist paradigm currently in vogue for analysing community, citizenship and belonging has tended to treat the construction of the 'other' as essential to the identity of the 'we'. Insiders can only know who they are by knowing who they are not. Belonging requires exclusion; community requires boundaries. Within this context, immigrants or non-Christians (these two categories are obviously different but overlapping) play four roles. First, their existence and flourishing cultural presence highlights the continuing importance of 'identity work' in order for the Christian majority to maintain their national hegemony. There is no room for complacency.

Second, the construction of the 'other' helps constitute the symbolic contours and boundaries of the 'host' community. By underscoring the beliefs, practices and languages of the outsider, greater clarity can be given to the culture of the Christian majority; the walls are fortified, and Christian children can locate without confusion their own belonging. Third, and somewhat contrastingly, the 'other' is used to validate the Christian education 'turn'. As Parliamentarians declared, Christian education was not just for the good of Christians, minority faiths wanted it too. Lord Bishop of Truro proclaimed,

> Those Asian parents of whom I speak are happy and eager that their
> children should experience that Christian worship.[45]

In the Commons, similar sentiments were heard. In fact the example
below proved so popular it was reiterated by several speakers in subsequent debates.

> ... Mr. Mustapha, the chairman of the Moslem Teachers Association,
> went into a school that he was inspecting ... and heard the head
> teacher say, 'We do not mention Jesus ...' Mr. Mustapha was so
> shocked that he went and told his imam. The next Saturday ... one
> heard Moslems saying prayers to improve the respect for the place
> of Jesus Christ in British schools.[46]

Yet, minority faiths are not simply *functional* to the reconstruction of
Christian national belonging. They also exist, finally, as a *problem* that
requires resolution. This problem takes two main forms: contagion and
incorporation. Contagion is important in highlighting the racialised
character of NCR discourse on religion.[47] The NCR identify the
danger of contamination in stories of Anglo children returning home
from school singing Hindi songs or chattering about Muslim holy festi-
vals. Contamination occurs through a syncretic approach which denies
the need to keep religions separate—epistemologically or ontologi-
cally. Mixing—racial, religious or cultural—carries the risk of
transmitting undesired traits into the host community.[48] Yet contagion
also implies desire. While religious miscegenation does not require the
reproductive mixing of genes, it shares with the Right's opposition to
homosexuality the belief that knowledge alone will seduce.[49]

How and to what extent should Jews, Hindus, Sikhs and Muslims
be incorporated within a Christian nation-state? What conditions, if
any, apply to their membership? While some on the NCR looked
simply to exclusion, Conservative Christians tried to reconcile the
tension between integration and separation. This is apparent in the
local variation built into the religious education provisions. First,
worship is intended to take its character from the majority faith

present in the school (by means of an exemption if the dominant faith is not Christianity). Second, religious education, despite its orientation towards Anglo-heritage learning, rather than a more general faith nurturance, provides room for some geographic flexibility. A DFE Circular 1/94, for instance, states that in order to minimise withdrawals, religious education should take into account the faith composition of the school population.[50]

The Conservative Christian project enables minorities to belong. Nevertheless, the disjuncture between minority faith and that of the nation-state means belonging is always partial. As guests, minorities must remember their status and not exceed their welcome. Good manners require conformity—at least on the surface—and deference to the host community's preferences.[51] The guest who feels at home—who draws attention to faults and suggests improvements—presumes too much. As one MP declared, 'I do not believe that ethnic communities who come here should expect their faith or social structure to change what has been the greatness of our own society'.[52]

In the previous chapter, I considered belonging on a continuum that extended from a relationship of community membership to one of ownership. This continuum is intersected by another concerning the degree or intensity of belonging. This second axis places those whose identity possesses the greatest correspondence with the nation-state at one end, those demonstrating the greatest divergence at the other. Yet, positions along this axis are not fixed; the degree or intensity of belonging can increase or decrease depending on how cultural affinity or discordance are expressed. For instance, those with the greatest compatibility can intensify their belonging through public expressions of cultural identity. The reverse is true for those at the other end—minorities—who must contain their identity within the private domain (see also chapter six). The more they demand public space and support, the more their capacity to belong is jeopardised. Successful privatisation or repudiation of difference, alongside public expressions of national loyalty and identification, offers the key to minorities wishing to belong more fully. Yet the erasure of ethnic and racial difference is rarely complete. For the Christian Right, the 'glass ceiling' of belonging means even compliant and assimilated outsiders will keep colliding against its impermeable surface.

Regulating the self

Despite references within parliamentary debate, statutory provisions and circulars, in the main, non-Christians remained peripheral to the law framers' concerns. The 'other' was not at the emotional centre of the debate, despite their role in identifying the problem and legitimising the solution. On the contrary, the main objective of law reform was to place Christians back at the heart of British policy and return Christian-heritage families to the hub of the nation-state. When the state speaks, it addresses them; their needs and concerns provide the democratic standpoint. To put it another way, part of the problem, for the Christian Right, was minorities' perceptions that they too were being equally hailed when the state addressed its public. Measures were therefore needed to make clear the identity of the public 'you'.

The ERA reframed the state's hailed public, in several ways. First, Christianity is the only religion actually named—the others remain generically identified. Second, while non-Christian children are expected to fit in with predominantly Christian assemblies, any derogation from Christian worship has to pay particular attention to the implications this will have for Christian pupils. Third, money can be spent on Christian prayer, but withdrawal by other faith members has to be at no expense.[53] Minority-faith parents have the right to provide their own worship in state schools, but they cannot use state (public) money to do so. We can see in this recentring of the Christian subject, a parallel with Foucault's analysis of nineteenth-century sexual regulation.[54] Foucault argued that the middle-classes first turned themselves into the subjects of regulation in order to reconstitute themselves as a distinct and special class.[55] In part, the same objective is apparent here in the need to recreate a distinct, national, Christian identity that perceives itself as both bounded and special. But the hailing of the Christian subject also has a disciplinary agenda based on instilling conservative moral values. While lapsed Christians are not the sole culprits of moral failing, their constitutive membership of the nation-state means that it is their lapses which are seen as jeopardising national identity. What England is depends on the behaviour of the English.

Excessive or Responsible Governance

The governmental premise that religion is a matter of public policy is not inherently surprising given the history of entanglement between the church and state in Britain. However, in the context of Conservative government policy during the 1980s and 1990s, the neo-conservatism underwriting religious policy contradicted the government's oft expressed emphasis on individualism and a contracted state (see chapter four). Yet, the religious education provisions of this period were not anomalous. Rather, they paralleled other juridificatory initiatives concerning public order, sexual expression and familial relations, similarly based on the premise that certain areas of life were the legitimate terrain of government intervention.[56]

Legitimating intervention

In contrast to US judicial dicta which treat children's susceptibilty as a reason for taking extra care not to indoctrinate,[57] in Britain the fact that children are impressionable lay behind the thinking that religious induction should occur at school. Since many families were unable to provide adequate socialisation, quasi-public bodies such as schools needed to assume the task of generating faith commitment. Yet how did the Christian Right constitute their demands as appropriate? How did they identify governmental intervention in this area as being within the boundaries of legitimate state action? Addressing these questions highlights both the specific mechanisms of legitimation used in relation to religion in schools as well as wider issues of governmentality.

The starting point is the existence of an Established church. In a nation with a state/religion divide, such as the USA, policies with a religious purpose immediately risk being construed as excessive— going beyond the state's legitimate remit. In contrast, the constitutional status of the Church of England gives policies privileging Christianity *a priori* legitimacy. Yet, this does not mean that government can do anything to advance Christianity and still retain legitimacy. There are other bases, for granting government policy validity. In the following discussion, I consider their effectiveness in relation to religious education reform.

For the Christian Right, legitimate state action existed in preserving national security, and the promotion of a Christian, pastoral tradition dedicated to forming morally self-governing individuals.[58] In the context of Christian education in schools, the combination of these principles took three forms: strengthening national cohesion; facilitating parents' interests; and improving children's moral well-being.[59]

> [I]t seems to me that there are three principal reasons for the collapse of moral standards in this country. First, there is the failure ... to support the family in any meaningful way ... Secondly ... there has been a complete failure on the part of the established Church ... to communicate the gospel in a manner which is both relevant and meaningful ... Thirdly, there is the failure of parents ... [children's] spiritual needs are met scarcely at all.[60]

Securing the nation has traditionally provided an acceptable rationale for government intervention. As well as safeguarding economic and territorial interests, and intervening to withdraw civil rights from people defined as a national threat, security also requires safeguarding the state's cultural identity and corporate health. Maintaining a distinct national identity requires the reproduction of nationhood. Drawing on Judith Butler's conception of performativity,[61] we can see nationhood as a corporate identity that is not constructed once and for all, rather it requires repeat performances to sustain itself. The room of praying children or the pile of 'committed' essays on Jesus's scriptural beliefs constitutes, for the Christian Right, a significant performative act of Britain nationhood. In this way, Christianity stands in for England; its micro, localised practices provide the 'I do' to a cultural contract through which child and nation are joined (see chapter six).

Since the early 1980s, parents' rights have also gained legitimacy in Britain as a justification for public policy decisions (see chapter five). In the context of religion, this was reinforced by a domestic and international emphasis on faith as familiarly located—children acquire the faith of their ancestors, while their faith is the property of, and subject to, the familial domain. During the ERA debates, the Christian Right attempted to validate law reform on the grounds of parental support. Several parliamentary members referred to parents' desire for new legislation.[62]

Speakers also drew attention to those parents keen for their children to receive adequate religious instruction, but unable personally to provide it. Lord Swinfen declared, 'I am sure that the vast majority of those who call themselves Christians and have children do not themselves feel capable of teaching their children properly about Christianity and how to be good Christians'.[63] A second, more covert, justification concerned Christian parents' apparent fear of losing their cultural authority in the face of growing minority demands. The statutory emphasis on Christianity within the ERA was to reassure parents that their culture would be protected; the government was acting on their behalf.

There are parallels here with the image of government as an agent or fiduciary, pursuing the interests of a reliant, principal class or constituency—here, parents. Yet, if the state functions as a fiduciary on behalf of parents, can it act on behalf of all parents unequally? As discussed, religious education law reform centred Christian parents and children. Similarly, forms of address during the ERA debate made clear that Parliament was scarcely speaking on behalf of non-Christians. Recognition of their needs reflected Christian tolerance[64]—a tolerance fetishised as the fragile, yet quintessential, symbol of Anglo-Christianity—it did not constitute the state's duty.

The third justification for law reform concerned the needs of young children, particularly young Christian children. Parliamentary speakers referred to the value of prayer in times of need. Baroness Blatch declared, 'I believe we owe it to those children to give them a [religious] framework. After all, school will be the only anchor in their lives. Therefore we have a duty.'[65] Spiritual nourishment functions as a legitimate element within a pastoral, governmental politics. To this extent, government can intervene to nurture its future subjects. Yet, what role does the state have when nourishing children spiritually conflicts with parents' interests, for instance, in those cases where parents are unwilling for their children to have a Christian upbringing?

In relation to religious education, the Christian Right split between those adopting a neo-liberal position, and those taking a more authoritarian approach. The first group adopted a pro-parent stance, affirming the right of withdrawal, and generally centring parents' wishes. In contrast, authoritarians, despite affirming parental authority, adopted a more proactive perspective, using children's 'right' to receive the Christian faith as a way of transcending other interests. For instance, leading activists Burn and Hart argued against local syllabus development on the grounds that 'local determination, far from enlarging our freedoms, has restricted them and denied many children the right to hear about the Christian faith'.[66] The law, thus, represents a compromise. On the one hand, it affirms the benefits to children of religious instruction, and refuses Christian-heritage parents, who want multifaith worship, the right to request a determination. On the other, it gives parents more opportunity to reject and modify Christian education than many authoritarian conservatives would like. Thus, while the substance of the law attempts to give children a particular, spiritual upbringing, this is moderated by a residual, neo-liberal emphasis on individual, here parental, rights.

Challenging government intervention

While the health and security of the nation, parents' rights and the needs of the child were deployed to present government interventions as legitimate, to what extent were these widely accepted? One of the most striking features of religious education reform was the degree of opposition it generated.[67] Resistance raged from LEAs maintaining or producing multifaith syllabi, to headteachers requesting determinations in majority Christian-heritage schools or engaging in the most superficial of 'Christianisations', to educators at all levels flagrantly refusing to abide by the law.

Yet, despite the quite surprising level of non-compliance—figures have been given for full compliance at less than five per cent[68]—in the main, opponents did not argue that promoting national identity, parental wishes and social stability were outside central government's remit. Their opposition rather took three forms: objection to the way national identity, parental goals and social cohesion were portrayed; in other words, they should not be based on a monocultural model. Second, a minority position—that religious activity per se in schools was an inappropriate means of procuring (legitimate) governmental goals. This position echoes American arguments where US courts have held that rather than being seen as a cohesive force, religious penetration of education can only be divisive.[69] Indeed, Justice Frankfurter in

McCollum v. *Board of Education* argued that it is *because* schools are the symbol of democracy and the most pervasive means of promoting a common destiny that religion must be kept separate.[70] The third objection wa to the *way* religion was dealt with: opponents adopting this position argued that religion in schools *could* be beneficial. However, placing too much emphasis on Christianity would simply create exclusionary school communities. At the same time, advocates of this perspective acquiesced in the government's depiction of national identity as Christian. Thus, they were caught in the similar bind to Conservative Christians, trying to juggle the reproduction of national identity with the (non-assimilationist) inclusion of other faiths.

Conclusion

Conservative racial and cultural policies of the 1980s, particularly in the field of education, spawned widespread critical debate as commentators saw in these policies the entrenchment and reproduction of a white, Anglocentric national identity. Yet, the religious education reforms of 1988 and beyond did more than promote Christian beliefs within a Protestant nation-state. They also functioned within a wider project of cultural hierarchy, conservative norms and pastoral government. The rhetorical articulation of Christianity to an elite classical tradition worked to displace other texts and narratives. With Christianity made central to Britain's traditions, institutions and culture, what room existed for political ideas, novels, art, theatre and science from secular, anti-theistic or other faiths? How could these be constituted at the heart of what it was to be British (or English), if Christianity had already (over)filled this space?

It would be easy, tempting even, to see this conservative Christian project—with its emphasis on tradition, hierarchy, discipline and passivity—as past, irrelevant from May 1997 when the Labour Party assumed governmental office. However, the power of these ideas did not dissipate. Discipline and duty proved key concepts within the Blair government's vocabulary; culture retained its conservative framing; and Christianity remained predominant, both as an ethos animating leading political figures (including the Prime Minister), and as a foundational building block of Britain's identity. The resilience of this last was demonstrated in controversies over Britain's Millennium dome. To clerical insistence that Christianity should be at the heart of the exhibition, the Minister responsible, Peter Mandelson, replied that the centrality of Christianity to 'Western civilisation' would not be neglected.[71] At the same time, the Labour government found itself in the same contradictory predicament as its predecessors, maintaining Christianity's pre-eminence while publicly affirming the equal citizenship of all faith communities. Yet how can equal belonging be achieved when national identity is culturally skewed? Indeed, can national identity ever be constructed in a way that allows people to belong equally or are inequality and symbolic exclusion inevitable once nation-states are given cultural definition, that is, when they are more than mere administrative spaces?

In addition to asserting a particular narrative of Britain, religious education reforms also proved politically significant in identifying criteria for government action. The use of national health, parental wishes and children's interests to promote the reforms may have been largely strategic, but in the process these objectives became legitimated as bases for state governance. Religious education reforms thus take their place within a web of policies (others include reproductive rights and child welfare) which are both validated by, and in turn validate, a pastoral government project. We can see this as a form of self-governance in which central government not only aims to restructure the identity of subordinate bodies but to re-present itself. Its emphasis on pastoral qualities, however conservative, superficially mitigates the socio-economic impact of its neo-liberal withdrawal of responsibility. Thus, religious education reforms promise inclusion within an Anglo-Protestant community to the economically excluded, provide solace through prayer for those facing times of trouble and teach discipline for the self-reliance necessary to survive the harsh realities of the market-place.

Yet government's construction of legitimate criteria for its actions also carries risks. For instance, the government may strengthen and give credibility to discourses that are then used against it. This is what happened in chapter five's conflict, when headteacher, Jane Brown, turned down ballet tickets to *Romeo and Juliet*, for reasons, amongst others, that it was incompatible with the school's equal opportunity policy. In this instance, local residents used the governmental rhetoric of parents' rights to defend their headteacher against Hackney council. At the same time, central government's capacity to determine which criteria for state action gain authority and legitimacy is open to dispute. In relation to religious education, however, opponents did not disagree with the criteria for intervention but rather with its content. They protested against daily prayers, the marginalisation of minority faiths, religious separation of children, while accepting, in the main, that government could (and should) act in a pastoral and representational character. Yet this interpretation needs complicating. Although educators did not object to government criteria for action, many opposed what they perceived as increasing intervention and curtailment of professional autonomy through a steady stream of education reforms. In addition, despite opposition to the most explicitly divisive aspects of the reforms, at a basic level, the assumptions upon which they were based were largely accepted—that Britain is and has been a Christian country; that Christianity is a beneficial normative structure; and that, it should be presented to children as a theological and cultural, rather than historically situated phenomenon. At this level, even given the high levels of documented non-compliance, governmental steering proved effective. The 1988 Act effected a modern resettlement of an archaic relationship. In doing so, it legislated Christian hegemony as 'fact', while giving that 'fact', thanks to its parliamentary passage, a spurious foundation within the demos.

Part Three

Challenging Inequality

(In)subordination and the
Reassertion of Authority

4 Governing Local Politics

Property, Community and Fiduciary Duty

This chapter explores the power of judicial review as a meta-governance practice. In particular, it focuses on the use of fiduciary duty to structure local government activities and identity according to neoliberal values. Judicial decisions in this area constructed progressive, redistributive, local government policies as excessive. While judges argued that council initiatives had exceeded the duty owed to local taxpayers, implicit (and sometimes explicit) within their decisions was a perception that local government was trespassing on the terrain of central government. Yet these cases do more than impose constraints upon local government practices, they also impact upon local government's identity in a manner that steers councils towards governing themselves. One mechanism is through reformulating belonging. As well as looking at the construction of community belonging within judicial discourse, I also look at belonging in relation to property ownership, namely, who do taxes belong to? What implications does this have for local government's identity and autonomy?

Structuring discretion

Over the past century, the courts have deployed a range of principles to structure the exercise of local discretion, their actions often provoking considerable opposition. Despite the fact that administrative law principles can be seen as legitimising and therefore enabling local government to exercise power, activists and commentators saw their application as restrictive and undemocratic. While it was generally accepted that central government, as an elected body, could restrict local government activities (at least within certain parameters), there was far less acceptance of the principle that courts could strike down policies, within local government's statutory discretion, on the grounds they contravened judicially derived principles of administrative law.[1] Particularly during the 1980s, when many local councils engaged in innovative policy development, the courts were perceived as carrying out a political vendetta, systematically outlawing local decisions. During this period, courts ruled against subsidised public transport, South African boycotts, bans on National Front hall rentals and gestures of solidarity in industrial disputes.

Fiduciary duty, then, was one amongst a collection of administrative law principles through which the courts could control local discretion. Unlike more abstract notions of political trust,[2] judicial deployment of fiduciary duty required local government to act in the interests of a specific class;[3] with a few exceptions, this class was identified as local taxpayers.[4] In reaching policy decisions, therefore, councils had to give special consideration to their taxpayers' interests. This did not mean local government actually surveyed the 'real' interests of local taxpayers, instead their interests were usually given a formalist interpretation. This required local government to spend taxes in a manner that was efficient, businesslike and non-discriminatory.

How important has local government's fiduciary duty (LGFD) proven to be? Some administrative lawyers have tended to be dismissive, claiming it is an anachronistic detail of little current significance, since few recent decisions have been based on its existence. My argument, however, is that, at the tail-end of the twentieth century, it remained important. First, it functioned as a taken-for-granted principle of local government law. Despite the fact it was rarely decisive, it made a regular appearance in a range of cases, giving particular weight to judicial rejection of redistributive municipal policies, such as subsidised transport and higher public sector wages. In doing so, it was used to assert neo-liberal norms and interests. More generally, it proved important in symbolising and condensing wider tensions regarding local government's role. LGFD places the question of local government's identity at its heart. Are councils primarily accountable to voters or to taxpayers? Is local government a political body or an agent acting on behalf of its 'contributors' or central government?

Fiduciary principles

The origins of fiduciary duty lie within equity and, in particular, within the development of trust law. Trust law concerns the division of legal and equitable ownership so that wealth or property can be managed by one class (trustees), while the benefit lies elsewhere. Because of the power trustees possessed as a result of ownership of the formal legal title, a framework of rules developed to restrict them gaining personal benefit while acting on behalf of beneficiaries. These included rules against 'self-dealing' (where the trustee contracts with him or herself), prohibitions on 'secret profits' (benefiting financially from trust action without the beneficiary's consent), and rules proscribing a conflict of interests (between duty and personal interest). Today, these restrictions do not apply only to trustees, they also apply to people owing a fiduciary duty.

Fiduciary principles largely developed to cover situations falling short of a trust as the latter term gained its modern, narrower meaning.[5] However, whether a fiduciary duty exists is a surprisingly complex matter, made more complicated by the fact that different judgments approach the subject in quite different ways. Some relationships are generally accepted as fiduciary ones, for instance, between a company director and her company, and a solicitor and her client. However, often whether a fiduciary duty is found to exist will depend on the factual relationship between the parties. The courts will therefore look for particular fiduciary elements: an undertaking to act on behalf of another; control over their property; reliance; or the exercise of power in a way that affects the beneficiary's interests, leaving her vulnerable.[6] These principles have been used to extend fiduciary duty to a whole set of new relationships, such as between doctors and patients, and between social workers and clients.[7] Fiduciary duty may also function in a remedial capacity. These are situations where it would be hard to identify a pre-existing relationship, but the courts wish to grant a particular, equitable remedy. In order to prevent unjust enrichment, for example, they will declare a fiduciary duty exists.

While the origins of fiduciary duty lie in trusts, commentators see fiduciary relations as becoming increasingly important and pervasive. Frankel argues that the United States is witnessing the emergence of a society based largely on fiduciary relations.[8] Fiduciary duty offers a way of regulating, and hence, facilitating, professional and expert conduct in an increasingly specialised society. Government can also owe a duty. Fiduciary principles have developed in the area of indigenous people's rights, in Canada and the USA, in particular. The basis and scope of this duty is the subject of a complex jurisprudence.[9] Nevertheless, the principle has been used to require governments to exercise certain powers over resources and land in the interests of indigenous communities.

The character of local government's duty

Translating existing fiduciary principles into the British local government context, we might expect a duty to be owed to two classes: first, to local government by its paid and unpaid officials—analogous to the duty company directors and employees owe to a company, second, from local government to particularly vulnerable constituencies: council tenants, social services clients, or children in residential care. In the USA, states have developed different rules to deal with the first situation, such as where local government officials trade, on behalf of their authority, with companies in which they have an interest. In a detailed analysis, Lawrence explores the regulatory frameworks used. He argues these range from a strict trustee standard to the more liberal, corporate director model that allows for some limited self-dealing.[10]

In the United States, self-dealing is not surprisingly a significant issue given the large number of local governments and the degree of business they each conduct. However, in Britain, self-dealing has received little attention. The criminal law may intercede in certain cases, but there have been few attempts to use equitable principles to define the legitimate boundaries within which self-dealing can occur.[11] This appears a surprising omission, particularly in light of the upsurge in tendering and contracting since the 1980s, rendering potential conflicts far more likely.

In relation to the second class—a duty to vulnerable people—fiduciary principles are slowly evolving based on standards of professionalism and confidentiality. However, the main fiduciary duty owed by local government is not to those who lack socio-economic power within the wider community. This does not mean the courts reject the relationship between fiduciary duty and vulnerability. Rather, in talking about the duty owed to contributors of taxation, judicial decisions portray taxpayers as a vulnerable constituency, at the mercy of local government expenditure decisions.

Conceptualising Local Government's Duty

In the main, existing research on LGFD focuses on the way the principle has been applied. Less attention has been given to its doctrinal conceptualisation. This is probably because writers in this area are more familiar with administrative and local government law than with principles of equity. Yet, the actual way fiduciary duty is conceptualised by the courts has considerable implications. If a different paradigm of fiduciary duty had been used, the courts might be talking about the fiduciary duty owed to socially vulnerable constituents other than— or rather than—taxpayers. This is not to suggest the courts have got it wrong, nor to ignore the historical trajectory which has produced the current paradigm.[12] Rather, it is to say that part of the problem of the way LGFD functions concerns the very conception of fiduciary duty itself. This conception both reflects the courts' understanding of local government and helps to reinforce it. First, the courts' use of a business paradigm to understand fiduciary duty structures notions of municipal excess in specifically neo-liberal ways. Second, the fusion of fiduciary and trust principles reinforces the construction of accountability according to a proprietary paradigm of belonging.

A commercial model

Despite the references to taxpayer vulnerability and local government's public identity, the courts have based their paradigm of LGFD on a quasi-contractual,[13] corporate model. Local taxpayers are implicitly equated with shareholders[14] who invest money in self-interested pursuit.[15] This analogy was expressed explicitly in *Prescott* v. *Birmingham Corporation*, a case concerning free travel for pensioners.[16]

There, discussing the fact that the only people who could complain about a 'trustee' running a public transport system and charging reduced fares were the beneficiaries or principals, Jenkins LJ stated:

> A similar situation might arise as between a company, or the directors of a company, running an omnibus undertaking with a similar right to charge fares, and the shareholders of such company ... [Quoting from another case:] [I]f it omit to exact the toll which is a consideration for the service, the shareholders would seem to be the only persons who can have a right to complain.[17]

Key elements within this fiduciary framework, then, are: entrusting property or other interests to another; who has discretion over their use; on the (agreed or accepted) basis that what is entrusted must be deployed for the principal's benefit.[18] Within this commercial paradigm, the fiduciary—here, local government—is perceived in two contradictory ways. On the one hand, councils, like company directors, are seen as actors with an agenda they would pursue were it not for legal restraint. At the same time, councils are seen as offering corporate, expert[19] action by means of which collective, private interests can be pursued. While this second image is based on ideas of trust and good faith, limitations are still imposed on the fiduciary's behaviour. These limitations are less concerned with constraining fiduciary self-interest, than in limiting the scope of their agency to those areas in which corporate action is deemed more effective than individual, private action. Thus, whereas in the first image, the fiduciary can pursue its own interests outside the scope of its fiduciary duty, in the second, the fiduciary does not exist as a corporate actor beyond that duty. We can therefore see, within this second image, a traditional narrative of government legitimacy and origins. In the formation of government, not all power is relinquished by the people, only that required for a more efficient, effective society. A government that exceeds its mandate in terms of the policies it develops, or that tries to appropriate more power, is constituted as despotic and illegitimate.

These two images of the fiduciary offer different conceptions of the limits on local government action. In the first, fiduciary duty provides the leash on local government's pursuit of its own interests. This leash has been variously interpreted, from requiring that councils prioritise their taxpayers' interests to stating that these interests form one set of considerations to be taken into account within the decision-making process. In the second image, council action is *defined* by its capacity to achieve, for taxpayers, services they could not achieve more effectively at an individual level. Yet, even if this second view is accepted, identifying which objectives can best be pursued through council action is deeply contested,[20] raising questions not only regarding the division between public and private, but also the allocation of functions between levels of government.

Since the 1980s, in particular, courts seem to have adopted the first image, both in recognising that councils can act beyond the remit of their fiduciary duty and in balancing the duty owed to taxpayers against that owed to other classes. However, underlying this approach are elements of the second image. This does not just relate to local government's duty to its taxpayers but to a more general notion of trust. In other words, local government must *never* pursue its own interests; its *raison d'être* is to act on others' behalf. In addition, the limits placed on its legitimate action are assigned on the basis that those activities permitted are the ones local government does 'best'.

Fusing fiduciary duty and trusts

The commercial norms expressed in the shareholder—company director paradigm of local government have been exacerbated by the trusts model to which it has been linked. The courts in the twentieth century have been chary of suggesting the taxpayer-local government relationship is one of trust. However, they have, in several instances, defined local government's duties as analogous to those of a trustee in charge of a trust fund (eg, see *Roberts*,[21] *Prescott*,[22] *Cumings*,[23] *Pickwell*,[24] and *St Albans C & DC*[25]). While the concept of trusts, like fiduciary duty, can be interpreted variously, the courts have chosen an interpretation which privileges the management of property on behalf of contributors. This meaning has been reinforced by the (con)fusion of trusts with fiduciary duty.[26] While both trust and fiduciary duty are intimately linked to a division between benefit and control, there are significant differences in their usual application.[27]

Trusts, particularly private ones, involve a distinction (at least conceptually) between settlor and beneficiary.[28] Indeed, trusts often function as a triadic relationship of settlor-trustee-beneficiary. Within the classical trust model, the settlor abdicates all rights in the property settled except for those retained within the trust deed. In contrast, fiduciary duty usually concerns a dyadic relationship in which the settlor and beneficiary are fused and there is frequently no clear *corpus* (trust property). In other words, the property interest at stake in fiduciary relations can be nebulous or even non-existent. In addition, a fiduciary model is unlike most trusts in that the principal (or contributor) often retains residual control over their interests, is able to direct or advise the fiduciary and has the capacity to renegotiate the relationship over time. What LGFD judgments have done, then, is to merge the *principal-centred* character of fiduciary duty with the *corpus* requirements of trust law. By combining fiduciary duty and trust law in this way, the rights of those who fund council services through taxation are emphasised, while the redistributive aspects (at least formally) of trusts, and the non or quasi-property basis of many fiduciary relationships are rejected[29] or ignored.[30]

Yet, as I suggested above, this corporate model of fiduciary duty is not the only paradigm possible. Other fiduciary frameworks are being developed, for instance, in the area of medicine and indigenous people's rights. Unlike the company director—shareholder model, these frameworks are less dependent on the principal class's proprietary interests,[31] or on the fiduciary's management of their assets.[32] I have discussed the possibilities posed by this alternative approach to fiduciary duty in more length elsewhere.[33] I mention it here simply to highlight the ideologies implicit within the paradigm used by the courts. In other words, the approach they adopted towards fiduciary duty was not inevitable, but the result of a particular history and understanding of local government. In the sections that follow, I explore this approach in more depth. My aim is to highlight the political character of the courts' interpretation of LGFD, particularly in relation to the identity, practices, and community of local government.

Taxpayers and their Interests

The courts' conceptualisation of fiduciary duty requires local government to act as a business. This is compounded by the courts' understanding of the interests of the beneficial class. Taxpayers' interests are equated with efficient, cost-effective services and business-like practice. Despite other changes in the application of LGFD, the interpretation of taxpayers' interests has remained largely frozen this century. Taxpayers are deemed in 1997 to want the same as those paying in 1927. Clearly, this ignores substantial changes in taxpayers' identity, in part the result of demographic shifts. The ratepayer can no longer be assumed to be a male head of household. Responsibility for paying local taxes is held by a far more diverse group of people, reflecting the existence of single-adult households, same-sex couples, cohabiting friends, as well as nuclear and extended families. It is also the result of more direct changes in government policy. For instance, since the early 1980s, more people have been brought into the net of local taxation—the result of Conservative government attempts to redistribute the impact of local tax increases. Alongside capping tax levels to protect payers, central government argued that local financial accountability would improve if all households felt the consequences of any rate rise.[34] Poorer households would be less inclined to vote for higher rates if they also became liable for the increase. Consequently, Conservative central government reduced rate rebates so more households were brought into the tax net, and then went on to individualise taxes through a *per capita* charge (replaced in the early 1990s by the council tax, a property tax with residual elements of a *per capita* strategy).

These shifts in taxpaying demography are significant because they question fundamentally the courts' construction of taxpayers as a single group with a unified set of interests unchanging over time. It therefore suggests the courts are not interested in identifying the real wishes of taxpayers but of using them to legitimate a particular set of neo-liberal norms. The lack of any real interest in taxpayers' interests was made particularly explicit in the little discussed case of *Cumings* v. *Birkenhead Corporation*.[35] This concerned a challenge by parents to the allocation of secondary schools for their children. Because their children had been

to Roman Catholic primary schools, they were only offered admission
to Roman Catholic secondary schools by the local education authority. However, parents' claim that this was a breach of the fiduciary duty
owed to them was rejected by Justice Ungoed-Thomas. He stated,

> The submission made before me was that, by limiting the expres-
> sion of parents' choice of schools, the defendant discriminated
> unfairly as between different classes of ratepayers ... the plaintiffs'
> submission appears to me to confuse the discriminatory application
> of rates ... with discrimination, not in the application of rates ... but
> in the course of acting as the local education authority ... as
> between classes of parents and children ... [36]

Discrimination between taxpayers is only relevant when it functions
as discriminatory application of the taxes. Taxpayers become their
taxes. This synecdochal role allows interests to be constituted homoge-
nously, despite the variety of people who pay taxes. Yet, in talking
about taxpayers—in making them stand in for local taxes—the courts
do two things. First they marginalise those taxpayers who do not wish
their council to be run on commercial lines and who do not see the
private firm as the paradigmatic organisational form. Second, they
reinforce a narrow conception of LGFD's scope. In this case, the court
is clearly concerned to restrict local government's fiduciary duty to
questions of expenditure. Where discrimination does not involve
spending, local residents qua taxpayers or others do not have recourse
to the courts as beneficiaries of a fiduciary duty. This does not mean
other forms of redress do not exist. As my discussion in chapter seven
makes clear, the courts have other ways of rejecting policies that
contravene judicial notions of the legitimate boundaries of local
government activity. However, it underscores the first of the two fiduciary images discussed above: only certain public actions are deemed
to fall within the scope of the duty, beyond these, providing the action
is lawful, local government can pursue other interests.

At the same time, the courts' restriction of fiduciary duty to questions of expenditure can be seen as disembodying taxpayers—reducing
them, as a class, to a column in a computerised ledger account.
However, the embodied taxpayer is brought back in two primary ways,

first, in relation to their taxes—who taxation belongs to is central to determining the kind of body local government is. Second, despite its metonymic role, the courts make constant reference to taxpayers' interests. In doing so, they constitute taxpayers and the wider community according to an individualistic, property-oriented paradigm of belonging.

Taxation—whose property?

Within a traditional model of political or democratic government, taxation *belongs* to the government; they can use the revenue as they wish, to pursue whatever political objectives are their priority. However, the introduction of fiduciary duty undermines local government's full ownership of its taxes.[37] It suggests instead that monies paid constitute a form of property administered by councils on behalf of their true owners: taxpayers. But why should taxation produce a residual right when, for example, council service charges do not? There is no requirement on local government to use revenue from directly provided services in any particular way. Those who pay to use municipal leisure facilities, for instance, cannot demand that the money they pay be used to improve the service, unless some form of statutory ring-fencing applies. Perhaps, charges are seen as *belonging* to local government because they are paid in exchange for a service. Customers receive benefit in consideration for the money expended; they therefore have no entitlement to anything further.[38] In contrast, local taxes are not paid as part of an exchange, except at the broadest political level. While we may receive services paid for out of our taxes, we cannot demand that we receive a particular benefit or, indeed, any personal benefit at all. Not surprisingly, taxes tend to be identified within neo-liberal discourse as an illegitimate 'taking'.

Within LGFD cases, the courts have moved between two approaches to the question of tax ownership. Early cases treated the rate fund as held on a kind of trust. Ratepayers had a beneficial interest but could not individually demand their share. Later cases moved away from this approach, in some instances stating explicitly that the money belonged to the authority[39] (although there are other recent cases where the courts still refer to contributors' money[40]). But does not the notion of LGFD inevitably imply that taxpayers retain an interest in their taxes even if they do not legally 'own' them? This may depend on how the basis to LGFD is conceptualised. If local government's fiduciary duty is based on an undertaking to act on behalf of contributors, taxpayers can be identified as retaining a residual property interest in the taxes they pay (the residual property right approach). If, however, fiduciary duty is based on taxpayers' vulnerability (power/vulnerability model), no residual ownership exists. The power and vulnerability model locates the fiduciary duty in the very fact that contributors have little or no control over the amount they pay in property taxes other than as voters. It is because local government is *government* that an obligation is placed upon it. In other words, it is because councils have the governmental power and authority to determine local tax levels—to extract money which ceases to belong to its payer—that a duty to consider the impact on future taxpayers is imposed.

Since the early 1920s, the courts have tended to oscillate between the two approaches. While cases in the latter half of the twentieth century treated the taxpayer as someone who should be protected from excessive (future) charges, other contemporary decisions suggested contributors retain some form of interest in funds already paid.[41] Yet, recognising this interest, however amorphous it may be, undermines the notion of local rates as taxation since the latter requires a complete cessation of ownership at the point of transfer.

Judicial interpretations of community

The second aspect of embodiment I wish to address concerns the way in which taxpayers as a class are understood. Taxpayers do more than simply legitimate market norms; they are also used to construct a particular image of the local community as individualistic and self-interested and as abstract, conservative and male.

Taxpayers as a class are constructed in two ways. First, by what they are not. While cases in the 1980s talked about the courts balancing interests, the notion of balancing taxpayers' interests against those of transport-users or council staff suggests the two groups are separate and not overlapping. The exclusionary character of the class of taxpayers was made particularly explicit in the 1991 case of *ex p. Knowsley MBC*.[42] There, Lord Justice Legatt suggested that, while disbanding the council's direct labour force might have immediate costs for community-charge payers in terms of redundancy costs, in the long run they could benefit. Evidently, taxpayers are not seen as members of the council's direct labour force, their family, neighbours or friends, nor local tradespeople reliant on their business.

At the same time, the figure of the taxpayer is intended to symbolise the generic and universal[43] juxtaposed against particularistic interests.[44] Transport-users, council tenants and employees may be owed a fiduciary duty but it is owed to them not as tenants or transport-users, rather as part of a larger community comprised of abstracted subjects. Yet as feminists and others have argued, this abstract subject is never neutral. She, or rather he, is ascribed particular characteristics—usually those of the dominant constituency. The taxpayer here is neither a socialist nor a feminist (*Roberts*[45]). Nor does he want local government practising philanthropy,[46] although, as *Prescott*[47] suggests, in outlawing subsidised transport for elderly people, *limited* benevolence may be acceptable—the taxpayer is evidently a donor rather than recipient of charity.

The notion of the taxpayer as simultaneously an exclusive and universal class feeds in to the courts' depiction of community. With a few exceptions (for example, Atkin LJ, *Roberts, ex p. Scurr,*[48] *St. Albans C & DC*[49]), most of the cases discussed in this chapter implicitly equate community with the taxpaying class. While many of the judgments refer to other classes: tenants, employees, transport-users and the elderly, taxpayers (as beneficiaries) remain paradigmatic. Their central positioning plays a normative role in challenging the specific communitarianism of electoral democracy, with its privileging of rights over obligations.[50] Because electoral democracy centres the voter, its image of community marginalises those who contribute financially but lack political franchise. Redefining community around the taxpayer reasserts that rights are contingent on obligations—freeriders do not belong—while commercial taxpayers, excluded from a modern suffrage-based image of community, become model members.[51]

As well as linking political accountability to financial contribution rather than electoral franchise, the taxpayer paradigm also depicts community itself along neo-liberal lines. In other words, communities are deemed to consist of self-interested individuals, lacking a collective conscience. *Ex p. Knowsley MBC*,[52] mentioned above, provides a good example of this. Here members of the community are deemed to benefit from the disbandment of the direct labour organisation because costs may be lowered. The social and economic cost of higher unemployment or of a decline in wages for local workers is ignored. The depiction of community by the courts is a minimalist portrayal. It reduces cultural values, norms and local concerns to the efficient use of taxes. It is also a despatialised conception (cf chapter three). Community interests are not only constituted ahistorically but as entirely unaffected by location. The fact that it is *local* workers who may lose their jobs or have their living standards brought down is treated as irrelevant.

This despatialising of local government is important. At a political level, a major justification for local democracy is geographical variation; local communities have different interests and local people know best what they are.[53] While parliamentary rhetoric in the previous chapter emphasised the importance of flexibility to allow for local variation in religious education, here no such allowance is made. Councils may be accountable to local taxpayers but these taxpayers have no spatial specificity or variation. At the same time, the courts' erasure of geography should not be overstated. In other cases, local conditions are considered. For instance, in chapter seven, I explore how the long history of hunting in the Quantocks played some role in the courts' judgment that hunting should be allowed to continue. Even in the cases discussed here, local conditions, such as industrial action or the election of a radical authority, enter judicial decisions. However, geographical specificity tends to occur at the level of context. The courts recognise, for instance, that local conditions will affect how councils balance different interests (for example, *Luby* v. *Newcastle-Under-Lyme*).[54] However, at the level of reading taxpayers' interests, or the character of the local community, geographical variation is almost completely ignored.

Fiduciary Duty in Judicial Review

While interpretations of taxpayers' interests have not changed since the early twentieth century, the weight and usage of fiduciary duty has undergone shifts.[55] Broadly, we can identify three phases (there are also many judgments which cut across this trajectory). The first period, until the middle of the twentieth century, placed considerable weight on local government's fiduciary duty, holding councils to be analogous to trustees. For instance, Lord Greene MR, in *Re Decision of Hurle Hobbs*, declared that taxpayers' interests are the 'real governing matter determining [local government's] action'.[56] This approach changed slowly, reaching its apotheosis in the 1980s when the courts declared that the interests of taxpayers must be balanced against other (non-fiduciary) interests.[57] In addition, the courts declared that they would not second-guess decisions,[58] providing a council could show it had considered the implications for local taxpayers and that the decision was neither unlawful nor blatantly unreasonable.

From the early 1990s, cases underwent a third, more radical shift in focus and approach. This change reflected the growth of compulsory competitive tendering and internal markets, as well as the decline in councils' financial, political and statutory capacity to subsidise public provision or augment salaries. Consequently, for the most part, these latter cases did not concern 'philanthropic' policies such as low rents and subsidised fares but licenses, leases and contracts. As a result, rather than judicial review focusing on whether the council had breached its fiduciary duty, LGFD was used *by councils* to strengthen their case against private contractors. Councils argued in court that their contractual and tendering decisions were in line with their fiduciary duty to get the best financial return, or to achieve the lowest costs for their taxpayers (for example, *Newcastle-upon-Tyne, ex p. Dixon*).[59]

Breaches: gifts, subsidies and discrimination

As a result of the particular way LGFD was applied in the mid-1990s, it tended not to form the target for legal challenge. Councils defended their contracts on, amongst other grounds, the fiduciary duty they owed, while opponents were left arguing that fiduciary duty should be given little weight when it came into tension with statute (for example, *Portsmouth City Council, ex p. Bonaco Builders*).[60] Most judicial discussion of LGFD breaches is therefore pre-1990. In the main, LGFD breaches tended to involve one of three things: 'excessive' tax increases, gifts to a particular class or discriminatory treatment. More fundamentally, the cases seemed to involve local government power being deployed to undercut or distort commercial market relations. For instance, *Roberts* v. *Hopwood*[61] concerned Poplar council's decision to pay above market wages, including and equal wages for men and women. In response, the House of Lords defined such payments as a gift. Thus, because they were not wages within the legal meaning of the term, they could not come within the council's wide statutory discretion. Similarly, Atkin LJ in the Court of Appeal stated, '[Local government] must determine the amount of wages as wages in an industrial system ... They are not to use the servant or his wages as a means of subverting existing institutions'.[62]

By itself, increased taxation has proven the least effective basis for a fiduciary challenge.[63] It does, however, provide the residual basis for other breaches, since the problem of 'profligacy', discrimination and 'gifts' is that they occur at the taxpayers' expense. Gifts or subsidies have come under particular attack for being particularistic—benefiting one group, such as transport users or council staff, over and above the general taxpayer class as described above. They have also been attacked as discriminatory—benefiting a class within a class. In *Prescott* v. *Birmingham Corporation*, Lord Justice Jenkins declared,

> In the absence of clear statutory authority for such a proceeding ... we would for our part regard [free travel for pensioners] as illegal on the ground that ... it would amount simply to the making of a gift or present ... to a particular section of the community.[64]

Other cases of discrimination relate to the way the financial burden is distributed between classes of taxpayers, as a result of subsidisation[65] or negligence.[66]

Yet not all discrimination falls within the scope of fiduciary duty. This is important for it highlights the stress placed by the courts on breaches involving financial resources rather than other forms of power. For instance, in the case of *Cumings* discussed above, Justice Ungoed-Thomas stated that although there was discrimination between classes of parents and children in the exercise of 'statutory duties and powers', this was independent of the application of the rates, and therefore not a matter of fiduciary duty.[67] Second, the notion of *acceptable* discrimination highlights the way in which judgments in this area are permeated by politics. For instance, in the case of *In re Decision of Walker*,[68] a special payment to male employees with children was deemed acceptable, partly because of the economic rather than 'philanthropic' reason for its introduction (distinguishing it from the earlier case of *Roberts* v. *Hopwood*),[69] but also because the council were not setting a lead as employers but rather following existing commercial practice.

> [A] local authority not only may, but ought to, have regard to the practices of private employers. ... [I]t may generally be assumed that a private employer is guided by commercial rather than philanthropic motives ... [T]he Birmingham Corporation, far from setting themselves up as model employers, are following the example of many of the joint stock banks and insurance companies. If local authorities were to be debarred from following a course which has commended itself to such profit-making employers, it is possible that they might be seriously hampered in their efforts to obtain the best services available and that the efficiency of local government would suffer accordingly.[70]

Other forms of acceptable discriminatory expenditure can be found in the early case of *Roberts* v. *Hopwood*. There, the court *required* local government to differentiate between men's and women's wages on the grounds that the labour market was currently structured so that women's labour could be purchased more cheaply than men's. While this particular form of discrimination would no longer be required or even permitted, there is still a basic principle that the courts will review discriminatory expenditure according to standards of reasonableness. This does not mean they will strike down any expenditure with which they disagree.[71] However, notions of what constitutes excessive unreasonableness are clearly highly political.[72]

A method of governing—business style

The concept of the gift and reasonable discrimination demonstrate two ways in which LGFD is permeated by political values. However, the promotion of particular norms does not depend on a fiduciary transgression. This point is often neglected by writers in the area who see the relevance of LGFD as entirely contingent on whether cases arise from its breach. In this chapter, I am equally interested in the principle's pervasive and naturalised status within legal argument and decisions even where it has no practical impact. Cases from the 1920s to the 1990s assert that local government's duty is to provide services on business lines. Repeatedly, the judgments deify business practice, juxtaposing it against some undefined bureaucratic 'other'.[73] This approach assumes a particular paradigm of business in which companies operate with absolute efficiency, according to short-term notions of profit. It also assumes that councils can operate as if they were private firms, and that this is an appropriate style for local government.[74] As I discuss further in chapters seven and eight, a business or managerial style is perceived as apolitical, in contrast to 'philanthropic' or socialist municipal practices. This value judgment is clearly apparent *In re Decision of Walker*[75] where the court referred to the *arbitrary* fixing of wages in *Roberts* v. *Hopwood*.[76] These wages were defined as arbitrary because they were fixed 'without consideration of any of those matters which *an employer, acting reasonably, would normally take into account*'.[77] The fact they were decided on the basis of progressive political beliefs did not make them any less arbitrary from this perspective, for ideology constitutes the antithesis of rational, economic principles applied in 'proper' management.[78]

Yet, do the courts really expect local government to behave like a private company? My focus in this chapter is on judicial dicta that inscribe local government according to a commercial business paradigm (this does not deny the substantial dicta that exist emphasising the *political* nature of local government).[79] However, even those judicial forces who privilege a business paradigm may be equivocal about fully applying commercial norms to local government.[80] Neo-liberal-ism may advocate the *marketisation* of local government through recharging systems, contracts and privatisation,[81] but local government as an unconstrained market actor is scarcely desirable. Local councils have the capacity to dominate markets as a result of their potential economic power, and ability to undercut through lack of a profit motive. In addition, political agendas lead councils to act commercially and non-commercially in anti-market ways. Consequently, although LGFD has been used principally to promote local government as a market actor, the courts have applied other principles, at the same time, to restrain local government's commercial activities.[82] One example is the judicial restriction on local government (speculative) activity in the financial markets (*Hazell*),[83] a second is the constraint placed on local government using its licensing powers as an income-producing asset without clear statutory authority (*Manchester City Council, ex p. Ling*)[84]. In both cases, the councils argued their actions were in pursuit of their fiduciary duty to ratepayers; in both cases these arguments were dismissed by the courts.

This use of fiduciary arguments by local councils in the 1990s highlights the way in which fiduciary duty is not simply a way of the courts saying 'no' to local government as appears the case from previous judgments. The marketisation of local government, however modified, does not simply confront councils but works through them. Yet, it would be wrong to assume that this means fiduciary duty is a facilitative technique. Rather, the shift here is one from direct governing to governing at a distance. The notion of governing at a distance identifies a process whereby government acts to structure the field of decisions rather than directly imposing rules or mandates.[85] In particular, it depends on actors governing themselves, internalising state norms, expertise and discourse in order to reach the 'right' decisions.

Despite the courts' reliance on district auditors, councils and taxpayers to initiate cases, the traditional judicial application of fiduciary principles to strike down council decisions can be seen as a form of governing directly. Governing at a distance, however, was also evident in local government's internalisation of fiduciary duty. Councils, in this sense, policed themselves. This was particularly apparent in the mid-1980s, when, as a result of high profile fiduciary decisions, councils ensured they went through the motions of giving adequate attention to financial and fiduciary implications.[86] But from the early and mid-1990s a more complex mode of governing at a distance became apparent. Councils were not simply formalistically considering their duty to taxpayers but using this duty to defend policy decisions which promoted economic efficiency, income maximisation and value for money.[87] Self-hailing as a fiduciary was no longer a rhetorical technique to obscure or gloss over controversial, redistributive initiatives but an interpellation that matched many councils' deeper sense of purpose.

Conclusion

As a taken-for-granted principle of administrative law, LGFD depicted, and helped to constitute, local government and its community according to a particular political logic. In exploring how this occurred, I have focused on several aspects: the application of fiduciary duty; conceptions of local tax ownership; taxpayers' interests; and the actual paradigm of fiduciary duty itself which identified the duty as being owed to the contributors rather than to the beneficiaries of local taxation.

Yet the impact of LGFD on local authorities has not been straightforward. On the one hand, fiduciary duty restrained council activity; on the other, authorities in the 1990s used it to defend their market practices. Similarly, fiduciary duty was used both to constitute local government as a market actor, while, simultaneously, being limited by the perception that local government, despite its duty to taxpayers, should not have the commercial freedom of other private actors (see also chapter seven). This was partly to protect private, commercial actors, and partly to subordinate local government within a hierarchical state framework. Thus, while councils were constructed as the servants of their taxpayers, they were also constructed as the subordinates of central government.

My analysis of LGFD therefore raises the question: what kind of body is local government? Judicial ambivalence over local government's governmental status functioned in various ways. First, the property relationship between local taxpayers and their taxes was used to undermine local government's authority. Within the 'residual property' approach, taxes were seen as not fully belonging to local government; as a consequence, councils' ability to use taxes to promote their political agenda was constrained. Moreover, the very ability of local government to function as a political body was called into question by denying them the right to 'tax'.[88]

The political identity and capacity of local government was also constrained through the use—implicit or otherwise—of a shareholder—company director paradigm. While some of the decisions discussed proclaimed local government's relative political autonomy, the notion of local government acting in pursuit of shareholder interests withdraws political discretion. Clearly, this model is not apolitical; as I explore in chapter seven, such managerial models of local government are highly politicised. However, their ability to appear apolitical is important. It is for this reason that I have stressed the ideological character of the beneficial class, and of the way in which their interests were judicially represented. To suggest local government owes a fiduciary duty to its contributors offers a seemingly positivist model of local government—it is simply doing what it must do. However, once we start to problematise the way in which taxpayers and their interests are constructed, and to ask why the duty is owed to taxpayers rather than other classes, the political implications of the framework being adopted become far more apparent.

LGFD in the twentieth century has become something of a judicial mantra—repeated often, but subject to little sustained consideration. Given that it has not been applied to other state institutions in relation to their 'contributors', should it continue to bind local government? Does it make sense for councils to owe a 'special' duty to their taxpayers or for taxpayers to be doctrinally exploited to legitimate neo-liberal and conservative values? There are two choices here; either LGFD should be declared dead or else revised so that the beneficial class or classes to whom a special duty of consideration is owed comprise those facing social, economic or physical disadvantage.

5 Declining Shakespeare

Governing School—Sex and Space

The previous chapter discussed how British courts constituted local government as excessive for making anti-market policy decisions, deemed outside its remit. Yet, implicit in my discussion was the issue of the courts' own excessive behaviour. How far should they go in structuring the actions of local government? The question of boundaries on legal authority highlights the difference between the conflicts in chapters four and five. When the courts declared that local government had gone outside its boundaries, local government, in the main, complied. However, in the conflict explored here, the subordinate body—a school—resisted their depiction as 'out of order'. Indeed, the school and its supporters went further to argue that it was the council that was behaving inappropriately, going far beyond its authority in a context of devolved powers. Both sides thus wielded 'excess' as a rhetorical tool: the school, according to its local education authority (LEA), was attempting to do something no state body should—challenge heterosexuality; while the local education authority, school governors and supporters declared, had exceeded the formal review powers allocated to it.

This is the story of Hackney Council versus Jane Brown, headteacher of Kingsmead School, whose rejection of ballet tickets for her primary school pupils in the autumn of 1993 made national headlines for days in succession. It became the biggest story of municipal lunacy since 'Baa Baa Green Sheep', and the banning of Enid Blyton from local libraries. For headteacher Jane Brown's refusal was not any refusal, nor was the ballet any ballet. This is a story of *Romeo and Juliet* rejected on the grounds of exclusive heterosexual love.

At one level, the rejection of ballet tickets by a London headteacher is a parochial tale in which a head's 'error of judgment' led to public castigation by her local authority and the subsequent mobilisation of support by governors, parents and others. However, the conflict can also be read within a wider educational context, as an example of what can happen when a school steps out of line. British educational history, as elsewhere, is replete with examples of local radicalism. London's William Tyndale School became a *cause célèbre* in the 1970s when teachers decided to educate pupils in ways that thwarted the role of schooling in the reproduction of capitalist relations.[1] Schools have also proven a focal point for radical work on gender and race. Yet, it is not always schools that take the radical stand in relations with their local authority. While William Tyndale provided an example of an LEA combating and censuring school-based radicalism, in other instances, the LEA has taken the initiative in attempting to develop and implement new ideas, often in the face of local opposition. For instance, as I discussed in chapter three, challenges to traditional Christian education largely came from progressive LEAs developing multifaith teaching.

This chapter, however, deals with an LEA, Hackney Borough Council, engaged in less progressive action. My analysis of how Hackney (a London authority with a reputation for disorder and 'loony leftism') attempted to enforce its will upon a disobedient school needs to be situated within the changes brought about by the Education Reform Act 1988 (see also chapter three). A taken-for-granted truth of the educational changes that occurred during the 1980s is that they shifted relations of control and belonging. The Education Reform Act (ERA) 1988, in particular, was supposed to have taken schools away from local education authorities, and, according to government rhetoric, handed them over to local communities (parents and business people) by extending governing body power.[2] However, the transfer was not as straightforward as that narrative might suggest.[3] In the case of Kingsmead school and Hackney Council, the local authority attempted to continue governing despite its loss of formal power.

An Act of Ideological Idiocy

Kingsmead Primary School is located in an economically deprived, geographically isolated, district of Hackney's East London. Until 1990, the school was governed by the Inner London Education Authority; post-abolition, Hackney council took control. The late 1980s and early 1990s was a turbulent period for the school with high turnover of teachers, and a poor official inspection. In 1992, Jane Brown was formally appointed to the headship of the school.[4] In June 1993, a visit by the inspectorate removed Kingsmead from the 'at risk' list, identifying good leadership and staff morale and a 'warm, caring environment'.[5] Then, in the autumn of 1993, Jane Brown received a call from Ingrid Haitink, on behalf of the Paul Hamlyn Westminster Week, inquiring whether Kingsmead would be interested in subsidised tickets to a ballet of *Romeo and Juliet*. Her attention on other matters, Jane Brown said no. The woman persisted. Brown considered a series of reasons why the ballet was unsuitable, including its place within an equal opportunities curriculum. She ended with the comment, 'I could even say its heterosexist'.[6]

Shortly afterwards, Haitink wrote to Hackney council describing general take-up of tickets.[7] The letter indicated disappointment that Kingsmead had refused to participate on grounds of the ballet's heterosexual content.[8] Several months after the letter had been filed by the council, it appeared in the London daily newspaper, the *Evening Standard*. Immediately, Hackney council geared into action. A press statement was issued asserting 'anger and disbelief'.[9] Pat Corrigan, Chair of Education, described Brown's objection as 'an act of ideological idiocy and cultural philistinism'.[10] As the media descended on Kingsmead School, the LEA quickly proffered a written apology in Jane Brown's name;[11] it referred to her dismay at distressing parents, pupils and staff by the 'unwelcome media attention'.[12]

> Because of the nature of her comment about the play [sic], it didn't take long for the tabloids to think she might be a lesbian. They looked up the electoral register, found she was sharing with a woman, then sieged the house.[13] (Trade union representative, interview)

Within a couple of days of the story's initial coverage, press insinuations began to circulate about Brown's relationship to the Chair of Governors at the time of her appointment; quickly the LEA shifted ground to query the process of her appointment.[14] Gus John, then Director of Education, declared: 'I have had to expand the scope of my enquiry substantially following fresh allegations in the media that there may have been a conflict of interests in the appointment...'[15] Brown was called to account for her relationship, an interrogation which extended to whether she had been coached for her job interview by a member of the appointments committee.[16] John declared if a prima facie case of misconduct was identified, he would recommend suspension.[17]

This direction followed,[18] but was rejected at a meeting of Kingsmead's governing body.[19] Governors' dismissal of the LEA recommendation received applause later that evening from a large meeting of parents. Initially critical of Brown's decision, parents turned their anger on the Director of Education for his lack of support.[20]

> At the time we thought Jane Brown was in the wrong ... we believed we should have been notified and given the choice ... At the end you'd have to pay for the tickets, Jane would have had to take £200 out of the school fund for a coach ... (Parent, interview)

As the attack escalated, a campaign to defend Jane Brown and Kingsmead School developed, and the Kingsmead Support Group was established. Backing came not only from local parents but also from Hackney Teachers Association, Hackney Lesbian and Gay Workers Group, and other feminists and lesbians.[21] One woman described getting involved after she 'saw on tele a Hackney dyke being attacked, forced "out"'. (Supporter, interview) Another gave her account of community mobilising.

> There must have been a hundred lesbians at Featherstone Street [a community building] in the first week of it breaking ... There were groups all over the country as well; and she'd got in the first four months, she got something like nine hundred letters and some of them were from Canada and Australia ... and she did get some

horrific hate mail in all of that as well ... And I felt it was a bit like Greenham, you know, a terribly, terribly small version of that obviously, but it had that permission to just get on and respond from your perspective within your community. (Supporter, interview)

Furious at the governors' refusal to support his recommended suspension, Gus John declared he would appeal directly to the Secretary of State.[22] John Patten, the Minister, had already condemned the ticket refusal as 'political correctness'.[23] However, given his promotion of devolved powers, intervening in support of an Inner London, Labour LEA, against a school headteacher with parental support, was more political 'hot potato' than he wished to carry. In exercising responsibility, parents had the right to choose badly—indeed, how else would they learn? Thus, despite press criticism, Patten declined to intervene on the grounds that the governing body had not displayed the requisite lack of reasonable behaviour.[24]

Hackney council continued its attack. The Director of Education sent a letter to all the borough's staff, condemning the 'spurious and fundamentalist dogmatism' which led Jane Brown to reject the tickets.[25] Yet, as the council's attack escalated, Kingsmead governors also grew more assertive. Having met to reconsider the recommendation to suspend Brown, and form a disciplinary panel,[26] governors once more refused to suspend or hand authority over to the LEA. However, after further LEA pressure, governors decided to take the matter into their own hands and establish an inquiry. Progress was delayed by the council challenging the panel's membership and terms of reference. Outing one of the inquirers, Hackney suggested she had shown bias in favour of Brown by sending a letter criticising the LEA to Gus John at the start of the episode. They demanded her removal on the grounds that the inquiry would otherwise lack legitimacy. The governors refused. The inquiry report was formally completed on 8 June 1995; it found, for lack of evidence, no case against Jane Brown.[27]

Governing Techniques

> The council wanted to distance themselves from the school, and
> have the power to change it. LMS[28] [Local Management of Schools]
> meant they couldn't do both. (Trade union representative, inter-
> view)

Hackney's attempt to reassert control over Kingsmead school functioned through the construction of proprietary relations of belonging
and of non-belonging. In order to explore the complex character of the
council's strategy, I draw on the three forms of governing as set out in
chapter one: governing directly, mid-way and at a distance. Governing
directly refers to a personalised, direct relationship of rule in which
the parties to the relationship are clearly visible. The demands of
governance are equally visible since they are externalised as commands
or prohibitions rather than being internalised by the governed subject.
In mid-way governing, the governing body attempts to structure the
actions of its governed subject; however, the governed subject sees the
rules being established as ploys or tactics rather than internalising
them as conduct. Mid-way governing tends to operate within situations of conflict. In contrast to direct governing, it often reflects a
breakdown in a formal, hierarchical relationship. The governing body,
unable to deploy effectively mandates, instructions and prohibitions,
is forced to use more indirect, strategic techniques that will generate
the outcomes it requires without being able to demand them specifically. Finally, governing at a distance guides the actions of subjects
through the production of expertise and normative inculcation so that
they govern themselves.[29] It also includes governing by establishing the
rules of conduct. Subjects internalise these rules in the sense that they
'know' their powers, duties, functions, responsibilities, and what is
appropriate or inappropriate behaviour. A key quality of governing at
a distance, as I am using it, is that it appears impersonal and anonymous. The rules established are both general in character and do not
appear to originate anywhere in particular.

Given devolved legal powers, several questions arise: did Hackney
move from direct to indirect forms of governing? If it could no longer

govern directly, was it able to govern at a distance? Or was it stuck with the difficulties and inadequacies of mid-way governing? The question of Hackney's methods of governing is linked to the issue of belonging. Was governing deployed as a means of maintaining or creating a particular relationship of belonging or non-belonging between the LEA and school? Or were belonging and non-belonging themselves deployed as strategies of governing? My argument is that both occurred. Belonging and non-belonging functioned both as strategies and as wider political projects. This dual role is important to understanding the complexity of the relationship between strategy and objectives, and to understanding how, for instance, *non*-belonging as a strategy could be used to achieve as an objective a particular relationship of *belonging*.

Alien, wilful, subjugated space

The spatialisation of the conflict between Kingsmead and Hackney council is a central focus of this chapter. From the perspective of Hackney, it involved a complex manoeuvre in which Kingsmead was simultaneously constructed as alien, wilful and subordinate space. The initial depiction of Kingsmead as alien space allowed the council to distance itself from Brown's actions.[30] Articulating a mainstream Labour agenda, members of Hackney council were determined to divorce themselves from any trace of their previous 'loony left' image: the devolvement of powers as a result of the Education Reform Act 1988 meant school decisions were the responsibility of schools not of the LEA. Yet the desire to appear respectable and responsible not only meant publicly separating themselves from the school's action but also demonstrating their ability to 'deal' with it. Thus, at the same time as saying 'This has nothing to do with us', Hackney reasserted its authority. As a result, the image of Kingsmead as alien space was overlaid by other representations linked to the process of redomestication or 'reigning in'. First, the school was constituted as transparent; Hackney could therefore act directly against the head within a hierarchical, managerial relationship.[31] Second, Brown and Kingsmead were joined together as wilful and brazen, clearly in need of disciplining. These contradictory processes of alienation and domestication wound through the discursive, disciplinary and legal techniques deployed by Hackney council.

Missed cultural opportunity

Rejecting *Romeo and Juliet* tickets on grounds of sexual orientation raises profound questions for progressive education. The conflict that ensued between the council and school was partly a product of their very different approaches to cultural equality. Brown's approach, in line with feminist and much anti-racist politics, involved focusing on how readers, in this case children, would interpret the text (through seeing the ballet). If their interpretation seemed likely to reinforce modern conceptions of inequality, viewing (or reading) would be a regressive rather than progressive educational decision.

The council, however, took a more assimilationist approach. 'Equal Opportunity is about working class estate dwellers ... in the neighbourhood around Kingsmead School having the opportunity to go to a renowned centre of cultural production where middle class and rich people go...'[32] For Hackney, the important issue was working class access to 'high brow' culture. In contrast to Brown, whose concern was the harm a problematic text could engender, the council stressed the benefits to working-class and minority ethnic children from being introduced to classical, English texts. 'Councillor Pat Corrigan, Chair of Education, said: "We want every Hackney child to have access to all the great works of art and literature. We positively encourage theatre, ballet and opera companies to come into our schools and work with our pupils...." Council Leader John McCafferty, who is himself an English teacher was quick to back the views expressed ... "I am currently teaching this great play to my 13 year old pupils. It is one of Shakespeare's best-known and best-loved plays."'[33]

Hackney's approach resonates with the celebration of elite English culture discussed in chapter three. There I explored how MPs and peers across the political spectrum asserted the importance and value of children learning and appreciating England's Christian, literary heritage. For Hackney's Director of Education, Gus John, British 'high' culture formed an integral aspect of challenging racism. '[Gus John] wrote a lot about the denial of culture for Black children, not only their own culture, but the culture in which they were expected to survive and succeed...' (Governor, interview)[34] At the same time, it is hard not to see this move by the council as, at least partly, a strategic ploy—supporting Shakespeare on the basis that to do otherwise would make Hackney appear to the wider public as still immersed in 'ultra left' politics. Shakespeare thus came to stand for respectable and responsible governance.

Ridiculing sexual space

Kingsmead was also identified as 'failing' space as a result of its inappropriate sexualisation. Despite the formal inclusion of sexuality within Hackney's equal opportunities policy, schools were not considered by the LEA to be appropriate arenas for equality of sexual orientation.[35] Schools should not actively challenge heterosexual bias nor promote homosexuality as an equally valid life choice; to do otherwise would transgress powerful social norms. Gus John declared: the idea a school is against heterosexism is explosive in the current context.[36]

Brown's reference to heterosexism, in conjunction with her own 'outed' sexuality, enabled Hackney to represent Kingsmead as space that had breached the sexual consensus and could no longer be trusted. Kingsmead was pursing its own agenda, at odds with the interests of local children and parents. Deploying a narrative of authentic community in which Kingsmead belonged to working-class residents on the local estate, Hackney portrayed the school as having been colonised by middle-class lesbians, who brought with them inappropriate practices and values. Gus John stressed the privileged, proprietary status of heterosexual parents when he declared, at a Kingsmead parents meeting on 25 January 1994, if it were not for heterosexual relationships, there would be no Kingsmead School.[37]

John's strategy of ridiculing Brown's decision, while emphasising parents' ownership of Kingsmead, was intended to function as a form of governing at a distance, mobilising parental disgust so that they would demand Brown's suspension.[38] This strategy failed. As a mechanism, however, for engineering more direct forms of governance, ridicule was not entirely ineffective. For although ridicule asserted Kingsmead's distance from the authority, at the same time, the *right* to ridicule affirmed the existence of, first, a relationship, and second, one that was asymmetrical. Indeed, ridicule largely targets 'uppity' behaviour—in this instance, an institutional body getting above itself. In doing so, it asserts the contingent character of institutional independence on obedience to received norms. In other words, non-belonging is not absolute but depends on good behaviour. Once the internalisation of governance norms breaks down, a school will be reigned in. Yet, the capacity to 'reign in' constitutes the body as never fully independent. Thus, the mocking portrayal of space as alien reconstitutes it as wilful, that is, space that has exceeded its authority and discretion. This very reconstitution functions as a form of domestication in which the school is produced as belonging to the authority.

Disciplinary strategies[39]

Hackney's focus on the oppressive aspects of Jane Brown's ticket refusal—her denial of equal access and of freedom—was intended to facilitate indirect governing and spatial distancing. Parents, to whom the school was now accountable, needed to take measures to ensure their children received the cultural resources they needed (rather than the ones politically correct professionals believed they should have). However, Hackney's use of disciplinary measures took a different turn. Here Brown and Kingsmead came to represent subordinate excess— a surplus of freedom—against which the LEA needed to reassert boundaries.[40] In other words, Kingsmead, through its head, had transgressed the prohibition on homosexuality's public status.

Hackney's disciplinary response took two forms: an investigation— in which accusations could be aired on the basis that the sifting of narratives would uncover the truth; and the subsequent recommended suspension. These actions, under the direction of Gus John, confirmed Hackney's continuing ability to govern directly. Initiating an inquiry, with its subsequent demand for suspension, constituted the council as 'in control'. This was made particularly evident by John's early behaviour when he called Brown to account for her actions, both in relation to her telephone conversation with Haitink and *vis à vis* her earlier headship appointment.[41] Any notion of headship professionalism and autonomy was thoroughly dismantled by this 'right' of a manager to demand recall of a telephone conversation held months previously, to scrutinise the offered 'confession' against another version, and then to declare gross misconduct on the grounds that they failed to tally.

At the same time, Hackney's action made visible the limits of its capacity to govern directly by provoking Kingsmead's governing body to assert its own legal powers. 'How Gus John refers to us constantly is that we are out of control ... We were out of control of the local authority, but we should have been, we were LMS, we didn't have to be controlled by the local authority'. (Governor, interview) Another governor stated,

> Gus John went on his own into the enquiry, and at the end of that he decided that Jane should be suspended, and we were like, 'Well, you've gone about three steps before us, because for one you shouldn't have been doing that investigating; and two, you can advise suspension but you can't make us follow it ... They wanted the power, they wanted the authority because they feel they are the authority. I don't think they knew the full extent of LMS themselves ... because the things they were asking to do, it was quite clear they had no power. (Governor, interview)

Despite its lack of formal legal power, and despite the fact its actions met with resistance, Hackney continued to place pressure on Kingsmead. Initially, a key objective was to compel the governors to withdraw their authority, so the council could suspend Brown and direct the investigation.[42] To engineer this, Hackney exploited technical legal provisions alongside a constant flow of information and 'advice'. This latter portrayed Kingsmead governors as 'out of their depth'. Given their lack of experience and expertise, the sensible choice would be to defer to Hackney's superior knowledge. This form of mid-way governance did not abate when governors initiated their own inquiry but continued throughout its term. Several interviewees described the intimidatory techniques used by the council, where educational background, senior management status, and masculinity were deployed to undermine investigating governors. 'It was only when we attended with a very senior barrister ... that [Gus John] changed his body language, his approach changed within seconds of this man walking into the room'. (Governor, interview)

The LEA's attempt to intimidate Kingsmead governors by portraying them as inexperienced entwined with other techniques of mid-way governance to produce a series of tactical manoeuvres. Interviewees described harassment, deflection, challenges to the terms of reference, and disputing of investigators' credibility.[43] 'He kept extending the terms of reference. He wanted to sidetrack and overwhelm us.' (Governor, interview)

> The LEA was trying to get us to investigate more of Jane Brown— they already had things to do with Jane Brown because of the appointment of a teacher. The LEA tried to introduce this at a later date—we refused to deal with it because the school was dealing with it ... We had real difficulty accessing the LEA; they said they didn't agree with the remit, wanted the questions before the interviews ... didn't see why we should have counsel and a solicitor... The LEA was trying to manipulate the investigation panel. First they complained about [one member] then [the other]. (Governor, interview)

Hackney's tactical engagements failed to generate compliance.

> They were telling us to jump, and we weren't asking how high. We were actually saying well, we don't want to jump. ... They started seeing us as defiant, like, you know, a child. 'You know, I'm the big boss, or I'm the parent and I tell you what to do and you do it. You don't question me. You don't argue with me. You just do it.' (Governor, interview)

Governors refused to concede that they were out of their depth, and resisted the council's attempts to control the disciplinary process. Consequently, each municipal tactic became an incitement for war as governors opposed the council's terms of reference, their choice of venues, and their determination of who would be present. Yet, while governors resisted LEA incursions, mid-way governance proved successful in one major respect. Although the LEA was unable to determine the investigative outcome or carry out disciplinary procedures directly, it did successfully compel the governing body to act, broadly identifying the issues to which the governors were forced to respond. As one governor described,

> The tickets we knew we had to address, that felt very straightforward. ... But once she was accused of being improperly appointed, you know that was very serious, a very serious thing ... For a whole range of reasons we had to and wanted to investigate that, and if it was found to be true we wanted to act on it, we had no doubts about that, absolutely no doubts ... However good a person is ... there's no way I want to be identified as having an all-girls' network ... you know, jobs for the girls ... (Governor, interview)

Arguably, this influence was less a product of mid-way governance than of governing 'at a distance'. In other words, governors complied in holding an inquiry, not because Hackney effectively pressured or persuaded them to, rather because of the authority of liberal norms of propriety, professionalism and due process. Yet, if we seek the origins of these norms, through which Kingsmead governed itself, they appear to have little to do with the council. They also cannot be said simply to originate with central government. Instead, they go to the heart of liberal rule. Institutions possess a *degree* of autonomy because they operate, at least formally, according to agreed public principles. It was thus not surprising that Hackney's deployment of them would prove successful. But Hackney also went beyond rearticulating and mobilising hegemonic, liberal, procedural norms. Their achievement was to link them to dominant political values so that it was Jane Brown's lesbianism and critique of heterosexism that became the subject of interrogation. While this did not receive unquestioning sanction from the investigators, they were unable effectively to mount a challenge. Several unsuccessful attempts were made to interrogate the council's action of leaking information to the press;[44] however, using the investigation as a mechanism through which heterosexual, educational bias, rather than Brown's behaviour, could be problematised proved impossible.

Legal techniques

The impact of disciplinary measures cannot be understood separately from the role played by law. Equally, the ability of governors to resist the council has to be located within the context of their new legal powers. At one level, law's impact appears straightforward: Hackney could not govern directly because Kingsmead no longer 'belonged' to the authority. Formal legal powers over school management and resourcing had shifted to the governing body. However, the wider impact of law is more complex. First, despite devolved powers, law contributed to the council's portrayal of Kingsmead as subordinate space within a supervisory relationship. Second, law facilitated and symbolised Kingsmead's alienation from the council—what had once been a relationship was now a battleground.

From the beginning, Hackney used its statutory powers to facilitate governing directly. This may seem a surprising point, since under the education reforms of the 1980s, LEAs possess few legal powers with which to compel schools to act. However, what Hackney did was not primarily to enforce legal rights, rather to identify legal powers that could be exercised if Kingsmead failed to act appropriately. Directions, therefore, were not themselves the product of legal authority, but issued as 'good practice' which, if ignored, would lead to the council exercising its residual authority against the school. For instance, when Kingsmead governors declared they would not suspend Jane Brown, the LEA drew attention to the council's residual legal responsibility to oversee school practice and staff behaviour.[45] If Kingsmead 'got it wrong'—failing to take proper account of LEA advice and thus failing to act reasonably—Hackney could take further action through the Secretary of State.[46] In this way, Hackney used the law as a framework within which negotiations could take place.[47] They also used it more explicitly to exert leverage. For instance, at one point Gus John suggested that if governors agreed to suspend Brown, they would be allowed to control the disciplinary panel, but that if they refused, the local authority had the power to take over the proceedings and carry out the suspension themselves.[48] (This threat was not enforced since the council lacked the legal authority to take over proceedings once Kingsmead governors called its bluff.)

Kingsmead governors did not respond favourably to the negotiating framework Hackney established and Hackney was repeatedly obliged to yield. However, while legal subordination did not prove an effective mechanism of direct control, it functioned more productively as a form of mid-way governance. While some areas of law assume a relationship between the parties only at the moment of breach or legal action, education law assumes a pre-existing legal and administrative relationship. Hackney's use of this relationship to assert a legal literalism—ensuring Kingsmead complied with a host of minor statutory requirements[49]—proved one of the more successful components of their strategic game-playing. The authority of law meant that although governors demonstrated proper conduct, they were forced to respond to the constant requests for information, and endure the repeated delay and insecurity such requests entailed.

Law was also relatively effective at a symbolic level in representing the alienated character of relations between the council and school once Kingsmead made it clear that they would not comply with Hackney's demands. From the moment Kingsmead sought outside legal advice, Hackney retorted with its own brand of legal formalism. Letters to the governors were sent by Hackney Legal Services rather than the LEA as had been the previous practice; governors were addressed as 'Dear Sirs' rather than by name; and the school was informed that all correspondence should now go between their respective lawyers rather than between the parties concerned.[50] These measures by Hackney council all highlighted the new, adversarial character of the relationship. Kingsmead's turn to law to resist Hackney's demands constituted a breakdown of loyalty and hence of the council's reciprocal obligations: Kingsmead was 'on its own'.

The alienation of Kingsmead can be seen as reversing the process of domestication described above. Here legal techniques were used to push the school away so that it would be governed at a distance according to impersonal legal norms. At the same time, it is hard to see these tactics as anything other than intimidating. Hackney council wielded the threat (and taste) of alienation in the expectation that Kingsmead would shy away from pushing the relationship to breaking point. However, the school's anger at Hackney, alongside its increased self-confidence, meant it was willing to accede to some cutting of ties.

Hackney's deployment of discourse, discipline and law challenge the notion that a loss of formal power produces an absence of will, desire and capacity to govern. Devolved legal powers might have caused Hackney LEA to govern differently; however, the Council's interest in governing remained firmly evident. Also apparent was Hackney's ability to structure Kingsmead's actions, although not always in the way intended. In the section that follows, I explore the strategies of Kingsmead supporters in more depth. In place of Hackney's right to govern, supporters asserted the rights of governors, staff and head; and in place of the council's proprietary relationship of belonging, supporters expressed a reciprocal conception based on loyalty, justice and trust.[51] Exploring supporters' portrayal of Kingsmead highlights the gap between their image of the school and that of Hackney's. For where Hackney portrayed Kingsmead according to the trope of alien, subordinate and wilful, Kingsmead supporters emphasised family, trust and home.

Kingsmead Resists: The Construction of Community

> It's not a bad thing [the LEA] are alienated if it means they stay away from the school if they can't do anything positive. (Ex-governor, interview)

Parents' rights

Parents formed one of the main constituencies supporting Jane Brown.[52] Reflecting a common hostility towards LEA bureaucracy[53] and its perceived excesses, compounded by their own interactions with the council as local authority tenants, Kingsmead parents claimed a relationship to the school that simultaneously disassociated it from the LEA. As one ex-governor put it: 'People felt it was their school; it was very heartening'. A major cause of parental hostility to the LEA was owing to the way parents saw the council as willing only to relate to the school hierarchically and only in disciplinary situations. When a more lateral, supportive relationship was required, the LEA remained absent. This perception is clear from the following extracted discussion which took place amongst a group of parents I interviewed.

It's our school. It's our children's school. It's the parents' school; I tell you the parents have done more for this school than anything the LEA ever have ... You ask who runs the fetes and who does the discos and all that? Do you ever see the LEA down here?...

The authority come in when they want to ban something. When they want to cut grants, they want to cut the supply teachers, take money away from the school, that's when the authority is here. But when you need them, when you want backing....

They won't come....

They won't come near our door. (Parents, interviews)

In distancing Kingsmead from Hackney, parents constructed a network of loyalty and community that placed Brown at the centre, as the locus of authority. 'She is headmistress in this building, looks after our children, and she should be allowed to do exactly what she wants'. (Parent, interview) 'Jane Brown takes a lot of interest—spends more time with the children'. (Parent, interview) Brown's affirmation and defence of Kingsmead as a community constituted according to norms of equality and respect, affirmed parents' own sense of ownership, motivating them in turn to defend their head. As one parent stated:

It was a lousy LEA because they didn't back her in the first place, they were behind whoever it was 100 per cent to get her out; that's the main reason, so you can't say they're a good education authority because she put her guts into this school and they were just prepared to kick her out and not think twice about it. (Parent, interview)

Supporters deployed three techniques—rhetorical, symbolic and physical—in rearticulating Kingsmead around Brown, and away from the LEA. These were a discourse of parental rights; the metaphorical deployment of family/home; and fortification. The mobilisation of parents' rights within the dispute was, one of its most surprising qualities. Watching the television news in January 1994, the story of a Hackney headteacher assailed for promoting lesbian and gay equality seemed fairly routine. However, the image of parents holding placards and being interviewed outside the school in *support* of the headteacher seized my attention. Something unusual was happening.

Parental rights functioned as a dominant element within Conservative government discourse during the 1980s (see chapter three), allied to an anti-professional, consumerist approach to education.[54] Expressing more than parental 'choice', it functioned as a signifier of a right-wing educational agenda in which parental common-sense would be deployed against the spectrum of 'radical', child-centred ideas.[55] In the mid-1980s, the rhetoric of parents' rights targeted lesbian and gay equality initiatives in education. In the London Borough of Haringey, an organisation hailing itself in the language of parents' rights—the Parents' Rights Group—was formed specifically to combat lesbian and gay educational work.[56] Yet at Kingsmead, eight years later, parents' rights were being expressed in support of a lesbian head who had rejected Shakespeare for its hetero-sexism.

It is important, however, not to over-estimate the oppositional character of parental rhetoric. Although parents publicly declared their support for Jane Brown, and used their formal educational status as parents to criticise the LEA, they did not support the grounds on which the *Romeo and Juliet* tickets had been rejected. Kingsmead parents did not invert the discourse of parents' rights but refined its hierarchy. Their priority was the common-sense right to a good head who, unlike some members of the local council, cared about the school; Brown's reputation as an excellent educator was the main theme of their argument. Consequently, Hackney's demand for suspension seemed to jeopardise educational quality in order to punish a silly decision. Parents perceived the former as far more important.

At the same time, despite government rhetoric of rights, parents, in the main, did not see themselves as having much power. As the group of parents, I interviewed, suggested,

No, we've got no rights ... They don't listen to you ... We like to feel that, well, we was behind her 100 per cent, but I don't think all what we'd done didn't really save her job ...

Although they rallied to defend Jane and Kingsmead school, they did not believe that the school belonged to them. Yet, in part, their defence of Jane Brown was owing to the fact she represented their aspirations for equality, respect and inclusion against a council that symbolised the apparent reality of their powerlessness.

Family and home

Despite scepticism about the extent to which Kingsmead was theirs, parents did, nevertheless, articulate a vision of belonging. However, given their scepticism, it is not surprising that their identification of belonging revolved around metaphors of family and home rather than ones of ownership. These kinship metaphors emerged in the process of community-building as parents defined themselves against the media and political establishment.

> We beat off the press, we beat off the media, we beat off Gus John, so we're not bad are we really? ... We found that we were a community ... We were all packed in this school and we all fought...And we still say now, if anything was to come up now...If she wanted to paint the school red, and they wanted it blue, then we'd still be behind her, and the day they dismiss her or suspend her or ... That would be the end of Kingsmead school. (Parents, interview)

In the process of communal self-definition, a trenchant familial discourse was expressed, as one parent articulated:

> I mean a majority of people that work in the school all live on the estate as do the children...and you just know everybody knows everybody ... It's just a big family ... They tried to break down the family and they just couldn't do it ... because we just stuck together as a family. (Parent, interview)

Parents depicted school space as familial, yet as home-space it excluded more than the media and LEA. While one parent interviewed referred to the exclusionary effects of estate racism, homosexuality also held an ambivalent place. In their writing, Johnston and Valentine explore the home as a place of hegemonic heterosexuality.[57] They argue that this generates difficulties for lesbians who are forced to leave their sexuality outside. While, at one level, Kingsmead parents accepted their head's sexuality, the majority of those I spoke to perceived lesbianism as less acceptable than heterosexuality and as inappropriate within the curriculum.

> As the kids were coming out of this school, the press were coming up to them and I know for a fact that they was like asking little boys if Jane preferred teaching little girls than little boys ... Up until that time my boy didn't know what a lesbian was or a homosexual or anything and I didn't want him to know, not at eight or nine years' old. ... I don't want my children thinking that sex between two women is right, because, I'm sorry, but I don't think it is ... I don't want it being taught at school ... Normal every day sex education should be taught in every school ... I don't believe that in sex education that you should be implying that it's okay if you go with a woman and it's okay if you go with a man. I don't believe that ... It shouldn't be pushed...and saying that this is an everyday thing, because as far as I'm concerned it's not. (Parents, interview)

Kingsmead might be family but, when it came to sexuality, parents saw the school as public space. Jane Brown's sexuality was her own, private business.

> Whatever Jane is, it's her own private business ... it's nothing to do with the way she runs the school.... We looked at it this way. She comes in here ... She does her job ... What she does when she goes home, behind her closed doors, that is her business. (Parents interview)

Indeed, the power of this belief was a major factor in the parents' attack on Hackney council, which they saw as undermining Jane Brown's right to privacy.[58] The privatisation of lesbian sexuality may appear a reactionary move given heterosexuality's accepted place within the Kingsmead community. At the same time, parents' attitudes also reflected a positive value on the private as an arena of personal control, reflecting, perhaps, their own experiences of life on a working-class estate where relations and activities are often too public and regulated.

Parents' portrayal of the Kingsmead community was also complicated by the representations of other school supporters, in the form of local feminist and gay activists. Hackney lesbian and gay trade unionists mobilised against what they saw as the expulsion of Jane Brown and, by implication, all lesbian and gay staff, from the municipal community. The council's actions suggested lesbian and gay employees did not belong, were not fully entitled to protection or loyalty from the local state. While trade unionists focused on personnel issues rather than the specific space of Kingsmead school, lesbian-feminist activists articulated a different strategy. As many said in interviews, 'This could be me'.[59] As well as personal identification, challenging educational heterosexism offered an issue around which they could mobilise, providing a space for lesbian activists alienated from modern queer politics. Local government homophobia targeted at a lesbian-feminist head provided a familiar battleground. Yet while lesbians mobilised defensively to protect a lesbian engaged in antiheterosexist work,[60] their tactics also provided a spatial, albeit impermanent, encoding. Like the parents, they located Kingsmead within a familial network; however, theirs did not prioritise heterosexuality. Rather, they constituted Kingsmead school as the focal point of a symbolic lesbian community.

A growing literature on lesbian geography has explored the character of lesbian space,[61] using as a critical starting point Castells' analysis that lesbians are far less territorial than their gay male counterparts.[62] Lesbian space may seem less apparent than that of gay men,[63] but this may be because the measuring rod is a male one, based on explicit gay insignia of place. Clearly, Kingsmead was not physically inscribed as gay in the way a pub might be flying a rainbow flag or marked by a pink triangle. However, at an imaginary level, lesbianfeminist educationalists placed Kingsmead at the centre of a network of political organising. Kingsmead was also no arbitrary reference point. Crucial to the specificity of its construction as lesbian space was the educational, public sector, professional (and, to a lesser degree, child-centred) character of its existing coding, as well as the vulnerable, state-attacked space it had become. Moreover, while lesbians nationally offered their support, the location of the conflict in Hackney was also relevant. Not only had many of the lesbian-feminists who joined the campaign lived or taught in the borough but, as well, Hackney functioned as London's best-known, lesbian-feminist neighbourhood.[64]

Lesbian feminists who mobilised around Kingsmead may have constructed it as their imaginary home, but to what extent did this impact on anyone else? Considerable effort was expended by Brown, amongst others, to ensure parents did not feel lesbian activists had appropriated the school or the campaign. Kingsmead must still be able to 'pass', and it largely did from the perspective of local parents. However, for council forces, the construction of Kingsmead as lesbian space was felt more strongly. Indeed, the LEA assumed the existence of a behind-the-scenes lesbian community from early on, evident in their initial proclamation of a lesbian 'mafia' responsible for Brown's appointment and, subsequently, in their unsubstantiated attack on one of the investigating governors for being part of a pro-Brown, lesbian clique.[65] It is doubtful though how much of this perception was the result of mobilisation by lesbian-feminist supporters. In the same way, while Kingsmead may have represented a surplus of lesbian sexuality for those following the story in the media, this had more to do with the media's 'outing' of key figures and Hackney council's press releases, than with supporters' actions.

Fortification[67]

The final technique used by Kingsmead supporters to express and structure belonging—with its creation of an inside and outside—was fortification. This did not take the form of literal walls; however barriers were constructed through parents, staff and supporters refusing to divulge hostile information, criticism or gossip, and through physically obstructing trespass: corporeal and ocular. Metaphorically and physically, Kingsmead was barricaded to stop outsiders—media and council—from penetrating and turning school privacy into 'free-for-all' public space. The doors were locked and curtains drawn. Jane Brown's body was also shielded. As she ran between buildings, she was flanked by supporters attempting to maintain some corporeal space free from photographic re-enactment. For parents, Kingsmead was threatened, not by lesbians but by aggressive, arrogant outsiders who believed they had the right to ask, photograph and print anything; in other words, by people who showed no respect for the familial structure of the school and who were willing to turn its private and hidden spaces inside out for commercial or political gain. 'The school bore the daily brunt of the media. A journalist from the *Sunday Express* stayed in a flat on the estate for a week to get dirt'. (Supporter, interview) While fortification focused on exclusion, at the same time, it identified those who belonged through their entitlement to enter and, simultaneously, to define and exclude trespassers.

Conclusion

This chapter both develops, and provides a counterpoint for, the discussion of local government authority in chapter four. There, I explored the way in which the courts used the principle of fiduciary duty to structure local government's identity and practice in neo-liberal ways. While law played a key role in both disputes, here local government refused to accept juridical disempowerment. Thus, they turned to a range of techniques to maintain control—discursive and disciplinary, as well as legal. In considering the difference between Hackney's response to Kingsmead school, and relations between local government and the courts, the traces of history are important. While councils, prior to the educational reforms of the 1980s, had considerable power over local schools, their relationship to the courts has always been a subordinate one. Thus, it is unsurprising that local government's tenacity and aggression proved far greater in relation to the former.

What is perhaps more surprising are the parallels between local government's strategy of subordination in this chapter and that of the courts in the previous one. In both cases, subordination entailed a double-manoeuvre to undermine institutional independence. First, hierarchical state relations were reaffirmed. The courts used fiduciary duty to reinscribe local government as subordinate to central government and statute; Hackney council depicted Kingsmead as subservient to the LEA. At the same time, relations of accountability were constituted between the subordinated institution and their community: taxpayers in the case of fiduciary duty; parents here. Yet, while the

body exercising meta-governance in both instances stressed the importance of accountability, this was given a formalist interpretation. As I
discussed in chapter four, little attention was given to identifying
taxpayers' interests properly. Similarly here, Hackney LEA constituted
parents' interests according to their own, rather than parents' agenda.
This portrayal was contested by Kingsmead parents who declared their
interests were not served by the castigation of a progressive headteacher, nor were they prepared to be the instruments of Hackney
council's struggle to maintain educational control. To this extent, they
differed from constituents who mobilised *qua* taxpayers to secure a
conservative, neo-liberal agenda. Here, ironically, parents, mobilised
by Conservative political rhetoric, chose to use their identity to
contest the project for which they had been hailed.

The accountability of governing institutions raises two further
issues, first, space; second, belonging. In my discussion of fiduciary
duty in the previous chapter, the courts' portrayal of local accountability evacuated the analytic domain of space. Accountability was
based on a relation of payment, it did not entail local representation
or the invocation of distinct, place-based interests. Indeed, the highly
formalised reading of taxpayers' interests highlighted the despatialised
character of the courts' approach. In this case, Hackney council
adopted, in contrast, a highly spatialised reading of Kingsmead school
to emphasise the specific working-class character of its authentic
community and to demonstrate the way in which the space had
become inappropriately constituted as 'politically correct' and lesbian.
Yet here too the formalised reading of parents' interests, the depiction
of lesbian feminists as geographical outsiders, and the assumptions
about Kingsmead's excessive sexuality reflect the *rhetorical* character
of Hackney's 'spatial turn'.

In relation to belonging, this chapter focused on the different paradigms generated by Hackney council and Kingsmead supporters.
Ultimately, despite local and national discourse surrounding devolved
powers, Hackney saw the school as belonging to them. They hailed
Kingsmead within a proprietary paradigm in which belonging meant
control and ownership according to a zero-sum relationship. Any
attempt by staff or governors to exert control was thus perceived as
threatening the council's position. In contrast, Kingsmead supporters

posed a relational, non-hierarchical model that emphasised reciprocality, consent and participation. Unlike the council, supporters treated belonging as positive rather than zero sum. Thus, involvement and commitment by others could be beneficial, not just threatening. At the same time, the forms of involvement demonstrated by the LEA undermined more communal approaches, partly because they represented an authoritarian governance that jeopardised local discretion and involvement; partly because they fractured the school community by introducing division and exclusion.

I do not wish to romanticise the community constituted by Kingsmead supporters. First, no single community was established; in addition, the familial relations expressed reflected their own forms of exclusion. To the extent that Kingsmead offered an inclusive project, this was largely the product of a fragile equilibrium maintained between the different groups involved. However, it also owes something to the ethos of the school which stressed the importance and collective responsibility of involving everyone, and of challenging *all* forms of inequality.

At a discursive or symbolic level, Kingsmead school thus offers us a model of a progressive, universalist community in which differences of race, gender and sexuality are supported and affirmed despite the countervailing tendencies of senior bodies. This inclusive project differs from the other political projects discussed so far in this book which have attempted to privilege *dominant*, particularistic interests such as Christianity, heterosexuality and private property. But what are its own limitations? How does a community-based politics of equality deal with the particularistic demands of minorities, when they are perceived as incompatible with the maintenance of a modern neighbourhood? This is the subject of my next chapter.

Part Four

Territorial Agendas
Space, Norms and Civil Governance

6   Out of Place

Symbolic Domains, Religious Rights and the Cultural Contract

This chapter is about the relationship between community and space. More particularly, it concerns orthodox Jews' attempts to create communal domains, eruvin, within urban neighbourhoods. The opposition such attempts engendered illustrate how the symbolic structures of one community can be perceived as threatening by others. At the same time, while often genuinely held, such perceptions can also be politically manipulated and exploited—evident in the previous chapter where Kingsmead school was strategically portrayed as overly (homo)sexualised by its local education authority. Both the examples of Kingsmead's sexualisation and the eruv's excessive religiosity are contingent on an assumption of dominant neutrality. However, they are also products of a reality in which sexual and religious practices are unequal.

For Jews, orthodox and otherwise, conflicts over symbolic space are imbricated within a history of persecution. For instance, in Poland, tensions between the Catholic church and Jewish community over the religious marking of public space came to a head over the establishment of a convent at Auschwitz.[1] While Catholics claimed this was their way of remembering the holocaust's horror and the suffering of religious Poles, to many Jews, the installation of a Christian edifice and community within Auschwitz symbolised yet a further attempt by the Polish church to appropriate the holocaust and erase its specifically Jewish implications.

The symbolism of the eruv offers, however, a different vantage-point from which to consider conflicts over the religious marking of public space. On the Sabbath, Jewish law forbids a range of labour. In addition to formal work, these include travelling, spending money and carrying objects beyond the home. The eruv relates to this last injunction. By creating a bounded perimeter which notionally extends the private domain, it provides a way for objects to be carried within a designated area.

Eruvin have become common in large urban districts in Canada, the USA, Australia and Europe, as well as Israel. Nevertheless, the requirement symbolically to enclose space, including, in many instances, miles of urban neighbourhood, and the dwellings of gentiles as well as Jews, has subjected several eruv proposals to intense scrutiny. In the USA, the American Civil Liberties Union (ACLU) has been particularly watchful to ensure eruvin do not violate the establishment clause of the First Amendment creating a wall between church and state.[2] Excessive entanglement depends on the level of state involvement, such as where new structures are needed to join to 'natural' or existing structures such as bridges or walls to complete the boundary.[3] In London, the need for additional poles and consequent requirement for planning permission to complete the 11-mile perimeter provided the focal point for opponents. They protested vociferously through the lengthy process of development control: from rejection by the local council, through the planning inspector's favourable recommendation on completion of his Inquiry, to subsequent acceptance by the Secretary of State.[4]

At the fore of the objections expressed during the planning process for the London eruv were aesthetic and visual concerns. Yet the environmental harm wrought by eighty additional poles and wire, in a London borough with many thousand, cannot alone explain the depth of emotion. Why did the eruv proposed for installation within Barnet's Jewish identified neighbourhood generate such a hostile reception, in contrast to the relative indifference shown by local communities in other jurisdictions? My argument draws on an earlier analysis which identified the eruv as threatening modernist norms and values.[5] Here, I want to link this threat to relations of belonging, framed in the language of a cultural contract.

Eruvin in Neighbourhood Space

> Driving under the gateways...to enter the Barnet Ghetto would be like entering a concentration camp.[6]

'Eruv' literally means 'to mingle', and can take several forms.[7] The one relevant here is the eruv that creates a mingling of space, enabling a relaxation of Sabbath carrying restrictions. According to Jewish law, Jews are prohibited from transporting objects between public and private domains during the Sabbath.[8] The creation of an eruv enables transportation to take place by turning the space between private domains into a single private arena.[9] However, the requirements for establishment are extremely complicated,[10] and subject to rabbinical dispute. For instance, what kind of perimeter is acceptable? How large a population can an eruv encompass? How should difficult structures within Jewish law such as busy roads and parkland be treated?[11] Past disagreements meant some eruvin were only recognised by certain rabbis. This was problematic since the legitimacy of any certain eruv depended on the authority of the rabbis granting it recognition.[12] In Toronto, the validity of the eruv boundary became increasingly disputed, thanks, in part, to the fact it encompassed a major highway. In the late 1980s, work began on a new perimeter, installed in 1996, in the hope it would prove more widely acceptable.

Although eruvin go back many hundreds of years, the modern movement gained force in the 1960s. Interest in eruvin has been linked to a growing orthodoxy amongst young people,[13] to the women's liberation movement, in particular, women's interest in participating more fully in religious life (eruvin allow them to push prams to syna-gogue or to place young children with families and friends while they attend);[14] and more recently to demands for disability rights. Eruvin also function as a sign of increasing confidence amongst the orthodox to create communal structures and facilitate an improved quality of life. Much of this confidence draws on the gains of other minority communities, such as African-Americans—one reason, perhaps, why eruvin seem to have proven more acceptable in the USA where there is a stronger tradition of minority cultural entitlement than in Britain.

The cultural contract

The concept of the cultural contract parallels the metaphorical social and sexual contracts developed in liberal and feminist thought respec-tively.[15] The contract is an imaginary settlement through which the consent of a community to a particular set of social and governance relations is identified. In this case, it relates to accepted norms of racialised and religious identity and expression, and to acceptable public and governance practices. The notion of a contract is important because of the idea of commitment and exchange. This does not mean a real relation of exchange exists, or that there is consent or a clearly delineated agreement. What matters is that these elements of a settlement are imbricated within the dominant, cultural imaginary, a framework which proved highly influential in shaping the beliefs, norms and values of eruv opponents.

In saying this, I do not wish to suggest that some people are duped by dominant ideologies, while others are not. First, even people who adopt a dominant perspective, often reshape it in particular ways according to their own experiences. Second, the social history and conditions of a community will affect the ways in which they view their environment, making some groups or classes more likely to acquire a minority or oppositional perspective. To understand why eruv opponents took the position they did, we therefore need to consider who they were. One of the most striking elements of the eruv controversy was the leading and active role played by non-orthodox Jews.[16] In the main, Jewish opponents came from a particular background: over 45, European, and middle-class.[17] Their stance towards the eruv and commitment to Enlightenment norms replicates a common theme of modern Jewish history.[18] For European Jews who took advantage of nineteenth-century emancipation and assimilated, cultural norms such as a public/private division, civic inclusion and formal equality functioned as both the means of integration as well as personal symbols of its achievement. Thus, many who integrated developed considerable hostility towards those orthodox Jews who remained visibly Jewish,[19] and 'culturally backward'. Their refusal to 'pass' drew attention to assimilated Jews' own roots and precarious sense of belonging.

The cultural contract eruv opponents elaborated has four main elements. First, it is predicated on an English, cultural essentialism (see chapter three). In other words, Britain's identity is defined by its history and heritage as Anglo-Christian. The cultural contract incorporates a commitment to maintaining this. Second, within this

Anglican settlement, minority practices are acceptable if performed privately. However, not all practices are deemed legitimate even where they remain private, for instance, those deemed non-consensual, against public policy, or as entrenching 'unacceptable' inequalities. The third element constitutes the British public as members of a national community based on rational, liberal values. Citizenship identifies an unmediated relationship between individual and state; any involvement by citizens with voluntary, private or civil organisations must be unco-erced and consensual. Finally, public space should reflect the values of the cultural contract. It is where the contract is both constituted and lived.

The rest of this chapter explores the way in which eruvin in general, and the London eruv in particular, were seen by opponents as threat-ening the four elements just outlined. In doing so, my objective is not just to provide a detailed reading of the menace eruvin were feared to pose, but, in addition, to use the eruv as a prism through which wider questions relating to governance, community and public space can be raised. In the discussion that follows, two aspects of the North London eruv are particularly important to bear in mind. First, the fact that it constructs a perimeter around public space; second, its requirement that poles and wire be installed to complete the boundary.

Privatising Space and Territorial Claims

The starting point for opponents of the London eruv, and the argu-ment they returned to again and again, was what they saw as the territorial agenda and practices of eruv advocates. 'The religious side is just a ruse ... They put up poles as a demonstration of their territo-riality—they don't need poles' (Objector, interview). To emphasise the territorial aspects of the eruv, opponents drew on the halakhic (Jewish law) principle that an eruv symbolically privatises space, made evident in the notional payment of rent. Adopting a zero-sum formu-lation of ownership, opponents argued if space now belonged to orthodox Jews, it could no longer belong to them. Through installing an eruv, orthodox Jews were both naming and fixing informal Jewish areas as Jewish, and then expanding outwards into non-Jewish areas.

'[The eruv] identifies a non-Jewish area as a Jewish area. The Jewish area is moving further out, away from Golders Green'. (Objector, interview) At the heart of this complaint lay the belief that eruv proponents were using the eruv as a strategic, territory-setting device through which to create their own zone. Feeding off widespread anxieties regarding ultra-orthodox behaviour in places such as Israel, opponents claimed that, within an orthodox zone, access, belonging, sanctioned behaviour and social relationships would be constituted according to orthodox Jewish norms rather than in the terms of their own cultural contract.

While the fears of opponents seem somewhat overstated, in at least two ways the eruv can be seen as having territorial implications. First, as one leading Barnet rabbi did acknowledge, the eruv was partly about developing a sense of community 'which has a boundary ... that comes into play on the sabbath'. Similar claims have been made in the USA, where the establishment of eruv perimeters in Miami Beach, St. Louis and Baltimore, amongst others, have been linked to the intensification of an orthodox community identity.[20] The authority that emanates from boundary-setting is particularly apparent in cases, such as Toronto, where prior to the 1996 eruv boundary, different perimeters were recognised by different rabbis. While recognition was ostensibly based on technical, halakhic grounds, it allowed rabbis to control the demarcation of their own community space. Thus, different congregations would operate according to different imaginaries of the boundaries and interior of belonging.

Second, the installation of a London eruv was likely to produce demographic consequences. This phenomenon has been noticed after the establishment of other eruvin. For instance, in the American city of Baltimore, the installation of a new larger eruv encouraged orthodox Jews to move into the area. The potential demographic shift from establishing an eruv in Barnet was a major concern for opponents. The fear of racial imbalance was summed up in rather worrying terms, by one opponent who declared the area's historic stability 'would be harmed if the proportion of Jews increased ... It is a matter of the right proportions and balance in the community'.[21] Opponents did not see this population shift as an incidental effect; rather they perceived the eruv as a deliberate strategy to increase the strength and numbers of

ultra-orthodox Jews.[22] 'They want to demographically alter the population of the area ... to deliberately move Jewish people into the area
to live together'. (Objector, interview) Opponents drew attention to
the fact that property advertisements in the *Jewish Chronicle* already
referred to properties as being within the boundary of the proposed
eruv. More than one interviewee suggested that this would have a
distortive impact on market values.

Assimilated Jews and gentile opponents thus perceived themselves as
becoming the new dispossessed. The cultural and demographic incursion
and entrenchment of orthodox Jewish space threatened to leave them
out of place: their cultural norms and values replaced by those of the
pre-modern, religious shtetl. As one opponent stated, 'People feel
they've taken over. This isn't my area anymore'. Yet, the position for
secular and liberal Jews was also more complicated than simply feeling
alienated by the eruv proposal. While, on the one hand, they saw orthodox Judaism as exclusionary, arrogant and presumptuous in its
expectations, at the same time, they felt equally angry at the prospect
of being constructed as 'belonging' within 'backward' Jewish space.

Public Expression of Minority Beliefs

Opponents perceived the eruv as territorialising and privatising public
space; they also expressed concern at the public expression of minority beliefs. This public aspect of the eruv was seen to undermine the
cultural contract in three primary ways. First, the eruv transgressed
the requirement that minority expression be contained within the
private domain.[23] Second, the eruv attacked the relationship between
soil and cultural identity. Third, the eruv would lead to a radical multiculturalism that would destroy British identity.

The public/private divide

Opponents perceived the eruv as transgressing the public/ private
divide largely through its identity as a spatial perimeter. In this way,
the eruv was compared unfavourably to religious structures such as a
church or mosque. According to one objector: 'A building is a discrete,

enclosed, limited thing'. Within church or mosque walls, only participants know what is taking place. With the doors closed, others are
protected from having to view rituals they may find offensive. In
contrast, an eruv, criticised for privatising public space, was seen, at
the same time, as also transgressing the divide by bringing inappropriate expressions of religious faith into the public domain.

This publicisation had three effects. First, it posed the prospect of
tainting space seen as belonging to and enjoyed by the whole community. Interviewees placed stress on the quality and significance of the
urban space involved. This was particularly apparent in relation to one
neighbourhood enclosed by the proposed eruv boundary: Hampstead
Garden Suburb (HGS). A highly regarded example of the early garden
suburb movement,[24] residents perceived HGS as almost 'sacred',
modern space (a view somewhat disparaged by other eruv opponents). Given the special quality of the area as aesthetically 'pure' and
socially harmonious, it would be unforgivable to impose an eruv upon
it. Second, the eruv was perceived as inappropriately visible. Yet, this
was largely the result of the publicity and media interest generated by
opponents. In most cities where eruvin exist, few residents other than
those who observe the boundaries can identify where they lie. Indeed,
this was a factor in the US courts allowing eruvin permission to be
established. In *ACLU of New Jersey* v. *City of Long Branch et al.*,[25] the
district judge stated that the largely invisible character of the eruv
boundary (combined with the secularism of its physical form) meant
residents would not have a religion imposed upon them. Third, by
enabling orthodox Jews to carry outside of their homes on the
sabbath, the eruv was seen as enabling private 'differences' to be
expressed in public. Yet, there is a contradiction here. While it is probably true that an eruv means more orthodox Jews are visible on the
streets between Friday and Saturday sundown, at the same time, the
eruv normalises orthodox Jewry, by allowing them to behave more
like the majority.

Cultural identity and soil

As well as breaching the public/ private divide, the construction of the
eruv, particularly the installation of poles, was seen to attack and

rearticulate the relationship between soil and cultural identity. The eruv 'disfigures' the land because it does not belong. It functions, metaphorically, like an inverted circumcision; where a circumcision cuts away, the eruv implants. The installation of poles means alien, deeply rooted markers are embedded within the soil. Paralleling those who critique circumcision for disfiguring the body, here implanting was seen as both assaulting and disregarding existing forms of belonging. This perception came to the surface in one instance, in particular, in relation to a Church of England school whose playing ground formed part of the eruv boundary.[26] Here, the prior, explicit ethnicisation of the soil was seen to make the concept of a 'Jewish boundary line' particularly inappropriate.[27] Opponents characterised orthodox Jews, during interviews, as intensely arrogant in their disregard for existing spatial meanings, and in their assumption that the transgression of Christian markings was acceptable.

In the association of orthodox neighbourhoods with cultural and social outsiderness, we can see a degree of embarrassment amongst more assimilated Jews: that their orthodox 'kin' failed to understand the relationship between soil and belonging. So absorbed were they in their own narrow 'lost' world, they did not know where they were, more particularly, that they were someplace else. Orthodox Jews, with their vision always tu(r)ned to the past, remain forgetful of the ways in which the land beyond Jerusalem is both meaningful and already 'taken'. In other words, it is not vacant space that can be inscribed from scratch. One of the paradoxes of the eruv is that despite being seen to give public space a religious facade, its actual relationship to land is arbitrary; although it entails a spatial marking, inscription relates to current demography rather than pre-existing physical or cultural geography.[28] An eruv can be stretched across almost any soil where a Jewish community exists. It is intrinsically a structure for a nomadic or diaspora people—a portable, private domain.

The slippery slope

The third problem opponents identified was one of the 'flood gates' opening. The establishment of a 'special' structure for orthodox Jews would lead other minorities to demand similar entitlements. 'It would be a slippery slope of ethnic minorities asking for things, wanting special facilities'. (Objecting councillor, interview) '[A]ny minority will see it as a green light for their own particular view to be expressed...'[29] Opponents saw the advent of a north London eruv as assisting eruv proposals elsewhere in Britain. Indeed, in the USA, where many eruvin exist, orthodox communities, in some instances, are driven to establish them for fear of losing congregants to areas where eruvin are already in place.[30] While this is scarcely yet a problem for Britain, eruv opponents saw the eruv as legitimising demands for other minorities' public expression.

Interviewees revealed a degree of consistency in their opposition to supporting minority interests. Most opposed state funding for minority ethnic provision, such as 'mother-tongue' classes, and expressed concern at the widespread emergence of minority religious structures with public visibility. In part, this concerned the role of government. Eruv opponents tended to argue that the state should only involve itself in universalist forms of provision. It also concerned the status of minority faiths in a nation with an established church. However, linked to the assertion of heritage-rights was a concern to protect the 'rational', and to maintain a hierarchy of cultural sense. Thus, the slippery slope climaxed, for several interviewees, with the vision of totem poles on Hampstead Heath, the horror of the pre-modern and uncivilised intensely vivid in this repeated trope.

A question of harm

In the eruv's functioning as a public, symbolic structure, opponents identified a range of harms that would transpire. First, public status would force otherness on the general public without their consent; second, installation threatened to bring violence into the community; third, the eruv's communalism jeopardised a universal, national citizenship; and, fourth, it proffered a disorder that would overflow the eruv boundaries.

Forcing otherness on to the general public undermined a key element of the cultural contract: the right to be protected from minority offence. There are clearly parallels here with the opposition expressed towards public expressions of homosexuality. Heterosexual demonstrations are so naturalised they remain unapparent—wearing wedding/engagement rings, talking about marriage/honeymoons/ dating, kissing/holding hands in public places. However, analogous signifiers of sexuality by lesbians and gay men, lacking a naturalised status, remain highly visible, and are construed as flaunting. One woman I interviewed, an active opponent of the eruv, while vaguely content with public installation of Christian symbols, expressed her concern at the public display of minority, religious symbols, such as large menorahs attached to lamp-posts along the high street. Yet it would be misleading to see her opposition as simply a generic hostility towards non-Christian faiths. For, in contrast, she spoke positively about occasions when her neighbour had brought around pastries baked to celebrate an Islamic festival. The difference about the latter was not only that it occurred within the 'privacy' of her home, but as well the related fact that it was grounded in consent. For this interviewee, it was largely the lack of active consent—the forced viewing of minority culture—which made her feel displaced and out of control.

One consequence of such feelings—a second danger of public, minority symbols—is violence. 'Anglicised Jews felt [the eruv] broke the rules of the game. They saw it as un-British … The eruv fulfils the Jewish stereotype of pushy and aggressive'. (Objector, interview) The perceived danger of violence not only threatened orthodox Jews but others as well who became assimilated into an anti-semitic vision of the aggressive, grasping other. As one councillor, opposed to the eruv, stated, 'A minority of the community having staked out and identified its precise territory leaves the whole Jewish community open to attack, abuse and vandalism'.[31] Equated with their orthodox kin, liberal Jews would be punished for having evacuated their assimilation even though this move was not one willingly taken. The eruv proposal 'outed' them, and much of their anger seemed to relate to this. Several interviewees living in HGS recounted how, as a result of the eruv controversy, questions of individual religious identification came up at local parties and gatherings. What had previously been of little interest, and remained unknown, was now the identity forced to speak its name.

Opponents argued that the harm resulting from defining people by their religious background, and responding to them on those terms, would be amplified by the eruv's actual installation. Its establishment would generate anti-Jewish feeling amongst local residents who had 'never previously had an anti-semitic thought'. (Objector, interview) In other words, several opponents, including Jewish ones, identified anti-semitism as a potentially rational response from an alienated *majority*. Yet, while one opponent suggested he knew several middle-class residents who would undermine the boundary's integrity, in the main physical violence was identified with 'elsewhere' (working-class bigots entering the borough, bringing with them the race hatred of London's East End).

In response, proponents dismissed the likelihood of violence, suggesting that opponents were raising it for purely rhetorical purposes. (There was also some suggestion that if violence or vandalism did occur, opponents would be largely to blame, either as the perpetrators or for whipping up hostility to the eruv proposal.) Yet, while some opponents may have intentionally exaggerated the threat of violence, their arguments reflected wider fears of religious and ethnic brutality. In this respect the eruv was seen as a provocation, or, at best, a careless indifference to the world-wide hatred and strife, ethnic communal claims generated.[32]

This fear of more widespread disorder and hostility was linked to two further issues. First, the eruv was seen as contributing to the jeopardising of a universal, national citizenship. The terms of the cultural contract require difference to remain private so that people can come together in the public domain as common citizens, albeit in hegemonically coded ways.[33] If difference is contained within the private domain, it can be safely expressed without Britain fragmenting into a series of disparate peoples or nations. 'Ghettos', by representing a restructuring[34] or refusal to privatise difference, threaten a common citizenship. A postmodern interpretation that marks them as interesting places of intense cultural expression and diversity is, I was told, dangerously naive. Ghettos represent troubled symbols of cultural ill-health and disequilibrium. Several interviewees cited the USA, where the capacity of cultural minorities to form local majorities enabled them to remain outside, and thereby undermine, universal(ising) citizenship identities.[35]

The dangers this might generate, opponents suggested, went beyond local anti-semitism; for ghettoes cannot be contained. While Barnet's eruv might appear to offer a container for difference, enclosing a large proportion of London Jewry within a single, symbolic perimeter, this perimeter was always in danger of splitting—literally and figuratively—contaminating the surrounding area. At one level, such contamination relates to the pre-modern norms with which the eruv is associated, at another, the contamination concerns the expression of modern, subnational territorialism. Thus, the slippery slope extends beyond totem poles on Hampstead Heath to the threat or fear of a Rwanda or Yugoslavia: symbols of nations and even supranational regions contaminated and fragmented by a racialised out-of-controlness.

Christian hegemony and religious law

> For the last 30 years, my wife and I have every Christmas put a very large tree in the front bay window of our house. This has, I venture to suggest, given a great deal of pleasure to the community...[36] The eruv will, I think, create exactly the reverse effect.[37]

So far I have talked about the importance of difference remaining within the private domain without making particularly explicit what difference I refer to. However, it is clear in this context that it is minority faiths that are largely expected to remain private in Britain. The dominant faith—Christianity—can legitimately be expressed within the public domain. Indeed, Christianity's expression within the public sphere is seen as playing a crucial role in the reproduction of traditional forms of belonging and national identification. The maintenance of Britain's Christian heritage was affirmed by eruv opponents, even Jewish ones. According to one objector, 'Christianity is fundamental to our culture and ninety-five per cent of the population'. (Interview)

The special place of Christianity needs to be kept in mind in considering eruv opponents' valuing of secularism. Secularism can be taken to mean religion's location within the private rather than public sphere.[38] It also signifies the rejection of religion as a foundation for policy-making or political decision.[39] Within Britain, however, the impact of secularism on different religions is clearly uneven.[40] Not only does secularism coincide with an established British church, but

Christianity is also less disadvantaged by the political subordination of religious bases for action than other faiths.[41] Like heterosexuality, Christian space 'has an air of neutrality...the epitome of rational abstraction ... [because it] has already been the focus of past processes whose traces are not always evident in the landscape'.[42]

Thus, when eruv opponents objected to religion functioning as a criterion for action, their target was non-Christian faiths. One woman I interviewed proffered an analogy: 'Suppose you have a wonderful bush at the end of your garden, but the person living behind you, who shares the bush, believes it represents evil; do you have to remove the bush just to comply with their religious beliefs?' While this raises generally interesting ethical questions regarding religion's status as a basis for action, equally significant was the specific illustrative context she drew on: a person from the Caribbean who believes in Voodoo. Thus, at the heart of her analogy is a criticism of action to accommodate seemingly 'irrational', *non-establishment*, belief systems. And there is fear. If 'irrational' beliefs such as Orthodox Judaism can legitimately demand action simply on the ground of being a belief, does any basis for distinction remain? This question reverberates with 'cultural relativism' anxieties; it echoes, for instance, my discussion in chapter three regarding British attacks on multi-faith teaching for their refusal normatively to privilege Christianity as the superior faith framework.[43]

Competing Governance

A key aspect of the cultural contract is the relationship between individual and state. This has several components. First, it takes a monist rather than pluralist view of law, seeing citizens as subject to the law of the state rather than to the laws of their subnational community. Indeed, as I discuss below, the very *legal* character of such normative systems is itself placed in doubt. Second, it means that citizens are governed directly by the state rather than through the mediation of civil structures. Third, while civil forms of governance are permitted, these must function voluntarily and by agreed membership. Fourth, the unmediated, singular relationship between citizen and state (sovereign) is crucial to the sustenance of the liberal nation-state.

Legal pluralism and the cultural contract

While opponents perceived minority faiths as irrational and potentially dangerous unless contained within the private domain, Protestantism appeared, by contrast, cool and level-headed. Unlike Western narratives of faiths such as Islam, Protestantism fulfilled the appropriate role for religion: to supplement and complement social life, not to provide a competing structure or set of norms. The acceptable domain for religion in Britain was morality, ethics and culture in relation to which, as I describe in chapter three, religion played a critical role. Christianity provided the cement of national belonging. Any absence or deterioration would leave a gap.

This defining of the legitimate realm for religion, based on the role played by Protestantism in a nation where the Church of England is the established faith, locates other faiths as hazardous. Judaism, for instance, has historically borne accusations that it fails to facilitate nation-state belonging, being at best neutral and at worst counter-productive in its demands for 'special' treatment and its extra-national loyalties. In addition, critics have perceived its legalistic form as threatening a monist, hierarchical notion of law.

In the context of the eruv controversy, opponents found themselves unable to accept the idea of Jewish law as they understood it. Opponents did not simply treat halakha as subordinate to secular, domestic law,[44] many dismissed its very legal status.[45] (This rejection carries particular significance if law is seen as the expression and projection of community identity, as discussed in chapter two). Jewish law was denied legal status for several reasons. First, it could not be true law since law was perceived to operate according to a singular hierarchy of state legislation and case law. Second, drawing upon a Christian imaginary, the role played by God in the construction of Jewish law meant that its laws were matters of faith and spirituality. According to one leading eruv proponent interviewed, opponents proved so unwilling and unable to comprehend halakha that they gave up trying to explain.

> Jewish law is very complicated. We were aware of trying to explain it to people who hadn't a clue ... It's hard to find ways of expressing the idea of the eruv ... Eventually we said we can't explain it or

you'll never believe it ... We presented it as a facility the community needs, to explain why we need it is our business. We just want you to respect the fact we understand it.

As a consequence of being perceived as not-law, opponents portrayed Jewish law as voluntary—grounded in choice and consent rather than obligation; and as indeterminate—lacking the fixity and clear meanings of 'real' law. At the same time, Jewish law was characterised as rigid and obscure in opposition to the mercy, forgiveness and accessibility perceived as emanating from the Christian tradition.

Opponents' conceptualisation of Jewish law produced two main responses to the eruv. First, the reduction of halakha to voluntary belief and closed principles meant one either believed in the singular, underlying purpose—here, not carrying on the sabbath—and complied, or one did not.[46] One of the most repeated accusations thrown at the eruv was hypocrisy: 'It allows people of a certain persuasion to break the law.' (Objector, interview) This criticism was reinforced by pointing to sections of the ultra-orthodox community who had publicly repudiated the eruv proposal.[47] Asserting halakha's interpretive closure, opponents claimed if the ultra-orthodox did not accept the eruv, then this must be the best reading. They rejected the possibility of equally valid competing interpretations, a recognition that would undermine law's hierarchy—internal and external.

At the same time, the perception of Jewish law as technically obscure and disputed (as well as voluntary) meant eruv requirements were deemed entirely plastic. In other words, an eruv could be constructed according to any measurement that suited both users and the wider community. For instance, several interviewees suggested an eruv might be more acceptable if it embraced the entire British mainland. When I replied that an eruv could only be of a limited size, enclosing a limited population, I was met with a shrug and rejoinder that since the whole thing was ridiculous, it was pointless to look for 'rational' rules. More broadly, eruv opponents approached the subject of Jewish law with the view that people should do what they want— carry if you want, don't carry if you don't. But they refused to accept that the decision whether or not to carry might be a legal one or one that could be legally enabled through highly detailed legal provisions.

Civil governance

The perception that the eruv undermines the direct relationship between citizen and state resonates with the role of pre-modern Jewish governance, which, to varying degrees, brokered and mediated the relationship between community and nation.[48] In addition, the eruv threatened to structure the lives of people who had not consented to incorporation. As one objector put it: '[W]ithin those physical boundaries around 80,000 people will be enclosed, the vast majority of whom have no desire at all to live within a private Jewish domain'.[49] But what does it mean to call the eruv—which is, at least on one reading, simply a perimeter wall—a governance body?

Bodies such as eruvin can be considered governing institutions because they structure space, activities, norms and resources according to a particular agenda, which may be explicit or simply identified through a textual analysis of institutional practices. This is governing out of order in the final meaning of the term, namely, governing from a position of normative order. Yet, although the eruv clearly impacts on the activities of observant residents within its boundaries, to define it as a governing body suggests a degree of agency that a wall does not possess. In a sense, it requires us to see the physical structure as a technique deployed by religious leaders and internalised by congregants. There is some evidence for this in the reasons behind the establishment of eruvin in Canada and the USA, where, as well as facilitating a sense of community, Jewish leaders saw the eruv as a means of encouraging and sustaining observant behaviour.

The eruv as a governing structure problematises any attempt to see direct, mid-way and distant governing as clearly delineated. Is the eruv a form of direct governing—does God require observant Jews not to carry beyond the eruv boundary? Or does it represent governing at a distance through orthodox congregants' internalisation of religious law? We might also see elements of mid-way governing, both in the eruv's basic purpose—to avoid some of the harsh restrictions on Sabbath activity—and in the complex manoeuvres undergone to enable eruvin to be established halakhically in modern spaces. How the eruv is seen may also depend on the observers' standpoint. For instance, to opponents, the eruv may be more likely to be comprehended as a form of direct, prescriptive governance, while users see it as an expression of collective self-governance. The eruv is therefore a complex structure articulating elements from different forms of governing. My three-fold categorisation of direct, mid-way and distant governing is useful here, not as a means of classification, but in drawing attention to the different, overlapping governing practices the eruv constitutes.

Territorial

The final aspect of the eruv to threaten the relationship between state and people, according to the terms of the cultural contract, concerned its territorial quality.[50] The articulation of space to a constituency whose primary allegiance was to its own members caused the eruv to jeopardise essential nation-work (cultural work carried out to reproduce nationhood). A key element in this jeopardising concerned the eruv's emphasis on borders.[51] Borders are important because they allow a discrete territory to be imagined—crucial to the production and reproduction of nationhood. According to Balibar, in his work on nationalism, external frontiers of the state have to be constantly imagined as a 'projection ... of an internal collective personality, which ... enables us to inhabit the space of the state as a place where we have always been—and always will be—'at home'".[52] In addition, borders function as a boundary that regulates entry and exit. A leading eruv proponent described these boundaries as vitally important to an internal sense of community. On the most sacred day, he suggested, it was vital that orthodox Jews knew where the boundaries of their community lay, and that they functioned within them. This restriction on observant Jews is more than symbolic since, if they are carrying or pushing wheelchairs or prams on the sabbath, they cannot travel beyond the eruv perimeter.

Will the boundary impact upon anyone else? Clearly, opponents identified the eruv perimeter as a symbolic wall that would keep the non-orthodox unwelcome and excluded. Anxiety that the eruv would constitute a form of 'home rule' within its borders was given added fuel when the main local newspaper, the well-respected *Hampstead and Highgate Express*, claimed to have received minutes from a group of Jewish zealots who planned to patrol the perimeter to ensure its sabbath integrity.[53] These minutes were subsequently dismissed by the Jewish Board of Deputies as a hoax;[54] however, their production and effectiveness both built upon and reproduced images of a Jewish militarised nation—a fortified, turbulent, Middle-Eastern Israel within suburban, staid, conservative, north-west London.

Is there however a contradiction between this analysis and my earlier discussion of the eruv as a structure that might contaminate surrounding areas? Can the eruv be both a highly militarised stronghold and a locus of disintegration? These two images may be compatible if we see fragmentation as threatening the British nation-state, while localised Jewish governance solidifies, drawing for its strength on modern coercive techniques. At the same time, we might see the eruv not as threatening the possibility of a British nation-state so much as its current identity. What it means to be British or English—the emphasis on a single sovereign, legal system, citizenship and public faith—is challenged by the govern/mentality an eruv is seen as posing. At the heart of British opposition to the eruv is a fear of change—that the British nation-state will culturally replicate the American model of opponents' imagination. But it is also a fear that there is no essential British identity. In other words, it is a fear that Britain can live with an eruv, that Britain's national identity may organically change without crisis or rupture.

Conclusion

Why did eighty poles and some thin, high, invisible wire generate so much fear, hostility and distress? My argument draws on an earlier discussion of the eruv as threatening a set of modernist, liberal norms. Here, I explore the extent to which these norms were articulated to a cultural contract according to which hegemonic forms of British belonging are constituted. The way in which the eruv breached this contract embraced four transgressions. First, the eruv was seen as privatising space that belonged to a wider public. Second, it flaunted minority beliefs, practices and loyalties in a way that provocatively disregarded the liberal public/private divide. Third, it resituated religious law within public decision-making, and constituted religious law as a legitimate basis for public action. Finally, it troubled modernist forms of nation-state governance.

Above all, and at its most simple, the eruv appeared to opponents as a form of territorialism or 'taking'. A neighbourhood cherished as rational, modern, safe, civilised and balanced appeared in danger of reinscription according to both premodern and postmodern forms of belonging.[55] Yet, seeing the eruv as displacing existing residents and undermining British nation-work has to be located within the context of modern anti-semitism. Analogous initiatives by other minority faiths may well have engendered similar levels of hostility. However, the specific character of what happened here is rooted in the orthodox Jewish nature of the eruv enterprise within a residential area with a significant Anglo-Jewish population.

One of the most interesting but not necessarily surprising aspects of the conflict was the role played by non-orthodox Jews. However, it is important not to forget the many opponents who were not Jewish; Christian and secular residents also opposed the eruv and several of the public displays of opposition came from local church figures. Nevertheless, the opposition of non-orthodox Jews was a distinctive aspect of the conflict. In considering the specific motivations and feeling that generated the intensity of their response, I would suggest that underpinning much of their emotion was a feeling of displacement. The eruv proposal extracted secular Jews from assimilation and relocated them in a wasteland of non-belonging: neither at home with observant Jewry nor part, any longer, of a universal citizenry. Their membership and loyalties recast as ambiguous, we can read their intensive, arduous opposition to the eruv as necessary Jewish labour, fulfilling their contractual obligations within the prevailing cultural economy.

7 Moral Perceptions and Management Concerns

Hunting, Land Rights and Legitimate Authority

This chapter brings together previous themes to explore conflict over deer hunting, political authority and rural space. My discussion develops the themes of this book in three ways. First, it explores the boundaries of appropriate governing in relation to local government, the courts and the hunt. The depiction of these bodies as excessive interrogates the legitimacy of gaining pleasure from culling; imposing ethically-grounded prohibitions; and judicial review of democratic practices.

Second, questions of belonging are linked to land ownership. In the eruv case, urban land was identified by its opponents as belonging to the general public according to the terms of an Anglo-Protestant cultural contract. Supporters of the hunt articulated similar views, arguing that countryside morally belonged to traditional users and farmers rather than to the state. The court also interrogated the possibility of local state ownership. Thus, a key question is the extent to which land can belong to (local) government beyond its status as territory. The third theme concerns the cultural and symbolic role of space. As I have said, rural space functioned as an object of conflict. However, I am also interested in three other questions: what does it mean to define space as 'public'? How were images of rural space deployed by protagonists? And what is the relationship between space and governance authority?

Opposition to deer hunting in Britain has been traditionally associated with two strategies. The first involves law reform: persuading parliament through pressure group activity to introduce legislation to outlaw hunting. (After experiencing limited success under conservative rule, attempts to change the law intensified post-1997 when

Labour came to office.) The second strategy is saboteuring: attending hunts to protest, cause obstruction or otherwise prevent the death of the hunted. This chapter concerns a third strategy—one that gained momentum in Britain from the late 1970s onwards, based on hunting's reliance on legal permission to cross land in pursuit of prey.

In the early 1990s, councils across Britain began to follow the lead of private and civic bodies and introduce bans prohibiting hunting across land they owned on the grounds of animal welfare and environmental management. One authority to do so was Somerset County Council in the west of England, it was a decision that did not go unchallenged. Within days of the policy being passed, the hunt applied for judicial review. The case went as far as the Court of Appeal, where the majority reiterated the high court's decision: local government as a public body did not have the authority to ban hunting on moral grounds.

The conflict over hunting provides a site for exploring the primary themes of *Governing Out of Order*. It is also interesting in its own right in offering a reversal of more conventional conflicts over property and land access which have focused on governmental 'takings',[1] and the rights of members of the general public to cross private land.[2] In this chapter, I explore the reverse: elite access to, and authority over, public space. The contested character of the land highlights the way in which the authority of both hunt and county council was grounded in control over the soil. The respective withdrawal of control that occurred—first, through the council's hunting ban, and second, through judicial review of Somerset council's decision undermined both bodies, reconstructing them as 'poachers'. The withdrawal of land-rights can thus be seen as a deliberate strategy of disempowerment. While the council was intent on asserting its authority and morality through the attack on hunting interests, the court was equally intent on subordinating local government to Parliament. Both the high court and subsequent Court of Appeal agreed Somerset's ban was *ultra vires*; a ban for reasons of cruelty was outside the legitimate remit of local government.

In addition, legitimate access to, and control over, land (rights) for both hunt and council were identified as contingent on 'good' management. Hunting's political legitimacy depended on demonstrating it was for the welfare of the deer; the council's legal right to ban depended on showing it was being done for land management rather than ethical reasons. Thus, land rights performed a complex function. On the one hand, they proved the basis of political authority; on the other, they were the reward for exercising authority appropriately. This dynamic is further complicated by the relationship between governance and management. If land rights mediate the relationship between governance and management, so that the former depends on demonstrating the latter, what are the political implications for the kind of governing agenda that can be articulated and developed?

Somerset's Hunting Ban

Hunting is often equated with other country sports such as game-shooting. However, in terms of property interests, hunting raises different issues. Shooting and stalking are traditionally articulated to ownership of the land on which the sport takes place.[3] Thus, conflicts revolve around attempts by private property owners to protect land from wider public access in order to safeguard game.[4] However, essential to hunting, particularly in recent centuries, with the break-up of chases, deer parks and royal forests, is the *liberty of free chase*, the right to enter and take produce from *another's* land.

The spatially transgressive character of modern deer and fox-hunting—their need to exceed geographical boundaries of land ownership—has proven both the site and an increasingly effective mechanism for challenging hunt power. From the late eighteenth century, several cases arose concerning the legal status of hunting where the hunt had neither a license nor informal permission to hunt across other people's land. The emergence of trespass principles in this area,[5] whilst historically treated with relative unconcern by many hunters for whom customary and sporting norms were more impor-tant,[6] made possible a political strategy in which hunting could be restrained through the purchase and unsympathetic deployment of sporting rights. The League Against Cruel Sports developed this strat-egy from the 1950s, with purchases escalating in the 1970s.[7] Pressure was subsequently placed on other large landowners, such as the

Cooperative Society and National Trust to follow suit.[8] Faced with a growing mosaic of inaccessible land, hunt supporters fought back, buying up sporting rights of land across which they wished to hunt. In Somerset, the key pro-hunt purchaser was the Badgworthy Land Trust;[9] it approached landowners selling land to see if they would donate or sell their sporting rights.

The decision by Somerset council, however, to enter the fray, using control over sporting rights to introduce its own ban shifted the conflict on to a different level. The specific background to Somerset County Council's ban goes back to the mid-1980s when the Liberal Democrat authority considered the possibility of banning hunting on a 148-acre strip of land owned in the Quantock Hills. Although the council also owned other land in hunting country, Over Stowey Customs Common was chosen because the council controlled the hunting rights (the council had limited regulatory powers to restrict hunting on land it did not own).[10] It also proved a strategic choice of land for a ban since the Common almost bisected the territory of the Quantock Staghounds (QSH), the local Somerset hunt. In 1986 Somerset deferred reaching a decision until further studies on the effects of deer hunting had been completed. In 1989, a Conservative administration, sympathetic to staghunting, won control of the council and the ban proposal was dropped. However, four years later, the Liberal Democrats returned to power. Although no mention of a ban was included in their manifesto, a report considering whether hunting should be banned was quickly completed for the July 1993 Environment Committee. The Committee decided that hunting should continue. On 4 August 1993, the issue came before full council. At a packed meeting and without a Liberal Democrat whip, the council voted by a majority to ban deer hunting across Over Stowey.[11]

Echoing a history of landed resistance to attacks on their authority over rural space,[12] the hunt quickly responded. Its determination to overturn the ban was strengthened by the rising number of similar restrictions being introduced by other authorities.[13] The application for judicial review against Somerset council was therefore an important test case for the future of hunting.[14] The High Court ruled on *R. v. Somerset County Council ex p. Fewings and Others*[15] in early February 1994. In a judgment highly favourable to the hunt, Justice Laws held that a local authority as a public body did not have an unfettered discretion; any action must be justified by public law. In this case, construing S. 120(1)(b) of Local Government Act 1972,[16] it meant a local authority could not take decisions about activities on its land on the basis of moral perceptions. Hunting could not be prohibited because it was morally repulsive. Although Somerset argued that its decision had not been based on moral grounds, this was factually rejected by the court. Justice Laws declared,

> A prohibition on hunting, which manifestly interferes with the lawful freedom of those who take part in the sport, could only be justified under the subsection if the council reasonably concluded that the prohibition was objectively necessary as the best means of managing the deer herd, or was otherwise required, on objective grounds, for the preservation or enhancement of the amenity of their area.[17]

The council appealed. In a majority judgment,[18] the Court of Appeal upheld Justice Laws decision. Sir Thomas Bingham MR gave the leading decision which focused on the council's failure to give adequate attention to the statutory power on which the land was held.

> The lack of reference to the governing statutory test was not ... a purely formal omission, for if councillors had been referred to it they would have had to attempt to define what benefit a ban would confer on the area and conversely what detriment the absence of a ban would cause.[19]

While the Court of Appeal was in agreement over the need to focus on statutory construction, it disagreed over the implication this had for the 'cruelty' argument. Bingham MR, taking the middle ground, argued that the cruelty argument was not *necessarily* irrelevant, providing it was considered in the context of benefit to the area (the statutory test), rather than as the expression of purely personal feeling.[20] Lord Justice Brown went further; he claimed 'the cruelty argument, as well as the countervailing ethical considerations, were *necessarily relevant* to the decision'.[21] The third judge, Lord Justice

Thomas took the most conservative position. Agreeing with Justice Laws, he declared that basing a decision to ban hunting on cruelty grounds went beyond the ambit of the statute on which the land was held.[22]

Hunt Governance and Land Rights

My interpretation of the conflict between hunt and council involves reading it as a contest over rural governance. The hunt's refusal to accede to the council's ban was more than simply a wish to carry on hunting. It also represented a rural body's fight to maintain its domain of authority against 'illegitimate' state interference. But what does it mean to call the hunt a governing body? Isn't it just a group of people who meet to chase, corner and shoot deer? As I have set out in earlier chapters (in particular chapter one), I use governing to refer to institutional activity which has social, political or cultural objectives embedded within it.[23] As my previous discussion of the eruv makes clear, not only state bodies govern; governance can also involve civil bodies, such as an eruv, school or, in this case, a hunt.

Discussing the hunt as a governing body does not mean that hunts identified themselves as such—with its connotations of overriding authority. They did, however, see themselves as playing a management role.

> Previous [council] committees ... had all recognised the contribution made by the sporting organisations ... that there were management contributions, and so on, which they played a part in. (Hunt supporter, interview)

Given, my interpretation of governance we can see the hunt governing in the way it regulated, structured and shaped a series of objects, terrains and discourses. Impacting in ways not fully intended (given its narrow agenda), its practices reveal the five aspects of power or government identified by Foucault: [i] a system of differentiation; [ii] objectives; [iii] application of power technologies; [iv] institutionalisation; and [v] rationalisation.[24]

Governance by the hunt

I have noticed in debates with the hunt fraternity that they behave as if they're the little sisters of mercy, trotting out now and again to rescue poor, injured deer. (Councillor, interview)

So my basic support of the field sports side is not as a hunter or fisher. It's because of what it's done in its responsibility in terms of conservation of the land. (Hunt supporter and ex-councillor, interview)

The principal object of the hunt's governance agenda, not surprisingly, concerned authority over the deer stock. This embodiment was, however, permeated by tension. On the one hand, hunting's role was identified as functional: the culling of vermin deer. Without such culling, the hunt argued, deer would destroy the local agriculture-based economy. At the same time, hunting was romanticised for nurturing beautiful, wild creatures. The Master of the QSH repeatedly claimed how much he loved the deer,[25] identifying hunting as responsible for sustenance of a healthy herd. One of the QSH main public arguments against a ban was that it would lead to less protection for deer. This argument has a long history. An early *Country Life* article dating from 1931, claimed that hunting assured the deer of protection until maturity and then death at the hands of *responsible* persons.[26] Without hunting, farmers would shoot deer in 'cold-blood',[27] with no attempt at 'responsible' species management. Alternatively, deer numbers would increase until starvation from lack of food created a new equilibrium.

The Somerset deer hunt, in common with many other British hunts, did not defend the sport on grounds primarily of enjoyment. Rationalisation for hunting instead took two other forms: sustainability and normalisation. Since deer no longer have 'natural' predators, the hunt must adopt this role to maintain the population at 'manageable' levels. Quality functions as both the objective and the means of sustainability, embedded within a bio-politics of fertility, mortality rates, social hygiene and healthy—although, in this case, not docile—bodies.[28] The hunt portrayed itself as sustaining herd quality through active eugenics, 'taking out' physically weak or aging animals or an overdominant stag.[29] 'The harbourer[30] goes out ... and selects an animal that should be hunted [for instance] elderly ones that are mating with their granddaughters'. (Member, QSH, interview)[31]

The hunt also rationalised their activity through a discourse of normalisation whereby deer were 'disciplined' to express a 'natural' wildness. Where there is no hunting, deer herds become tame;[32] they are willing to take food from humans, and no longer see them as a threat. By reminding the deer that humankind represents danger, hunters claimed, deer are kept alert and on guard—natural rather than domesticated. Normalisation also extends to the hunters. Given deer numbers need controlling, this should take place through the primordial form which pits man against beast, rather than by 'men in white coats'. (Member, QSH, interview)[33] In discussing other forms of culling, hunt members criticised the anonymity, rigidity and pleasurelessness of modern, bureaucratic practice in which there was no relationship with the deer[34]—no love, excitement or passion—just a remorseless, disinterested elimination of objects targeted for destruction. A similar argument is made by American hunters regarding the culling work of sharpshooters.[35] Embedded within this discourse is a perception of hunting as life-affirming—legitimated, even, through the consent of the hunted.

Although the deer proved the primary target for the hunt's governance remit, the QSH also expressed authority in relation to the organisation of land, community, economy and self. This does not mean the hunt was able to *control* the physical, social and economic environment, rather that it played a role in structuring its character. As one hunt supporter stated in interview,

> I support hunting because of the conservation of the land. The countryside is as it is because it's managed and that's sports related. Nobody can resource the countryside like sporting related activities.

The governance techniques deployed by the hunt linked authority over the landscape closely to authority over the construction of community, the local economy[36] and management of the self. Within rural areas, where the range of communities, employment opportunities, and

leisure activities found in urban areas do not exist, hunts have traditionally offered a highly visible, well-organised, social, cultural and
economic structure.[37]

> The role of the hunt in the community is very big ... A lot of events
> are organised by the hunt. [Otherwise] there's not very much for
> people to do. (Hunt opponent, interview)

In addition to organising social activities, deer hunting has historically
helped shore up rural hierarchies, despite the repeated modern references to working-class participation—the local postman who followed
the QSH was a frequently cited individual.[38] At the hunt, people know
their place; the structure of the hunt as an organisation has also tended
to reinforce the authority of members of the landed gentry. In part this
reflected their dominance within the hunt organisation. However,
given the fact that deer hunting is a sport that relies on access to large
areas of land, hunts' dependence on the co-operation of large
landowners reinforces the social and political authority already linked
to property ownership.[39]

As well as offering a community framework that incorporates local
residents within an intricate social and economic matrix, the hunt also
helped structure the identity and status of outsiders.[40] Its influence in
identifying who does and does not belong is important, for it also
determines who can represent the past (see chapter three)[41] and thus
the essence of the present within a locality. Yet, the cultural authority
of the hunt should not be overstated. It cannot maintain complete
control over interpretations of the rural, nor even over its own
conventions. A good example of this is 'blooding'.[42] Identified by
outsiders as a quintessential expression of the barbarism of hunting,
members of the QSH told me that, as a result, it was now rarely, if
ever, performed.

Finally, the hunt engages in the governance of self. This point was
made by several interviewees concerned that the sport was being inac-
curately equated with leisure and amusement rather than discipline
and skill. Their emphasis on self-regulation and aspiration to rigid
norms echoes other examples, such as the management of sexuality
and faith, where the dominant class set themselves apart through their

self-discipline. Traditionally linked to training for war,[43] the self-discipline of hunting is articulated to an idealised paradigm of the masculinised sportsman.[44] He demonstrates, first, the skills of primordial man that remain in our collective memory but need to be revisited if not entirely lost; second, the 'civilised' skill of the chess-game, a careful plotting and strategy of one brain against another, of man against deer; and, third, self-control, even in the ultimate moment of primordial excitement: the rout, capture and taking of another life.

Authority, legitimacy and access

I have discussed the ways in which the hunt operates as a governing body in some detail as the notion of the hunt as a governance body may seem counter-intuitive; however its existence as such is central to my discussion. In considering the impact of loss of hunting access on the hunt's governing authority, it is also important to bear in mind the hunt's status within the complex inter-organisational network making policy for the Quantock hills and deer in the early 1990s. Thus, in considering the ways in which its authority was undermined, the impact of the ban on the hunt's ability to contribute authoritatively to wider decision-making processes is important.

Somerset's ban affected the ability of the QSH to hunt, but it also had a greater effect. The withdrawal of land rights[45] challenged the hunt's status and capacity to act as a governing institution because that status and capacity largely rested on access to land. Hunting's relationship to land rights has a long history.[46] Defined by its legal relationship to the land (in contrast to poaching), hunting offered a means of expressing and asserting elite power over the rural.[47] While, traditionally, consent played a minimal role in maintaining the hunt's authority, in the 1990s the retention of credibility is crucial. As a consequence, hunts have increasingly had to justify their culling on grounds the public find acceptable: the welfare of the deer, local economy, resourcing land management, etc. Yet, these discourses are not alone enough. The legitimacy of the authority exercised by the hunt also comes from the land—from an intens(iv)e, knowing, surveying and shaping of the landscape. Such knowledge of the soil's contours and produce are the product of intently crossing the land: necessary preliminaries for a successful hunt. Thus, the hunt articulates a close, almost organic, relationship to the soil in which the ability to recognise minute changes generates the right to represent and speak on the land's behalf.

Conjoined to the land, the hunt provides the most natural, experiential form of knowing. Unlike other forms, it is already there, inscribed in the very character of the landscape.[48] There are interesting parallels here with environmental trust doctrine and the development of principles of stewardship which hold that property owners have responsibilities to present and future generations.[49] For instance, the notion that the hunt has moral representation rights as a result of activity-generated rural knowledge uncannily echoes Justice Douglas in the US Supreme Court decision of *Sierra Club* v. *Morton*.[50] There, in a dissenting judgment, he stated that those who enjoyed and used the land were its legitimate spokespeople and should be able to speak on its behalf.[51]

Challenging Traditional, Rural Governance

Access to land is clearly central to the hunt. This is not simply in order to sport; it also concerns the hunt's ability to govern with authority and legitimacy. This relationship between hunting and the land begins to clarify why Somerset's ban appeared so threatening; at stake was more than a useful strip of hunting ground. Yet it does not fully explain why Somerset chose to take this action. To understand this decision we need to consider two additional factors: first, the rise in local government activism, particularly around animal welfare and rights; and second, the value of land as a governance technique.

Local state activism

In the 1970s, Somerset council began to develop a more significant governmental role in relation to the Quantock Hills.

> Some hunt people say 'What is the council doing here anyway'?
> They [that is, the hunts] are dinosaurs, looking back to the 1940s

and 50s when there were few visitors, and commoners managed the
hills. Now the public want to use the hills and there are other new
pressures. The local authority's role is to manage pressures. We've
been involved in the hills for over twenty years, in a variety of ways,
through management plans etc. Our role ... is to talk to everyone
and take a strategic view. There were conflicts in the early 70s, with
increased visitor use, and the villages having pressures for new
developments. The County Council took on a brokerage role, and
the warden service began in 1973. (Council officer, interview)

An upsurge in local government activity to regulate and promote the
countryside for purposes of tourism and leisure coincided in the south-
west of England with another development: local government
activism. In the 1980s, activism mainly took shape in urban authorities, where the new urban left focused on affirmative action,
international solidarity and alternative economic development.[52] In
the late 1980s, however, this began to subside. In the 1990s, attention
shifted to animal welfare.

Urban councils had introduced animal welfare policies in an *ad hoc*
fashion since the 1970s.[53] Indeed, several city councils had introduced,
ultimately symbolic, hunting bans. However, from the mid-1980s,
rural authorities became increasingly active. The emergence of hunt
bans alongside prohibitions on the use of animals in circuses and the
attempted restraint on live animal exports[54] were all attempts to use
local government power to promote a particular ethic of animal
welfare and environmental consciousness.[55] Based on the belief that
people other than landowners and farmers had a legitimate interest in
the way countryside animals were treated,[56] councils attempted to
make the issue of life and death a public rather than private matter.

It is important not to over-romanticise Somerset's ban. Key considerations in reaching the decision related to land and deer management,
both of which the hunt were perceived as undermining. While some
councillors probably deployed a management discourse in order to
make their decision appear less 'political' (a tendency strengthened by
the court judgments), the opposition of several others does seem to
have rested primarily on management grounds. Nevertheless, despite
environmental management concerns, it is clear from interviews and

documentation that the 'cruelty' argument was pivotal. According to the courts it was the pivotal factor. The following discussion is therefore based on the assumption that a major reason for the ban concerned the perception that hunting was unacceptably cruel. Somerset's decision was thus more than an isolated attempt to control a strip of land, albeit less than 'the hunting of hunters' that opponents declared.[57]

Land/property as site of rural conflict

Why did Somerset tackle hunting through the withdrawal of use rights—a form of metaphorical enclosure?[58] A range of other governmental techniques was possible: regulatory, service delivery, propagandist, or price-based.[59] Why did the council reject these in favour of a strategy based on eliminating hunting from public land; one that involved governing at its most direct? Three different reasons are plausible. First, Somerset's political agenda: a ban challenges the legitimacy of hunting in a way that restrictive licensing, for example, does not. Denied access, hence the authority to speak on behalf of the soil, the hunt's ability to govern is jeopardised. Denying the hunt access to *public* land also interrogates its very membership of the local community. A body used to playing a key role in determining relations of belonging and exclusion suddenly finds the terms of its own belonging in doubt.

Second, a ban has physicality. Chris Clarke, Somerset council leader, declared, 'because of our ownership of this strategic piece of land, any vote we take will have a *real* impact'.[60] In interviews, several councillors emphasised the importance of implementing policies that would have a material manifestation, in contrast to what they saw as the excessive symbolic nature of predominantly urban initiatives such as Nuclear Free Zones. As one interviewed councillor put it,

> Nuclear Free Zone is a rather stupid concept because it's just a gesture ... It further erodes the credibility of local government. The question is can you really do something about the crime you're complaining about?

Third, a ban involved exercising the authority that emanates from private ownership rather than public regulatory power.[61] Private ownership, in this context, can be equated with governing directly— through clear statements of permission and prohibition—rather than with the more indirect, strategic and internalised mechanisms of governing mid-way and at a distance. The decision to exercise private land ownership also highlights the geographical location of the conflict. Historically, rural areas have demonstrated considerable antipathy to state intervention. The state is seen as an outsider: physically, socially and ideologically. In contrast to the authority and legitimacy that comes from an organic relationship to the soil, state regulation appears parasitic, lifeless and colonising.[62]

By using sporting rights to regulate activities on their land, Somerset attempted to behave like a private body. The council hailed itself 'as landowners...', arguing it was this designation that gave it the right and authority to impose a ban.[63] As one leading councillor interviewed stated, 'people who have land or property can decide whether things happen on their land'.[64] Legitimate decision-making power thus comes from private rights, rather than public justification. In addition, ownership control offers a legitimate weapon in restricting the land rights,[65] and wider legitimacy, of others. The adoption of a land ownership strategy by the council was therefore less an attack on private landowner rights,[66] than a decision to deploy and enforce them. However, reliance on private property rights was a double-edged sword. Somerset's authority as a governance body was explicitly diminished in the performative act of ownership by the court's denial of their landowner rights. Justice Laws declared,

> I would say that a public body enjoys no rights properly so called ... Where a right so [i.e., morally] to act is asserted by a subordinate body, whose powers by definition are not at large, the court will presume against it...[67]

His words were echoed by Thomas Bingham, Master of the Rolls,

> The reference ... to the council 'as landowners', and the statement ... that it was for every landowner to decide what activities he

wished to allow on his land, appear to equiparate the positions of private and local authority landowners. This in my view reflected a failure to appreciate the overriding statutory constraint.[68]

A defective landowner

The courts' construction of the council as a defective or inferior[69] landowner has three parts. First, judgments problematised the very possibility of public ownership. How can land legally 'belong' to a body which, as described by Justice Laws, lacks the very possibility of rights?[70] In considering local government's land, we need to distinguish between land as territory and land as property.[71] In the main, British politics does not treat local government's territorial interests with much seriousness. While councils are consulted on boundary changes, for instance, they have little power to stop them. Nevertheless, territory is important to local government: at the level of identity, authority, and as the terrain subject to its regulatory capacity.

The *Fewings* decision, however, did not concern territorial belonging, the council was not using its regulatory powers to ban hunting on private land within its boundaries (a far more difficult act) but concerned a public body's capacity to engage in legal ownership.[72] Usually, British courts treat local government as capable of possessing use and exclusion rights, as well as rights of alienation (that is, of sale or transfer).[73] While these rights are basically contingent on the pursuit of statutory objectives, problems of ownership are rarely raised. Judicial challenges to the notion that land can belong to local government emerge when authorities use their land in controversial ways, particularly when they exercise rights of exclusion against status quo forces or practices in clear pursuit of a political agenda. In *Costello v. Dacorum D.C.*,[74] it was considered perfectly legitimate for a council to purchase land in order to evict travellers. However, where an authority refused to give the local rugby team use of a council-owned stadium in protest at their refusal to discipline members who had participated in a South African tour, the court declared that they had exceeded their rights as land owners.[75]

Implicitly, despite the emphasis on councils as public bodies, the courts judge their actions against the standard of the private landowner who is assumed to act for non-political reasons. Councils are, then, penalised when they use their land for reasons not analogous to this paradigm. Consequently, the problem is not councils engaging in 'self-seeking exploitation',[76] but rather using land ownership to assert a 'territorial' agenda: mandating discriminatory spatial access or use to reinforce the political identity, character or authority of their regime. Ownership is thus contested when councils use their land to promote 'instrumental ideologies',[77] such as animal rights, workers' solidarity, or anti-racism. Dawn Oliver argues that the courts intervene in these cases because councils are using their power excessively to penalise people behaving in disliked but legal ways.[78] Yet, the notion of penalty assumes a right or legitimate expectation to hunt across public land, use a council rugby stadium or have one's newspapers stocked by local libraries. Since it is doubtful to what extent such access is a 'right', and since such rights can legitimately be withdrawn for other reasons: managerial and resource-based, for example, it is not clear why local councils should not be able to refuse permission where the activity contravenes their agreed, political agenda.

The second aspect of the illegitimate landowner concerns judicial imaginings of the rural. The courts undermined Somerset's authority in relation to Over Stowey by imagining the landscape in ways that negated the council's legitimate control. Public space suggests universal access and use, as well as public ownership. But public space inevitably will not be accessible to all activities or people. The most obvious reason is simply competing use.[79] Land used for golf cannot be used simultaneously for motorbike riding. In the case of the Quantocks, it was similarly suggested by hunt opponents, that rambling and hunting represented competing uses between which the council could legitimately arbitrate. However, the fluid and apparently adaptable nature of rambling as a pastime rendered this argument ineffective. The courts were not prepared to treat the Quantocks as a site upon which a legitimate decision about competing and incompatible uses had to be made. This does not mean, however, that the space was not constructed in an exclusionary manner. Rather than exclusion being driven by the demands of competing activities, it functioned in the identification and imagining of the land.[80]

Different writers have explored the exclusionary imagining of rural space.[81] In the case of the British countryside, its historical and cultural representation as the source of essential England[82] has led it to be inscribed as racially white and non-immigrant.[83] While neither court engaged in racialised representations of the rural, their judgments implicitly reproduced the exclusionary character of the countryside in a way that affirmed the QSH spatial imaginary and simultaneously undermined Somerset council's legitimate authority. In a historical narrative of the present, the court portrayed hunting as firmly rooted within Quantocks soil. Justice Laws declared, 'The hunt has been an established part of the scene in the area in question at least since the 1920s...'[84] Swinton Thomas LJ explicitly placed the commencement of hunting, by the QSH, four years prior to the council acquiring the land.[85] In this way, judicial dicta echoed Fewings, Master of the QSH, who declared the ban was 'a lot more than stopping hunting ... it's the whole tradition of the Quantocks'.[86]

Imagining public space structures the boundaries of appropriate practice. Justice Laws, for instance, described the 'land which is the subject of the council's prohibition' not by name but through its relationship to what is important: 'the territory over which red deer are most regularly hunted by the staghounds'.[87] Hunting becomes integral to this imagining of the Quantocks in a way that would be unlikely for off-road driving or motorbike riding. Given the latters' relative lack of status, it is unlikely their presence would be embedded within an imaginary of the hills. More likely, a ban would be defined as proper environmental management for dealing with a nuisance. Imaginings of space thus produce a fundamental polarity between 'nuisance'[88] and 'freedom'. This dichotomy is not concerned with relations between competing activities, as one might expect, but rather with the relation between activity and cultural imaginings of space. As Bingham MR stated in discussing *Costello*, where the eviction of travellers had been upheld under the same statutory provision raised in the *Fewings* case, '[t]his case is perhaps too obvious to give much help. The council acquired the land to remedy a nuisance.'[89] Nuisance becomes defined by its discord with a dominant spatial imaginary, freedom by its harmony.[90]

Sharing Management Discourse

> The only legitimate issues from our point of view were in terms of
> management and conservation. They were certainly not to look at
> whether stag hunting was correct, we would have seen it certainly
> as outside of our mandated responsibilities as a local authority.
> (Hunt supporter and ex-councillor, interview)

The third way in which the courts challenged the legitimacy of
Somerset council as landowner was through the status accorded to
management rationale. Despite the fact the wording of the key statutory section determining the way Over Stowey could be governed by
the council—S. 120(1)(b) of the Local Government Act 1972—refers
to the 'benefit, improvement or development of their area',[91] the
courts insisted on the interpretive claim that fulfilment of statutory
objectives meant land being used for 'management' purposes. In other
words, land rights, thus governance authority, became contingent on
demonstrating 'good' management.

Interviewing participants on both sides of the conflict, the significance of management discourse as a technique of legitimacy became
quickly apparent. The QSH emphasised that hunting was integral to
the good management of the deer (as a species)[92] that, without it, both
deer and environmental management would spiral out of control.
Similarly, the council defended its ban on management grounds.
Somerset were not opposed to culling; their criticism of the hunt was
that they failed efficiently to contribute to it. The council's critique of
the hunt revolved around two themes. First, the hunt did not assist in
deer governance. A key aspect of the council's argument was that the
hunt was neither necessary nor helpful to successful population
control—since the hunt could (and indeed preferred to) spend all day
chasing a single animal. In addition, the hunt did not choose the deer
most needing to be culled. Rather, Somerset claimed, reiterating a
widely held belief, the QSH chose a strong animal for a good chase.[93]

Second, Somerset disputed the hunt's commitment to wider governance norms such as environmental management. In building up its
critique, the council presented extensive evidence of damage to land
and fauna caused by the hunt, as well as the harm caused to other

users. 'In 1987, we looked at the performance of the hunt and decided it was a nuisance.. Four hundred vehicles up there, often out of control, nasty, disrupting quiet enjoyment' (Councillor, interview). Juxtaposed against a discourse of management, the hunt was depicted as articulating an anti-govern/mentality that undermined planning and husbandry. The hunt was out of control; motivated by a lust for the chase and kill,[94] it thrived on the blood, flesh, and skin of the shot deer.[95] Even opponents who saw this representation as overwrought, criticised the hunt for their refusal to submit to the democratic authority and culture of local government. According to one councillor interviewed, 'the hunting community is the last vestige of medieval and rural anarchy'.

Other opponents questioned the legitimacy of the hunt's reliance on self-regulation,

> They believe they're not answerable to anyone—above the law— just answerable to their own bodies, but nobody polices their own rules. (Hunt opponent, interview)

The hunt might obey their own rules, but, it was argued, paid little attention to the common good. At the heart of this criticism, we can see a dichotomy between public and private governance. Despite its deployment of private governance techniques, the council's concern was for others, the hunt only for itself.

Yet, despite their shared stress on the need for management, the QSH and council could not reach agreement. Each report or factual detail generated incited its counter. Are deer more successively culled by rifle? Can they feel terror from a hunt?[96] How much damage do deer cause? What effect does hunting have on the economy and deer population? Do other forms of crop protection exist? Arguments and substantiations, predating the Somerset conflict,[97] reverberated endlessly as each side wielded data that defended its activities and authority.[98] The reason why agreement could not be reached is, perhaps, obvious. Despite the deployment of management discourse by both sides, other issues were more fundamental in shaping underlying attitudes: namely, is it acceptable to cull for pleasure? Should local government be able to proscribe activities on ethical or moral grounds? Management discourse obscured these issues; it also generated further problems.

Clearly, management can function as an open-textured concept articulating different meanings.[99] However, the positivist, apolitical interpretation given to the term by all sides had serious implications. One of the effects of basing land rights on good management, constructing pleasure or morality as antithetical criteria, is that governance bodies, in this case Somerset council, become obliged to conform to existing, hegemonic norms.[100] This is not simply a domestic experience. Similar problems have confronted the Inuit people, whose demands for increased political responsibility and autonomy have been met with the requirement that first they demonstrate 'satisfactory' wildlife management.[101] The naturalised, seemingly apolitical, character of this demand facilitates its effectiveness. It is a form of governing in which subjects are clearly expected to govern themselves, and in which conflicts are blamed on technocratic or professional failure rather than being seen as involving essentially contested values.[102]

As well as constructing and requiring compliance with a particular set of norms, making governance contingent on good management also has another drawback. It runs the danger of contracting the *imagined* boundaries of political governance. This is more than a semantic point. In this chapter I have interpreted governance far more broadly than management: as concerning authority within an area as well as the structuring of resources, discourses and terrain. Management, in contrast, within the conflict, was interpreted as relating to the efficient and effective planning and use of resources for human gain and consumption. Thus, the broader remit or possibilities of governing become lost through the emphasis on management. Governing came to mean managing; other possibilities, if they were even considered, became construed as well beyond local government's remit.

Conclusion

Political activism by local government in recent years is well known. What has been less apparent are the interests within civil society affected by state intervention. In this study, Somerset council's attempt to extend its remit in animal welfare brought it into conflict with the longstanding activities of the Quantock Staghounds. As a micro apparatus of power, the QSH were not colonised by the council's action, but surpassed; their involvement in the management of the deer herds and countryside rejected. Since they were not offered co-option, they fought back, refusing to acquiesce in Somerset's attempt to set the wildlife agenda.

I have focused on land rights as providing both the terrain and techniques of struggle. For the hunt, access to land was crucial in order for hunting to take place. However, land rights were also a foundational basis for the hunt's authority and legitimacy as a governance body, involved in governing landscape, community, economy and rural, cultural imaginary, as well as the deer. The council's choice of strategy—targeting land access—thus signalled a major attack. Yet, Somerset's decision to use land rights as a governance technology also reveals something of the complex relationship between land and rural state governance, in particular, that authority is seen to emanate from land ownership rather than from public regulatory power. The status of private ownership and its separation from public authority was here reinforced by the two court decisions. Statements about local government's subordination to statute and Parliament combined with a narrow reading of S.120(1)(b) to render local state ownership contingent on hegemonic norms of appropriate governmental activity. Juridically, this concerned the legal status of the council's decision, however, the hunt's political credibility—and thus long-term access to land—was also dependent on demonstrating its essential contribution to the good management of the deer (as well as its economic and social value).

While 'management' is conceptually contested, various assumptions were apparent in the way it was deployed within this conflict. Problematic in their own right, these generated additional problems thanks to the way hunt, court and council equated governance with management. The emphasis on management as the only legitimate basis for local government environmental interventions eliminated a space within which other govern/mentalities could be legitimately expressed. Somerset did not entirely accede to this political reductionism; the council attempted to maintain a wider governance agenda in asserting its right as a democratically elected body to develop ethical policies. However, its simultaneous articulation of a positivist, managerial agenda subordinated a more oppositional set of objectives and rationalities.

Part Five

Conclusion

8   Towards Governing Out of Order

[N]o political act embodies ... a standard [of consent] perfectly prior to its institution. If it did, it would not be a *political* act, but one of administration or execution; because it does not, a political act always lacks full legitimacy at the moment of its production ...The paradox of politics/ sovereignty resides in this temporal gap between act and consent ...The temporal gap contains an element of arbitrariness not eliminable from political life.[1]

In Favour of Excess

Governing Out of Order, presents a series of images of governmentality at the close of the twentieth century. In doing so, I have chosen focal or flash-point moments that highlight my key themes of space, belonging and excessive governance; however, my perspective so far has been analytical rather than normative. I have offered interpretations of institutional and cultural power-clashes but have refrained from setting out any basis for resolution. Yet, the normative questions raised deserve consideration. Should councils be able to ban hunting on ethical grounds? Should governments be able to require the promotion of Christianity within schools? Should religious communities be able to claim symbolic ownership of public space? When do governing bodies go too far?

One way of approaching these questions is through the terms of constitutionalism which seeks to allocate and balance political power between governmental institutions. Constitutional politics asks: what powers should local government have? What forms, if any, of direct democracy should exist? What formal authority should be allocated to the president or sovereign? My intention in this final, brief chapter is not to replay this debate. I wish to address the question of governance power and authority from a different angle. In asking how we approach the question of the boundaries of institutional activity, I want to argue for a framework based on governing to excess. Broadly this requires an anti-essentialist, institutional perspective which positively recognises the capacity of governing bodies to embody a range of ideological conflicts, and to transgress the boundaries of mainstream, political practice. I thus argue against a normative approach which places rigid limits on institutional activity through conceptions of appropriate constitutional order. This form of limiting occurs in several ways. One is the legal device of *ultra vires*—where decisions are reviewed and rejected on the grounds they are beyond the powers of the institution. The imposition of order can also operate through political mechanisms, such as subordination (see chapter five), and bottom-up resistance (see chapters two and three). In the first, senior bodies attempt to maintain the status quo through the reassertion of hierarchy in the face of insubordination; in the second, the status quo is defended by lower level actors against the power-acquisition attempts of more senior bodies.

In this chapter, I want to make a case for governing 'out of order' and to advocate that institutions contest the boundaries of their authority. Such contestations can, and indeed have, taken three forms. First, they include taking decisions perceived to lie within another body's domain, for instance, local policy-making in the area of international relations or economic development.[2] Second, they involve institutions extending their existing remit, for instance, central government taking fresh steps to promote Christianity (chapter three), or taking decisions over conventionally accepted areas of jurisdiction on controversial grounds, such as animal rights (chapter seven). Third, they involve venturing into areas perceived to be outside the auspices of institutional governance per se, such as the advocacy of lesbian and gay equality (chapter five).[3] Boundaries should not be transgressed simply for the sake of doing so. My argument in favour of governing 'out of order' is based on four premises: political reality; political responsibility; political clarity; and political innovation.

Political reality

Ultra vires actions and insubordination are a political fact. Indeed, what kind of polity would we have where the boundaries of governance were not being contested? Part of the difficulty in thinking about these issues is that terms such as *ultra vires* impose a legal framework and imaginary upon political conflict. Concerned with legal rather than political capability, *ultra vires* normalises both the need for, and capacity to achieve, a division of political power. I do not wish to argue against the allocation of responsibility and legal capability altogether. However, a precise, formal division does not reflect the current situation within the British polity where responsibilities overlap, where statutory and political authority is both transferrable and subject to constant renegotiation, and where, as a result, considerable uncertainty can exist regarding institutional remit and responsibility (see chapter five). Partly this reflects the state of politics at the end of the twentieth century, but it also goes deeper. Institutional excess is both a political reality and an inevitability because of an inability to *fix* institutional behaviour. While institutions are not blank pages, they also do not have an essence that can be fully 'known'. Given their overdetermined relationship to their environment, they will always be out of control, behaving in unexpected and undesired ways. I am therefore wary of any suggestion that institutional responsibilities can be divided up in a clear, fixed manner.

One consequence of the inherent fluidity of institutional role and practice—the lack of an essential, institutional truth—is to question a political strategy that places great weight on identifying, and then implementing, a specific, 'correct' institutional arrangement or patterning. In saying this, I wish to underscore two points. First, institutional agency is mediated by a vast range of interconnected variables. I write this in the aftermath of the British Labour government's 1997 election victory, in a new political environment where people are hoping for constitutional change, and where there may be much searching for blueprints on how to reallocate political power. Yet, while progressives in London have argued for a new city-wide authority, progressives in Toronto, Canada, have campaigned against the amalgamation of local governments into one greater Toronto body.[4]

This does not mean one set is wrong. Rather, it suggests that institutional impact is contingent on specific circumstances rather than on a more abstract conception of how different bodies operate.

Second, despite the existence in Britain of a formal political hierarchy, even a sovereign Parliament cannot fully determine the behaviour of its institutional subordinates. Power is not a resource that one institution or text can collect in and then (re)distribute.[5] Thus, I would modify Clarke and Newman's claim that '[t]he state delegates—through a variety of means—its authority to subaltern organisations ... empowered to act *on its behalf*'.[6] First, changes function from the political baseline or resource allocation that currently exist. In addition, while certain forms of power can be withdrawn and reallocated—legal and financial resources, for instance—others, such as expertise and institutional authority, are harder and slower to dislodge (see chapter five). Power resources are not discrete bundles that can be given and taken away. They grow and change according to their context in ways that can only be controlled awkwardly by the centre. For instance, in the 1980s, central government withdrew many of local education authorities' (LEAs) power resources.[7] However, short of abolition (used in several instances), it proved far harder for the state to stop other forms of power from filling, at least to some degree, the remaining gap, as authority, experience and expertise were deployed by LEAs to compensate for their loss of legal and financial controls (see chapter five).

Political responsibility

Exceeding the boundaries of institutional order is a political reality. This should be validated and extended where to do otherwise would be to abdicate a more important responsibility. The hierarchical model of British governance allows institutions to disclaim responsibility through reference to someone else's orders. The premise of my argument is that this abdication of responsibility is not ethically acceptable. Since institutions exercise a governing role, they need to take responsibility for the effects of their actions and inactions, regardless of whether the issue in question is one over which they have substantial *legal* power. While it might be counterproductive to hold a subordinate body fully responsible for decisions made largely by more senior bodies, and in this way to release the latter from culpability, any participating institution needs to recognise its own agency and choice over whether or not to act. Institutional disobedience—exceeding the law—is in many ways analogous to individual non-compliance.[8] It is sometimes asserted that governing institutions have a greater duty to obey the 'law'. However, I would argue that the nature of their power and responsibility, along with their capacity to withstand political pressure, blame and penalties, makes their duty to obey laws that contravene institutional normative beliefs, less, if anything, than that required of individuals.

This may seem an extremely hazardous argument, in danger of undermining democracy, national sovereignty and the possibility of governing. Yet, instances of institutional defiance and illegality over this century, such as those demonstrated by local government, have not, in the main, had such perilous effects.[9] While some chaos did result from municipal acts of defiance,[10] this was often because of the political forces that gathered in response rather than caused solely by local government itself.[11] For the most part, defiance had other political effects: public attention, legal reform, administrative penalties, and political acquiescence. Yet, in arguing for institutional illegality as an act of political responsibility, I am not suggesting that it is the answer to all disliked acts of metagovernance. The contexts in which illegality offers a suitable strategy, as well as the form it might take, are questions that can only be addressed within a specific political situation. In addition, what becomes defined as illegal cannot always be known prior to the act or decision; while the most authoritative declarations of illegality usually come from the courts, the obtaining of such declarations is contingent on a range of different factors.[12]

Political clarity and innovation

My third basis for advocating governing out of order is that of political 'clarity'; in other words, the quality of political disputes is higher where the ideological bases for institutional decisions are made explicit. These ideological bases are increasingly obscured or 'mobilised out' by moves that define them as *ultra vires* or insubordination, in other words, by forms of meta-governance which police the reasons for a decision rather than examining the substance of the decision itself. As my discussion of the hunt, in chapter seven, demonstrates, councils may lawfully be able to ban hunting for land-use objectives, but not for reasons of morality. Similarly, the purchase of particular library newspapers can be halted for reasons of economy, but not as a way of impacting upon the newspaper company's industrial relations.[13] Thus, for local government, in particular, there is a real pressure to obscure ideological reasons for policies, and to substitute instead seemingly neutral factors such as economic or managerialist concerns. In the section below, I develop this argument in more detail.

Finally, I want to argue in favour of transgressing governing boundaries for the reason that institutions provide a useful arena not only for political debate—facilitated by ideological explicitness—but also for experimentation. In saying this, I do not mean that all transgressions are inherently positive.[14] However, the ability of governing institutions to put new ideas to the test is one of their key qualities and the reason why I have focused on *governing* bodies rather than other organisations or actors. My analysis has highlighted four forms of social and cultural experimentation: the promotion of Christianity within schools (chapter three); lesbian and gay equality (chapter five); religious symbolism within public space (chapter six); and hunt-free rural land (chapter seven).

The rest of this chapter develops my argument for governing out of order. To some, it may seem as if I am intent on advocating a breakdown in governing. Rendering underlying ideologies explicit, appropriating other bodies' functions, engaging in institutional disobedience, political experimentation—these do not sound like the practices of sound, healthy governance. However, my aim is not to advocate deep crisis, which often simply enables another governing structure to step in, rather we should recognise first the fluid, politicised, and responsible approach to institutional governance that *already* exists within many practices defined as excessive; second, that these need encouraging and extending rather than decrying or being dismantled.

Ideologically Visible Governing

It is not a vote for outdated dogma or ideology of any kind.
(Tony Blair, acceptance speech, general election, 1 May 1997)

Most of the struggles explored in this book concern attacks on institutions perceived as engaged in ideological governance. This does not mean that governance can be *non*-ideological—all governance is based on certain interpretive and normative frameworks; rather the important point is that governance can *present* itself as non-ideological. When bodies transgress this no-ideology rule, or when they can be strategically depicted as such, they become vulnerable to attack.[15] Previous chapters have identified four techniques used to construct, and contest other bodies' 'ideological' behaviour, and to achieve self-identification as non-ideological. These are positivist administration or managerialism (see chapter seven); the assertion of institutional hierarchy and constitutional norms (see chapters four, five and seven); political accountability (see chapters two, four and five); and the use of historical narrative (see chapter three).

Positivist forms of governance—with their 'end of ideology' resonance—became increasingly pervasive in Britain from the late 1980s. Epitomised in the above quotation from Tony Blair, they are based on the notion that proper governing comes from the pursuit of good management (with its uncontentious economic norms) rather than from ideology. In my discussion of deer hunting (chapter seven), the authority given to management rationale by the courts, hunt, and even by the council, as the basis for making land-use decisions, provides a clear example of this approach. Implicit advocacy of a positivist approach is also evident in the courts' rejection of socialist philanthropy as a legitimate local government objective, substituting business norms instead (chapter four), and in Hackney council's dismissal of an 'ideological' approach to equal opportunities (chapter five).

If the policies of opponents can be identified as ideological or excessively political, then it becomes possible to define one's own preferred methods and paradigms as non-ideological. If non-ideological policies are possible, they must be preferable since scientific expertise, objectivity and economic rationality generate 'better' administration than policies based on morality or political bias. Yet, positivism does not deny altogether the need for political decisions; the question becomes which bodies are suited to take them.

Although several institutions derive their legitimacy from the electoral process, it is unclear whether any body, other than perhaps Parliament, possesses sufficient legal sovereignty to pursue explicit ideological objectives. The limitations on local government acting 'ideologically' were spelled out by the courts when they overturned Somerset council's hunt ban (see chapter seven). According to Justice Laws, local government is a creature of statute, it cannot act according to norms or beliefs that do not find substantiation in positive law.[16] In a sense, local government is depicted as Parliament's agent—implementing its enacted wishes within the locality (see also chapter four).

While accountability up the institutional hierarchy has been deployed to restrict subordinate bodies from pursuing explicit, ideological politics, accountability has also been articulated laterally. For instance, courts have held local government accountable to local constituents, such as taxpayers (chapter four). Does this form of accountability offer more opportunity for ideological action since local government can claim legitimacy on the grounds it is acting according to local wishes and interests?

Taxpayer accountability has not provided a counter-discourse to local government's subordination to Parliament and statute since it has primarily functioned as a technique for interpreting legislative discretion (see chapter four). Where Parliament is unclear, the assumed wishes of local taxpayers come to the fore. But this does not make ideological governance possible; or, rather, it does, but it steers ideological practice in a particular way. As I discussed in chapter four, taxpayers were assumed by the courts to want efficient, cost-effective, business-like services. It was this set of 'common-sense' assumptions that defeated local redistributive policies and social justice initiatives. Similarly, in education, where the community was equated with parents' wishes, right-wing assumptions about parental interests were used by opponents to attack multi-faith and sex-equality initiatives (see chapters three and five).

It may seem as if I am treating the promotion of ideologically explicit change as arising only in relation to a progressive or left-wing agenda. Clearly, this is not the case. The attempt by British right-wing forces to use education legislation to embed Christian norms and values within school practice can also be seen as an example of explicit ideological politics (chapter three). While the norms and meanings conveyed came within a broadly defined common-sense— Anglocentric, Christian hegemony—the strategy nevertheless aimed to engender explicit, ideological change by reconstructing Britain as a Christian community. Perhaps because it came from central government—an institution with more legitimacy to promote ideological politics—religious education reform offers an example of legitimate ideological pursuit. By this, I do not mean that the law was not criticised. Government policy promoting Christianity in schools encountered intense resistance and opposition. However, as I discuss in chapter three, little of the resistance challenged government's right to intervene. In other words, the construction of a new religious settlement was seen as a legitimate government objective.

Yet this permission is complicated by the fact that, despite its promulgation by central rather than local government, the perception of religious education policy as politically 'in order' was heavily contingent on its representation as reestablishing *past* norms, values and practices. Proponents vigorously argued that promoting Christian values in schools was not new. Legitimised by the historical, Established character of the Church of England, and earlier education law, religious education policy was constituted as a renewal of commitment, aided by stricter enforcement measures targeting non-compliers. In chapter three, I question this portrayal of Britain's past. Yet, whether or not such conservative Christian representations are largely mythical is, here, beside the point. What I want to emphasise is that, even in this instance of Parliamentary instigation, ideological policies were couched in the language of continuity rather than change.

Explicitly ideological governance then appears, from the studies in this book, to be constrained. Bodies are obliged to couch policies in the language of historical continuity, good management, or community accountability, in order to obtain legitimacy. In some instances, this is simply a matter of presentation or discourse; in other cases, it makes particular initiatives impossible, for instance, where policies cannot be reframed within more apolitical terms. But why does this steer against ideological governance matter? I suggested above that ideologically motivated governing should be promoted, or at least facilitated. I want now to explore this argument further.

In defence of ideology

My starting-point is the belief that governance is inherently ideological.[17] In other words, all techniques, forms and objectives of governing emerge from, and articulate, particular frameworks and values. The ideological character of governance is also apparent in the fact policies impact upon, and are shaped by, social relations in asymmetrical or unequal ways. If we accept this starting-point, the notion of non-ideological governance is simply illusory, deflecting attention from the social agenda and effects of governance practices. Explicitly ideological governance, in contrast, draws attention to the substantive reasons for pursuing a particular policy. It also identifies what I would call— at least at a formal level—'good' reasons for policy initiatives or decisions. Thus, rather than seeing ideological considerations as somehow second-rate, or even sordid, I would argue that ideology is a legitimate and productive basis for decisions since it highlights the relationship between decisions and goals, and frequently makes sense of otherwise incomprehensible initiatives. Increasing Christianity's profile within schools, for example, is far more understandable when placed within a project of reaffirming a homogenous English identity and conservative community norms than within the more 'managerial' discourse of reducing teenage violence.

Defending ideological governance may seem more legitimate if it is reframed in the language of ethics—making decisions on the basis of a particular vision of the good life and of good conduct. This is because ethical decisions tend to be seen as beneficial, with a positive value judgment attached. However, I am using both ethical and ideological as analytical rather than normative concepts. I do not assume that the ideological or ethical bases for governance decisions are ones I would support or consider necessarily progressive. Rather, both terms identify the construction of policy rationales in ways that emphasise underlying values and objectives.[18]

Rendering the ideological bases for decisions visible is beneficial because it focuses attention on 'key' considerations. However, ideology goes beyond a question of motives to raise the possibility of public bodies *explicitly* pursuing ideological objectives. This is a public good for two further reasons. First, it generates a more politicised climate producing greater communal and individual agency. Recognition that social and political arrangements can be contested and altered places a greater responsibility on communities in relation to current socio-economic practices. If things can be different, those who do not like existing arrangements have an onus placed upon them to generate change. Second, a highly politicised climate, in which people debate issues, consider new possibilities, and attempt to prefigure change, offers a learning-oriented and creative environment. This is not to say that ideological governance is necessarily politically beneficial. From a progressive perspective, policies that emerge explicitly to pursue neo-conservative values will have other less positive effects, counteracting the benefits generated by anger and political action. These include demoralisation, diffusement of energy, disempowerment and, eventually, exhaustion. These last have been witnessed all too clearly in British politics over eighteen years of Conservative rule. It is also possible that heightening ideological conflict may lead people to adopt views they did not otherwise hold. In other words, we are not carriers of fixed ideological commitments. Our views on questions of race, sexuality, nationalism, and religion, for instance, are consequently open to being moulded or reorganised. This is a danger of ideological politics.

However, advocating that values and norms be centred within institutional governance is not the same as arguing for a free market in political practice, were this even possible. Within the polity we can decide that certain speech acts and institutional decisions are unacceptable on a range of grounds that might include protection from harm, equality, legitimate expectations and democratic accountability. However, these are decisions that need to be taken, rather than eliminated through formalist mechanisms such as *ultra vires* and institutional subordination.

Meta-governance and Innovation

My argument so far has focused on one aspect of governing out of order: making ideologies or norms and values explicit. I want to go on here and consider two further aspects. The first involves challenging the policies and practices of other bodies. The second concerns institutional experimentation with new initiatives.

While meta-governance in the form of review is often a way of asserting hegemonic institutional arrangements, this is not always the case. For instance, review can come from a subordinate body acting outside its conventional remit, for instance, where a school criticises or condemns government policy. This form of scrutiny might be condemned as insubordination or *ultra vires*. Its value, though, is in introducing new considerations or criteria through which institutional practices can be evaluated and explored. In addition, it enables voices to be heard that otherwise might be marginalised. For instance, as I discussed in chapter five, Kingsmead governors attempted to include the behaviour of Hackney LEA within the terms of the inquiry established to investigate headteacher, Jane Brown's conduct. The attempt was not successful. Nevertheless, it highlighted the way a school's review of its LEA can centre an alternative, potentially more expansive, reading of the authority's equal opportunities policy, and place the practices of senior LEA officials under the scrutiny of lesbian and working-class women.[19]

Whether review asserts or inverts institutional hierarchies, framing the issue as one of review rather than policy development makes the reviewed body rather than the reviewer the object of political scrutiny. This is clearly apparent if we consider judicial review, where attention is nearly always focused on the behaviour of the body before the court rather than on the court's right to judge. Other bodies, such as local government, are less able to assert their authority to review. However, attempts to do so are important. For instance, in the deer ban example, if the issue had been successfully constructed as one of reviewing the hunt, this would have kept the focus away from the council's ability to prove the ban came within their authority. Instead, the question would have been whether the hunt could justify its sport—politically if not legally—according to the discursive terms by which it was being judged. This attempt to establish the hunt as the object of review was carried out by Somerset council. However, as I discuss in chapter seven, the hunt's response to municipal efforts to place its practices under review was to shift the focus back upon the council by drawing upon the superior review powers of the court. An alternative strategy for the hunt might have been to reframe the terms by which they were evaluated. Given the success of their decision to call upon the courts, this second strategy proved less important. However, it was apparent in the hunt's attempt to shift the discourse from questions of pleasure, pain[20] and animal rights to the macro-discourse of bio-management— regulating deer numbers through hunting in the interests of agricultural protection and animal welfare.

The second form of institutional excess concerns the development of new policies, either in unexpected areas or through extending traditionally accepted areas of involvement. The character of institutions as governing bodies means they have the capacity not only to debate new ideas, but also to put them into effect—whether it is paying men and women equal wages (chapter four) or denying children access to homophobic texts (chapter five). Institutions function as effective surrogates for political debate and action because of their governance status. This works in two ways. First, even highly localised bodies possess a degree of authority, legitimacy and power. Second, the web-like relations through which they are linked[21] means channels of communication and (re)action exist. Institutions listen to each other, maybe not always well, but better than they often listen to others. Central government, for instance, may pay little heed to radical, multi-racial ideas articulated in a local community newsletter, but they pay far more attention to the same ideas expressed by a local authority or even by a school.

Institutional excesses, as I suggested earlier, are a political fact of life. Indeed, to call them excessive or transgressive is to accept their identification by opponents. The boundaries of legitimate institutional practice are not fixed once and for all, but are constantly being remade. Overstepping institutional boundaries functions as a marker of change, and as such produces conflict; at the same time, rhetorical claims that parameters have been exceeded emerge in the process of political contestation. Many political actors, particularly in Britain in the late 1990s, identified overstepping boundaries as a symptom of irresponsibility. However, as I have argued, institutional transgressions or excesses are just as likely to be the reverse. While they may indicate authoritarian rule, they may also characterise a reflexive, engaged political climate, where institutions take responsibility for the conditions that face them, whether these conditions be social problems such as poverty amongst refugees residing in their area or the actions of other bodies. For instance, as I discussed in chapter two, Canada's use of legislation to protect its fish supplies against over-harvesting by other nations, while deemed by some an irresponsible contravention of the parameters of domestic law, was supported by others who perceived Canada's action as demonstrating a far more important and overriding issue: the need to conserve fish stocks.

Similar contests emerge around the other policies I have explored in this book. Was the British government acting responsibly when it legislatively reestablished Christian teachings within maintained schools despite the degree of intervention this required in educational policy and practice? Was the eruv a responsible means of supporting orthodox, Jewish observance, given opponents' perception that it was a religious appropriation of secular neighbourhood space? In each of these instances, what is defined as responsible by one side is perceived as irresponsible by the other. This does not make the question of responsibility irrelevant. Rather, it suggests it is a much more profound, complex question than advocates of 'legality at all costs' sometimes suggest.

The Limits of Excess?

So far my discussion has explored different ways of governing out of order. However, I am not interested in advocating transgressive behaviour for its own sake, and in all circumstances. First, there is a place for institutional divisions of responsibility, even if these divisions are transgressed, evaded and rewritten in certain circumstances. Second, there is a need for boundaries to be placed on institutional activity as a whole. What do I mean by this? *Governing Out of Order* tells the story of political play between institutions. Yet, it is not intended to glorify institutions. I have argued here for the explicit politicisation of institutional practice, and for the transgression of boundaries, but I do not wish to underestimate the inevitable limits and constraints within which governing bodies function. An extensive literature exists exploring the ways in which different state arenas contain and restructure radical ideas.[22] Governing institutions within civil society are also not necessarily any more progressive as my discussion of the hunt and eruv demonstrates (see chapters six and seven). I therefore do not advocate institutional politics as a replacement for other political arenas. Rather, I identify governing institutions as forming collectively an important network of actors. Institutions not only engage in politics in their own right, but, in addition, through their power, structures and resources impact upon the choices, strategies and goals of other political forces.

Yet, given that are institutions are not the only political players does allowing them to extend their remit as wide as they like run the risk of erasing altogether a domain or series of life-choices[23] free from governmental interference. This is an important issue in a period where political debate is targeted at pushing back the state and increasing the domain of civic freedom. However, raising the issue of a domain free from institutional governance is not as straightforward as it might first appear. In this book, I have built on existing critiques to problematise the notion of a private, ungoverned realm in four ways. First, I contest the notion of a clearly delineated division between the state and civil society. Second, I treat civil bodies, such as the hunt or eruv, as exercising governance. Third, I argue that such civil bodies are as liable as other governing bodies to behave in autocratic, unaccountable ways. Fourth, while not all areas of life are subject to direct control by an institutional body, if we include governing at a distance (see chapters one and five), few, if any, areas are left untouched.

In addition, the boundary between institutional activism and individual and collective agency is not a clear one. This is not a zero-sum relationship in which the more governing institutions do, the less other actors are capable of performing. Governing institutions can give resources to and empower individuals and groups in a myriad of different ways—both intended and unintentional.[24] Conversely the agency of governing institutions, while mediated by institutional structures, processes and discourses, rests on the agency of the individuals involved. As authoritarian regimes have aptly demonstrated, if people are denied agency, institutions will fail to demonstrate it also. Thus, the capacity of governing institutions to demonstrate social responsibility and innovation is not antithetical to the capacity of individuals and communities to exercise agency but, rather, depends upon it.

Reference Notes

Preface

1 See D. Cooper, 'Defiance and Non-compliance: Religious Education and the Implementation Problem', *Current Legal Problems*, vol.48, 1995; D. Cooper, 'Strategies of Power: Legislating Worship and Religious Education', in M. Lloyd and A. Thacker (eds), *The Impact of Michel Foucault on the Social Sciences and Humanities*, Basingstoke, Macmillan, 1996.

Chapter 1

1 See *R. v. Somerset County Council, ex p. Fewings* [1995] 1 All ER 513 (High Court); [1995] 3 All ER 20 (Court of Appeal).
2 See S. Hall, *The Hard Road to Renewal*, London, Verso, 1988, ch.8; see also C. Hay, *Re-Stating Social and Political Change*, Buckingham, Open University Press, 1996, ch.7.
3 One might contest whether discretion has really been reduced or whether simply new norms are being advanced.
4 The term governance is used in a range of ways. Kooiman, for instance, defines governance as 'the pattern or structure that emerges in a social-political system as [the] 'common' result or outcome of the interacting intervention efforts of all involved actors. This pattern cannot be reduced to one actor or group of actors', see J. Kooiman, 'Findings, Speculations and Recommendations', in J. Kooiman (ed.), *Modern Governance*, London, Sage, 1993. While I find this a helpful definition, the focus of this book is on relations between *particular* institutions rather than on the wider network of governing bodies. I therefore also use the term governance to mean the techniques and practices deployed by specific bodies in the process of governing.
5 See for example, Z. Eisenstein, *The Female Body and the Law*, Berkeley, California, University of California Press, 1988; D. Herman, *The Antigay Agenda: Orthodox Vision and the Christian Right*, Chicago, University of Chicago Press, 1997.

6   The term civil society carries a range of different meanings, and has been subject to extensive feminist critique, see for instance the essays in M. Thornton (ed.), *Public and Private: Feminist Legal Debates*, Melbourne, Oxford University Press, 1995. In the discussion that follows, I mainly use the term to identify the realm in which people meet in 'everyday' encounters, and come together to form communities, organisations and other groupings, see also J. Habermas, *The Structural Transformation of the Public Sphere: An Inquiry into a Category of Bourgeois Society*, Cambridge, Mass, MIT Press, 1989.

7   Private governance can also refer to practices through which companies govern themselves. This inward-looking orientation is not the focus of my discussion.

8   See generally J. Kooiman (ed.), *Modern Governance*, London, Sage, 1993.

9   Few bodies define their own action as excessive. Even when radical policies are initiated, these are usually presented by institutional proponents as falling within the boundaries of political or legal acceptability. Alternatively, state and civil bodies may demonstrate how seemingly provocative initiatives are integral to their role or history (this is explored further in chapter eight). I also discuss this issue further in D. Cooper, 'Institutional Illegality and Disobedience: Local Government Narratives', *Oxford Journal of Legal Studies*, vol.16, 1996.

10   See H. Dreyfus and P. Rabinow, *Michel Foucault: Beyond Structuralism and Hermeneutics*, Chicago, University of Chicago Press, 1982; G. Burchell et al. (eds), *The Foucault Effect*, Chicago, University of Chicago Press, 1991; M. Dean, *Critical and Effective Histories: Foucault's Methods and Historical Sociology*, London, Routledge, 1994; A. Hunt and G. Wickham, *Foucault and Law: Towards a Sociology of Law as Governance*, London, Pluto Press, 1994; J. Simons, *Foucault and the Political*, London, Routledge, 1995; A. Barry et al. (eds), *Foucault and Political Reason*, London, UCL Press, 1996; T. Dumm, *Michel Foucault and the Politics of Freedom*, London, Sage, 1996.

11   C. Gordon, 'Governmental Rationality: An Introduction', in G. Burchell et al. (eds), *The Foucault Effect: Studies in Governmentality*, Chicago, University of Chicago Press, 1991, p.8.

12   For those seeking some background knowledge, the following works may be useful: M. Barrett and A. Phillips (eds), *Destabilising Theory: Contemporary Feminist Debates*, Cambridge, Polity Press, 1992; M. Billig, *Banal Nationalism*, London, Sage, 1995; P. Fitzpatrick (ed.), *Nationalism, Racism and the Rule of Law*, Aldershot, Dartmouth, 1995; S. Watson and K. Gibson (eds), *Postmodern Cities and Spaces*, Oxford, Blackwell, 1995; A. Barry et al. (eds), *Foucault and Political Reason*, London, UCL Press, 1996; and J. Clarke and J. Newman, *The Managerial State*, Sage, London, 1997.

13   For discussion of these new governance forms, see M. Clarke and J. Stewart, 'The Local Authority and the New Community Governance', *Regional Studies*, vol.28, 1993; J. Kooiman (ed.), *Modern Governance*,

London, Sage, 1993; R. Rhodes, 'The New Governance: Governing Without Government', *Political Studies*, vol.44, 1996.

14 For a selection of approaches, see M. Weber, *From Max Weber*, H. Gerth and C. Wright Mills (eds), Oxford, Oxford University Press, 1946; R. Miliband, *Marxism and Politics*, Oxford, Oxford University Press, 1977; N. Poulantzas, *State, Power, Socialism*, London, New Left Books, 1978; S. Franzway et al., *Staking a Claim: Feminism, Bureaucracy and the State*, Cambridge, Polity, 1989; B. Jessop, *State Theory*, Cambridge, Polity, 1990; W. Brown, 'Finding the Man in the State', *Feminist Studies*, vol.18, 1992; C. Hay, *Re-Stating Social and Political Change*, Buckingham, Open University, 1996, ch.1.

15 D. Cooper, *Sexing the City: Lesbian and Gay Politics within the Activist State*, London, Rivers Oram, 1994.

16 See L. Althusser, *Lenin and Philosophy and Other Essays*, London, New Left Books, 1971. For the wider debate, see R. Miliband, *Capitalist Democracy in Britain*, Oxford University Press, Oxford, 1982; N. Poulantzas, *State, Power, Socialism*, London, New Left Books, 1978; B. Jessop, *State Theory*, Cambridge, Polity, 1990.

17 See for instance, Z. Eisenstein, *The Female Body and the Law*, Berkeley, California, University of California Press, 1988; R. Pringle and S. Watson, 'Women's Interests and the Post-structuralist State', in M. Barrett and A. Phillips (eds), *Destabilising Theory: Contemporary Feminist Debates*, Cambridge, Polity, 1992. For an interesting and useful discussion of the state, see also T. Mitchell, 'The Limits of the State: Beyond Statist Approaches and their Critics', *American Political Science Review*, vol.85, 1992.

18 *Power in Struggle: Feminism, Sexuality and the State*, Buckingham, Open University Press, 1995, ch.4.

19 L. Althusser, *Lenin and Philosophy and Other Essays*, London, New Left Books, 1971.

20 As I discuss in chapter six, defining an eruv as a governance structure is somewhat controversial. Formally, an eruv is a notional boundary that extends the private domain within which observant Jews can carry on the sabbath.

21 See M. Foucault, 'Afterword - The Subject and Power', in H. Dreyfus and P. Rabinow, *Michel Foucault: Beyond Structuralism and Hermeneutics*, Chicago, University of Chicago Press, 1982, pp.222, 223.

22 Foucault states, 'I wish to suggest that one must analyze institutions from the standpoint of power relations, rather than vice versa', in 'Afterword - the Subject and Power', ibid., p.222. See also M. Dean, *Critical and Effective Histories: Foucault's Methods and Historical Sociology*, London, Routledge, 1994, p.179.

23 In particular, I adopt an 'internal' perspective in *Sexing the City*, op.cit., ch.3–6.

24 For instance, see J. Clarke and J. Newman, *The Managerial State*, London,

Sage, 1997, p.86. See also V. Lowndes, 'Change in Public Service Management: New Institutions and New Managerial Regimes', *Local Government Studies*, vol.23, 1997; R. Rhodes, *Understanding Governance: Policy Networks, Governance, Reflexivity and Accountability*, Buckingham, Open University Press, 1997, p.67.

25 Clarke and Newman distinguish institutions from organisations, see J. Clarke and J. Newman, *The Managerial State*, op.cit., p.86. I use both terms as relatively synonymous, although I prefer 'institution' since this has stronger connotations of governing beyond its own 'body', than the term 'organisation'.

26 See J. Keane, *Democracy and Civil Society*, London, Verso, 1988; D. Held, *Political Theory and the Modern State*, Cambridge, Polity, 1989; N. Chandhoke, *State and Civil Society*, New Delhi, Sage, 1995.

27 See Z. Eisenstein, *The Female Body and the Law*, op.cit., p.18; see also D. Rayside, 'Homophobia, Class and Party in England', *Canadian Journal of Political Science*, vol.25, 1992, p.121.

28 See for instance J. Kooiman (ed.), *Modern Governance*, op.cit.; R. Rhodes, 'The New Governance: Governing Without Government', *Political Studies*, vol.44, 1996.

29 N. Rose, 'Governing "Advanced" Liberal Democracies', in A. Barry et al. (eds), *Foucault and Political Reason*, London, UCL, 1996. See also N. Rose and P. Miller, 'Political Power beyond the State: Problematics of Government', *British Journal of Sociology*, vol.43, 1992; N. Rose, 'The Death of the Social? Re-figuring the Territory of Government', *Economy and Society*, vol.25, 1996 (cf B. Curtis, 'Taking the State back Out: Rose and Miller on Political Power', *British Journal of Sociology*, vol.46, 1995); and the discussion of Kickert's term, 'steering at a distance', in S. Ball, 'Education Policy, Power Relations and Teachers' Work', *British Journal of Educational Studies*, vol.41, 1993, p.111.

30 N. Rose, 'Governing "Advanced" Liberal Democracies', op.cit., p.46. See also N. Rose, 'The Death of the Social? Re-figuring the Territory of Government', *Economy and Society*, vol.25, 1996; M. Valverde, '"Despotism" and Ethical Liberal Governance', *Economy and Society*, vol.25, 1996.

31 N. Rose, 'Governing "Advanced" Liberal Democracies', op.cit., p.45; see also T. Popkewitz, 'Rethinking Decentralization and State/ Civil Society Distinctions: The State as a Problematic of Governing', *Journal of Education Policy*, vol.11, 1996.

Governing at a distance is therefore different to the notion of self-governing, which suggests a greater degree of independence or autonomy - not just in relation to how norms and objectives are met, but in establishing such norms and objectives as well; on self-governance, see W. Kickert, 'Complexity, Governance and Dynamics: Conceptual Explorations of Public Network Management', in J. Kooiman (ed.), *Modern Governance*, London, Sage, 1993.

32 There are echoes here of autopoietic analysis which suggests that successful regulation does not impose itself on its targeted object but incites or motivates the targeted field itself to act; see generally, G. Teubner (ed.), *Dilemmas of Law in the Welfare State*, Berlin, de Gruyter, 1996; G. Teubner (ed.), *Juridification of Social Spheres*, Berlin, de Gruyter, 1987; G. Teubner (ed.), *Autopoietic Law: A New Approach to Law and Society*, Berlin, de Gruyter, 1988.

33 A better analogy might be a game that is so well-known players immediately slip into the appropriate roles, conduct and relationships without thinking.

34 See discussion of intergovernmental management, R. Rhodes, 'The New Governance: Governing Without Government', *Political Studies*, vol.44, 1996, pp.664–5.

35 This point is made very clearly in the collection edited by J. Kooiman, *Modern Governance*, op.cit.

36 See R. Elmore, 'Backward Mapping: Implementation Research and Policy Decisions', *Political Science Quarterly*, vol.94, 1979–80; J. Sorg, 'A Typology of Implementation Behaviors of Street-Level Bureaucrats', *Policy Studies Review*, vol.2, 1983; D. Robertson, 'Program Implementation versus Program Design: Which Accounts for Policy "Failure"?', *Policy Studies Review*, vol.3, 1984; G. Teubner, 'After Legal Instrumentalism?', in G. Teubner (ed.), *Dilemmas of Law in the Welfare State*, Berlin, de Gruyter, 1986; J. Masson, 'Implementing Change for Children: Action at the Centre and Local Reaction', *Journal of Law and Society*, vol.19, 1992; R. Mayntz, 'Governing Failures and the Problem of Governability: Some Comments on a Theoretical Paradigm', in J. Kooiman (ed.), *Modern Governance*, London, Sage, 1993; D. Cooper 'Defiance and Non-compliance: Religious Education and the Implementation Problem', *Current Legal Problems*, vol.48, 1995.

37 Within an extensive literature, see for instance, M. Gottdiener, *The Social Production of Urban Space*, Austin, Texas, University of Texas Press, 1985; J. Agnew et al. (eds), *The Power of Place*, London, Unwin Hyman, 1989; D. Harvey, *The Condition of Postmodernity*, Oxford, Blackwell, 1989; E. Soja, *Postmodern Geographies: The Reassertion of Space in Critical Social Theory*, London, Verso, 1989; R. Shields, *Places on the Margin. Alternative Geographies of Modernity*, London, Routledge, 1991; J. Duncan and D. Ley, *Place, Culture and Representation*, London, Routledge, 1993; S. Lash and J. Urry, *Economies of Signs and Space*, London, Sage, 1994; D. Massey, *Space, Place and Gender*, Cambridge, Polity, 1994; D. Bell and G. Valentine (eds), *Mapping Desire*, London, Routledge, 1995; S. Watson and K. Gibson (eds), *Postmodern Cities and Spaces*, 1995; T. Creswell, *In Place / Out of Place: Geography, Ideology and Transgression*, Minneapolis, University of Minnesota Press, 1996; N. Duncan (ed.), *BodySpace*, London, Routledge, 1996.

38 For a good example of this cross-disciplinary approach, see N. Blomley, *Law, Space and the Geographies of Power*, New York, Guilford Press, 1994.

39 See for instance, J. Cream, 'Child Sexual Abuse and the Symbolic

Geographies of Cleveland', *Environment and Planning D: Society and Space*, vol.11, 1993; J. May, 'Globalization and the Politics of Place: Place and Identity in an Inner London Neighbourhood', *Transactions of the Institute of British Geographers*, vol.21, 1996.

40 T. Creswell, *In Place/Out of Place: Geography, Ideology, and Transgression*, University of Minnesota Press, Minneapolis, 1996, p.12; see also N. Blomley and J. Bakan, 'Spacing Out: Towards a Critical Geography of Law', *Osgoode Hall Law Journal*, vol.30, 1992; P. Jackson, *Maps of Meaning*, London, Routledge, 1992; E. Darian-Smith, 'Law in Place: Legal Mediations of National Identity and State Territory in Europe', in P. Fitzpatrick (ed.), *Nationalism, Racism and the Rule of Law*, Aldershot, Dartmouth, 1995.

41 See for instance, H. Benyon and R. Hudson, 'Place and Space in Contemporary Europe: Some Lessons and Reflections', *Antipode*, vol.25, 1993.

42 See for instance, Y. Shilhav, 'Spatial Strategies of the "Haredi" Population in Jerusalem', *Socio-Economic Planning Sciences*, vol.18, 1984; 'The Haredi Ghetto: The Theology Behind the Ghetto', *Contemporary Jewry*, vol.10, 1989.

43 See for instance, K. Delhi, 'Creating a Dense and Intelligent Community: Local State Formation in Early 19th Century Upper Canada', *Journal of Historical Sociology*, vol.3, 1990.

44 See for instance, D. Engel, 'Litigation Across Space and Time: Courts, Conflict, and Social Change', *Law and Society Review*, vol.24, 1990; J. Holm with J. Bowker, *Sacred Place*, London, Pinter Publishers, 1994; I. Wollaston, 'Sharing Sacred Space? The Carmelite Controversy and the Politics of Commemoration', *Patterns of Prejudice*, vol.28, 1994.

45 See also T. Creswell, *In Place/ Out of Place*, op.cit., pp.5, 37.

46 See N. Blomley and J. Bakan, 'Spacing Out: Towards a Critical Geography of Law', *Osgoode Hall Law Journal*, vol.30, 1992.

47 See for instance, A. Cohen (ed.), *Belonging. Identity and Social Organisation in British Rural Cultures*, Manchester, Manchester University Press, 1982; W. Kaplan (ed.), *Belonging. The Meaning and Future of Canadian Citizenship*, Montreal and Kingston, McGill-Queen's University Press, 1993.

48 See for instance, I.M. Young, 'The Ideal of Community and the Politics of Difference', in L. Nicholson (ed.), *Feminism/Postmodernism*, London, Routledge, 1990.

49 See D. Massey, 'A Place called Home?', *New Formations*, vol.17, 1992; E. Probyn, *Outside Belongings*, New York, Routledge, 1996.

50 For discussion in a Canadian context, see W. Kaplan, *Belonging: The Meaning and Future of Canadian Citizenship*, Montreal and Kingston, McGill-Queen's University Press, 1993.

51 For a useful collection of essays in this area, see P. Fitzpatrick (ed.), *Nationalism, Racism and the Rule of Law*, Aldershot, Dartmouth, 1995.

52 For further discussion, see D. Cooper, 'Talmudic Territory? Space, Law and Modernist Discourse', *Journal of Law and Society*, vol.23, 1996.

53 See generally, H. Kean, 'Managing Education—the Local Authority Dimension', *Journal of Education Policy,* vol.6, 1991; M. David, *Parents, Gender and Education Reform*, Cambridge, Polity, 1993; R. Deem and K. Brehony, 'Governing Bodies and Local Education Authorities: Who shall Inherit the Earth?' *Local Government Studies*, vol.19, 1993.

54 See for instance, K. O'Donovan, *Sexual Divisions in Law*, London, Weidenfeld and Nicolson, 1985; C. Pateman, *The Disorder of Women*, Cambridge, Polity, 1989, ch.6; N. Lacey, 'Theory into Practice? Pornography and the Public/Private Divide', *Journal of Law and Society*, vol.20, 1993; M. Thornton (ed.), *Public and Private: Feminist Legal Debates*, Melbourne, Oxford University Press, 1995.

55 See also M. Crawford, 'Contesting the Public Realm: Struggles over Public Space in Los Angeles', *Journal of Architectural Education*, vol.49, 1995; J. Howard, 'The Library, The Park, and the Pervert: Public Space and Homosexual Encounter in Post-world War II Atlanta', *Radical History Review*, vol.62, 1995; S. Low, 'Spatializing Culture: The Social Production and Social Construction of Public Space in Costa Rica', *American Ethnologist*, vol.23, 1996; H. Parr, 'Mental Health, Public Space, and the City: Questions of Individual and Collective Access', *Environment and Planning D: Society and Space*, vol.15, 1997.

56 For a slightly different approach which argues for the importance of separating the content of actions from the spaces in which they occur, see L. Staeheli, 'Publicity, Privacy, and Women's Political Action', *Environment and Planning D: Society and Space*, vol.14, 1996.

57 J. Weeks, *Invented Moralities: Sexual Values in an Age of Uncertainty*, Cambridge, Polity, 1995, p.131.

58 'Public' can also be in this context a euphemism for the state, although arguably the overlap is not complete. For instance, some state bodies, such as a secret security service, might not be identified as public.

59 This should not be overstated; administrative law also includes decisions recognising the essentially political and public character of local government.

Chapter 2

1 For wider discussion of related issues, see G. Hardin, 'The Tragedy of the Commons', *Science*, vol.162, 1968; R. Roberts and J. Emel, 'Uneven Development and the Tragedy of the Commons: Competing Images for Nature-Society Analysis', *Economic Geography*, vol.68, 1992; E. Schlager and E. Ostrom, 'Property-Rights Regimes and Natural Resources: A Conceptual Analysis', *Land Economics*, vol.68, 1992.

2 See generally M. Billig, *Banal Nationalism*, London, Sage, 1995.

3 I offer here a brief account of events, for a more detailed version, see D. Herman and D. Cooper, 'Anarchic Armadas, Brussels Bureaucrats, and the

Valiant Maple Leaf: Constructing British Nationhood through the Canada-Spain Fish War', *Legal Studies,* vol.17, 1997.

4 See generally, S. Abrams, 'European Economic Community: Entry of Spain and Portugal', *Harvard International Law Journal*, vol.27, 1986; I. Aurrecoechea, 'Some Problems Concerning the Constitutional Basis for Spain's Accession to the European Community', *International and Comparative Law Quarterly*, vol.36, 1987, p.14; F. S. Gadea and S. M. Lage, 'Spanish Accession to the European Communities: Legal and Constitutional Implications', *Common Market Law Review*, vol.23, 1986, p.11; I. Aurrecoechea, 'The Role of the Autonomous Communities in the Implementation of European Community Law in Spain', *International and Comparative Law Quarterly*, vol.38, 1989, p.74.

5 See R.R. Churchill, *EC Fisheries Law*, Dordecht, ND, Martinus Nijoff, 1987; A. Karagiannakos, *Fisheries Management in the European Union*, Aldershot, Avebury, 1995. For an early history of the CFP, see J. Farnell and J. Elles, *In Search of a Common Fisheries Policy*, Aldershot, Gower, 1984.

6 S. Abrams, 'European Economic Community: Entry of Spain and Portugal', op.cit.; pp.256–7; A. Karagiannakos, *Fisheries Management in the European Union*, op.cit., pp.116–17.

7 J. Farnell and J. Elles, *In Search of a Common Fisheries Policy* op.cit., p.22.

8 A. Karagiannakos, *Fisheries Management in the European Union*, op.cit., p.115.

9 See P. Davies and C. Redgwell, 'The International Legal Regulation of Straddling Fish Stocks', *British Yearbook of International Law*, vol.67, 1998. Greenland halibut is a groundfish that straddles the border between Canada's exclusive fishing zone and adjacent international waters.

10 See *Reuters European Community Reports*, 10 March 1995.

11 *The Financial Times*, 27 March 1995; The *Guardian*, 28 March 1995.

12 *Independent*, 29 March 1995; *The Times*, 30 March 1995; *The Times*, 31 March 1995.

13 The letter was then issued from the desk of the French Presidency of the EU Council of Ministers, rather than from the European Commission itself. See *European Reports*, 1 April 1995.

14 *European Reports*, 8 April 1995.

15 *European Reports*, 12 April 1995.

16 *European Reports*, 14 April 1995.

17 It was formally adopted by the EU Council of Ministers (Portugal voting against) on April 17, and confirmed by Agreed Minute on 20 April. See *European Insight*, 21 April 1995.

18 *The Financial Times*, 18 April 1995.

19 Earl of Clanwilliam, *Lords*, 30 March 1995, col.1767 (italics added). See also, Lord Stodart, ibid., col.1764 and 22 March 1995, col.1224; Austin Mitchell, MP, *Commons*, 13 March 1995, col.564.

20 See *Lords*, 7 February 1995, col.103–4.

21 Lord Stoddart, *Lords*, 30 March 1995, col.1764.

22 Michael Colvin, MP, *Commons*, 13 March 1995, col.564.

23 The Earl of Kinnoull, *Lords*, 30 March 1995, col.1761.

24 See B.R. Burg, *Sodomy and the Pirate Tradition*, New York, New York University Press, 1983.

25 D. Herman, *The Antigay Agenda: Orthodox Vision and the Christian Right*, Chicago, University of Chicago Press, 1997.

26 See *MacLeans*, 27 March 1995; Graham Riddick, MP, *Commons*, 13 March 1995, col.567–8.

27 See Earl of Kinnoull, *Lords*, 30 March 1995, col.1761–2. See also Canadian Ministers comments about 'baby' and 'immature' fish in *Maclean's*, 27 March 1995.

28 See generally, G. Mosse, *Nationalism and Sexuality*, New York, Howard Fertig, 1985.

29 Lord Willoughby de Broke, *Lords*, 30 March 1995, col.1769.

30 Lord Morris, *Lords*, 30 March 1995, col.1771.

31 Margaret Ewing, MP, *Commons*, 13 March 1995, col.565; also Gwyneth Dunwoody, MP, ibid.

32 Lord Willoughby de Broke, *Lords*, 30 March 1995, col.1769.

33 Lord Onslow, *Lords*, 22 March 1995, col.1225.

34 For discussion of the relationship between gender, race and nationalism, see G. Mosse, *Nationalism and Sexuality*, op.cit, ch.7; A. Brah, 'Reframing Europe: En-gendered Racisms, Ethnicities and Nationalisms in Contemporary Europe', *Feminist Review*, vol.45, 1993, p.9; C. Enloe, *The Morning After*, Berkeley, University of California Press, 1993; N. Yuval-Davis, 'Gender and Nation', *Ethnic and Racial Studies*, vol.16, 1993, p.621; A. McClintock, '"No Longer in a Future Heaven": Nationalism, Gender, and Race', in G. Eley and R. Suny (eds), *Becoming National*, New York, Oxford University Press, 1996; N. Yuval-Davis, *Gender and Nation*, London, Sage, 1997.

35 My thanks to Didi Herman for this phrase.

36 *Commons*, 13 March 1995, col.561.

37 Allan Rogers, MP, *Commons*, 13 March 1995, col.568.

38 *Lords*, 30 March 1995, col.1775.

39 See generally, L. Hagendoorn, 'Ethnic Categorization and Outgroup Exclusion: Cultural Values and Social Stereotypes in the Construction of Ethnic Hierarchies', *Ethnic and Racial Studies*, vol.16, 1993, p.26; N. Yuval-Davis, *Gender and Nation*, op.cit.

40 See William Waldegrave, MP, *Commons*, 28 March 1995, col.829; Theresa Gorman, MP, ibid., 29 March 1995, col.1014. David Harris, MP, ibid., 28 March 1995, col.828 describes Bonino as having 'gone completely over the top'.

41 See G. Seidel and R. Gunther, '"Nation" and "Family" in the British Media Reporting of the "Falklands Conflict"', in G. Seidel (ed.), *The Nature of the Right*, Amsterdam, John Benjamins, 1988.

42 *Lords*, 30 March 1995, col.1772.

43 See M. Billig, *Banal Nationalism*, op.cit., p.91.

44 It is not particularly surprising that Quebec is erased in depictions of Canada. Nominally Catholic, Quebec's identity is as much forged through being un-English as it is through being Quebecois. Moreover, with little shared culture, Quebec has historically shown no allegiance to Britain. Indigenous peoples, other immigrant communities, and non-Anglo ethnic groups are also erased in the representation of Canada. See for instance, Jane Jenson, 'What's in a Name? Nationalist Movements and Public Discourse', in H. Johnstone and B. Klandermans (ed.), *Social Movements and Culture*, London, UCL Press, 1993.

45 Theresa Gorman, MP, *Commons*, 29 March 1995, col.1014; also Teddy Taylor, MP, ibid., 28 March 1995, col.829, 13 March 1995, col.562.

46 Lord Stoddart, *Lords*, 22 March 1995, col.1224. On the Falklands war and political discourse generally, see J. Aulich (ed.), *Framing the Falklands War: Nationhood, Culture and Identity*, Milton Keynes, Open University Press, 1992.

47 Earl of Onslow, *Lords*, 22 March 1995, col.1225.

48 Austin Mitchell, MP, *Commons*, 13 March 1995, col.563.

49 Peter Hardy, MP, *Commons*, 13 March 1995, col.568.

50 See, Lord Morris, *Lords*, 30 March 1995, col.1771; also John Wilkinson, MP, *Commons*, 18 April 1995, col.23.

51 See generally P. Fitzpatrick, *The Mythology of Modern Law*, London, Routledge, 1992.

52 *Commons*, 18 April 1995, col.26. See also Earl of Onslow, *Lords*, 22 March 1995, col.1225.

53 For a useful discussion of the way in which Quebec and the Rest of Canada is constituted in gendered and sexualized terms, see C. Stychin, 'Queer Nations: Nationalism, Sexuality and the Discourse of Rights in Quebec', *Feminist Legal Studies*, vol.5, 1997.

54 G. Mosse, *Nationalism and Sexuality*, op.cit., p.13.

55 See John Wilkinson, MP, *Commons*, 18 April 1995, col.23; Graham Riddick, MP, ibid., 23 March 1995, col.567; Lord Willoughby de Broke, *Lords*, 22 March 1995, col.1223; Lord Shaughnessy, ibid., 22 March 1995, col.1224.

56 Michael Jack, MP, *Commons*, 13 March 1995, col.564.

57 See P. Davies and C. Redgwell, 'The International Legal Regulation of Straddling Fish Stocks', op.cit.

58 For sympathetic coverage in the mainstream press, see *Independent on Sunday*, 12 March 1995; *Financial Times*, 18 March 1995; *Independent*, 19 March 1995, 29 March 1995. Coverage in the tabloid press was rabidly anti-Spanish and pro-Canadian.

59 *Commons*, 18 April 1995, col.24.

60 See C. Stychin, 'A Postmodern Constitutionalism: Equality Rights, Identity Politics, and the Canadian National Imagination', *Dalhousie Law Journal*,

vol.17, 1994, pp.61–82.

61 In this regard, science is a double-edged sword. While it makes possible actuarial calculations that quantify sustainable fishing, it is also responsible for the increased 'efficiency' of vessels and fishing techniques that have largely generated the problem. See Earl of Clanwilliam, *Lords*, 30 March 1995, col.1766; Lord Morris, ibid, 30 March 1995, col.1771; *Macleans*, 27 March 1995.

62 T. Kuehls, 'The Nature of the State: An Ecological (Re)reading of Sovereignty and Territory', in M. Ringrose and A.J. Lerner (eds), *Reimagining the Nation*, Milton Keynes, Open University Press, 1993, pp.139–55. See also J. Anderson, 'The Shifting Stage of Politics: New Medieval and Postmodern Territorialities?' *Environment and Planning D: Society and Space*, vol.14, 1996, p.149.

63 See A. Owers, 'The Age of Internal Controls?' in S. Spencer (ed.), *Strangers and Citizens*, London, Rivers Oram, 1994; A. Paliwala, 'Law and the Constitution of the "Immigrant" in Europe: A UK Policy Perspective', in P. Fitzpatrick (ed.), *Nationalism, Racism and the Rule of Law*, Aldershot, Dartmouth, 1995; C. Hadjimichalis and D. Sadler, *Europe at the Margins: New Mosaics of Inequality*, London, Wiley, 1995; D. O'Keeffe, 'The Emergence of a European Immigration Policy', *European Law Review*, vol.20, 1995, p.20.

64 E. Renan, 'What is a Nation?', in H.K. Bhabha (ed.), *Nation and Narration*, London, Routledge, 1990, p.11.

65 See my discussion in *Sexing the City: Lesbian and Gay Politics within the Activist State*, London, Rivers Oram, 1994, pp.114–15.

66 Allan Rogers, MP, *Commons*, 13 March 1995, col.568. See also Nicholas Winterton, MP, ibid., 18 April 1995, col.25.

67 See Michael Jack, MP, *Commons*, 13 March 1995, col.565, 568; John Wilkinson, MP, ibid., 18 April 1995, col.23, 28 March 1995, col.832; Hartley Booth, MP, ibid., 13 March 1995, col.570; Baroness Elles, *Lords*, 30 March 1995, col.1765. See generally, G.R. Johnson, 'In the Name of the Fatherland: An Analysis of Kin Term Usage in Patriotic Speech and Literature', *International Political Science Review*, vol.8, 1987, pp.165–74.

68 *Commons*, 28 March 1995, col.829.

69 Gary Streeter, MP, *Commons*, 28 March 1995, col.829.

70 Baroness Elles, *Lords*, 30 March 1995, col.1765.

71 *Commons*, 13 March 1995, col.568.

72 Allan Rogers, MP, *Commons*, 13 March 1995, col.568.

73 G. Delanty, *Inventing Europe*, Basingstoke, Macmillan, 1995, p.98.

74 R.L. Doty, 'Sovereignty and the Nation: Constructing the Boundaries of National Identity', in T. Biersteker and C. Weber (eds), *State Sovereignty as Social Construct*, Melbourne, Cambridge University Press, 1996, pp.124–5.

75 Ibid.

76 For instance, in relation to Grenada, and South African sanctions during the Thatcher years of the 1980s, Britain revealed a much more ambivalent rela-

tionship to the Commonwealth. Thanks to Carl Stychin for raising this point.

77 *Commons*, 13 March 1995, col.562.

78 G. Marks et al., 'European Integration from the 1980s: State-Centric v. Multi-Level Governance', *Journal of Common Market Studies*, vol.34, 1996.

79 See for instance, Nigel Spearing, MP, *Commons*, 13 March 1995, col.569.

80 M. Billig, *Banal Nationalism*, op.cit., p.141. For critique of this view see J. Anderson, op.cit.; Preuß, 'Two Challenges to European Citizenship', *Political Studies*, vol.44, 1996, p.549.

81 A. Barry et al., 'The European Community and European Government: Harmonization, Mobility and Space', *Economy and Society Review*, vol.22, 1993, pp.314–26.

82 R. Munch, 'Between Nation-State, Regionalism and World Society: The European Integration Process', *Journal of Common Market Studies* vol.34, 1996, p.385; see also D. Morley and K. Robins, 'No Place like Heimat: Images of Home(land) in European Culture', *New Formations*, vol.12, 1990; K. Reif, 'Cultural Convergence and Cultural Diversity as Factors in European Identity', in S. Garcia (ed.), *European Identity and the Search for Legitimacy*, London, Pinter, 1993. Some writers have argued for the creation of a European political citizenship rather than a European cultural identity, see for example, J. Habermas, 'Citizenship and National Identity: Some Reflections on the Future of Europe', *Praxis International*, vol.12, 1992, p.1; J. Habermas, 'European Citizenship and National Identities', in B. Van Steenbergen (ed.), *The Conditions of Citizenship*, London, Sage, 1994; A.S. Nørgaard, 'Institutions and Post-Modernity in IR. The "New" EC', *Cooperation and Conflict*, vol.29, 1944; C. Gamberale, 'European Citizenship and Political Identity', *Space and Polity*, vol.1, 1997, p.37.

83 K. Wilson and J. Van der Dussen (eds), *The History of the Idea of Europe*, Milton Keynes, Open University Press, 1995, p.184.

84 Viscount Mountgarret, *Lords*, 7 February 1995, col.104.

85 Lord Stoddart, *Lords*, 7 February 1995, col. 103–4.

86 *Lords*, 30 March 1995, col.1769–70. See also A. Barry et al., 'The European Community and European Government: Harmonization, Mobility and Space', *Economy and Society Review*, vol.22, 1993.

87 I. Hont, 'The Permanent Crisis of a Divided Mankind: "Contemporary Crisis of the Nation State" in Historical Perspective', *Political Studies*, vol.42, p.172.

88 For an alternative approach to power and marginalisation as a result of European integration, see C. Hadjimichalis and D. Sadler (eds), *Europe at the Margins: New Mosaics of Inequality*, London, Wiley, 1993.

89 *European Report*, 8 April 1995.

90 *Lords*, 22 March 1995, col.1225. See also, Lord McAvoy, ibid., 23 March 1995, col.477.

91 Lord Stoddart, *Lords*, 30 March 1995, col.1763.

92 G. Delanty, *Inventing Europe*, Basingstoke, Macmillan, 1995, p.46.

93 Lord Stoddart, *Lords*, 30 March 1995, col.1763.

94 Earl Howe, *Lords*, 22 March 1995, col.1223.

95 Baroness Chalker, Lords, 16 March 1995, col.52; Earl Howe, ibid., 22 March 1995, col.1223; William Waldegrave, MP, *Commons*, 28 March 1995, col.827. See also Douglas Hurd MP, quoted in *The Times*, 16 March 1995.

96 *Commons*, 18 April 1995, col.25.

97 For example, see Allan Rogers, MP, *Commons*, 13 March 1995, col.568.

98 Michael Jack, MP, *Commons*, 13 March 1995, col.477; William Waldegrave, MP, ibid., 28 March 1995, col.827, 829.

99 Michael Jack, MP, *Commons*, 13 March 1995, col.477.

100 William Waldegrave, MP, *Commons*, 18 April 1995, col. 21–2.

101 A. Murphy, ' The Sovereign State System as Political-Territorial Ideal: Historical and Contemporary Considerations', in T. Biersteker and C. Weber (eds), *State Sovereignty as Social Construct*, Melbourne, Cambridge University Press, 1996, p.98.

102 *Commons*, 18 April 1995, col.25–6.

103 *Commons*, 29 March 1995, col.1014.

104 See Michael Jack, MP, *Commons*, 23 March 1995, col.477.

105 William Waldegrave, MP, *Commons*, 28 March 1995, col.827.

106 P. Fitzpatrick, *The Mythology of Modern Law*, op.cit., p.115.

107 Earl Howe, *Lords*, 22 March 1995, col.1223.

108 See Lord Stoddart, *Lords*, 30 March 1995, col.1764.

109 M. Billig, *Banal Nationalism*, op.cit., p.41.

Chapter 3

1 E.R. Norman, 'The Threat to Religion', in C. Cox and R. Boyson (eds), *Black Paper 1977*, London, Maurice Temple Smith, 1977, p.101.

2 *Lords*, 3 May 1988, col.503.

3 I. Goodson, '"Nations at Risk" and "National Curriculum": Ideology and Identity', *Cultural Diversity and the School*, vol.1, 1992; S. Ball, 'Education, Majorism and "the Curriculum of the Dead"', *Curriculum Studies*, vol.1, 1993; J. Beck, 'Nation, Curriculum and Identity in Conservative Cultural Analysis', *Cambridge Journal of Education*, vol.26, 1996.

4 See for instance M. Poole and J. Sachs, 'Social Assimilation or Cultural Mosaic?', *Cultural Diversity and the School*, vol.1, 1992; I.T. Leonetti, 'From Multicultural to Intercultural: Is it Necessary to Move from One to the Other', *Cultural Diversity and the School*, vol.1, 1992.

5 For instance, see discussion in G. Sorenson, 'Religion and American Public Education', *Education and Urban Society*, vol.28, 1996.

6 See M. McCarthy, 'People of Faith as Political Activists in Public Schools', *Education and Urban Society*, vol.28, 1996.

7   See for example, *Wallace* v. *Jaffree* (1985) 472 US 38, 86 L Ed 2d 29, 105 S
    Ct 2479; see also M. McCarthy, 'People of Faith as Political Activists in
    Public Schools', *Education and Urban Society*, vol.28, 1996, p.317.

8   See J. Burn and C. Hart, *The Crisis in Religious Education*, London, The
    Educational Research Trust, 1988, p.5; C. Hart, 'Legislation and Religious
    Education', *Education and the Law*, vol.5, 1993.

9   See also A. Bradney, 'The Dewsbury Affair and the Education Reform Act',
    Education and the Law, vol.1, 1989, p.51.

10 F. Naylor, *The School Above the Pub*, London, The Claridge Press, 1989,
    p.106.

11 See Baroness Cox, *Lords*, 26 February 1988, col.1454.

12 E.R. Norman, 'The Threat to Religion', op.cit., p.101.

13 *Lords*, 26 February 1988, col.1455.

14 Cited in J. Burn and C. Hart, *The Crisis in Religious Education*, op.cit.

15 See The Hillgate Group, *The Reform of British Education*, London, The
    Claridge Press, 1987, p.4.

16 See E.R. Norman, 'The Threat to Religion', op.cit.; S. Ball, 'Education,
    Majorism and "the Curriculum of the Dead"', op.cit.

17 F. Naylor, *Dewsbury: The School Above the Pub*, op.cit., pp.120–1. For explo-
    ration and development of a more progressive approach to religious educa-
    tion, see R. Jackson, *Religious Education. An Interpretive Approach*, London,
    Hodder & Stoughton, 1997.

18 For advocacy of a relational approach, see J. Hull, *Mishmash: Religious
    Education in Multi-cultural Britain—A Study in Metaphor*, Birmingham,
    University of Birmingham and the Christian Education Movement, 1991.

19 Baroness Cox, *Lords*, 26 February 1988, col.1456.

20 E.R. Norman, 'The Threat to Religion', op.cit., p.100.

21 J. Burn and C. Hart, *The Crisis in Religious Education*, op.cit., p.8.

22 Anthony Coombs, MP, *Commons*, 23 March 1988, col.403.

23 *Commons*, 23 March 1988, col.416.

24 *Commons*, 23 March 1988, col.416.

25 Viscount Tonypandy, *Lords*, 21 June 1988, col.646.

26 See M. Durham, *Sex and Politics*, London, Macmillan, 1991.

27 Lord Swinfen, *Lords*, 26 February 1988, col.1473–4.

28 *Lords*, 26 February 1988, col.1485.

29 For discussion of the evangelical politics of the Christian Right in the USA,
    see S. Diamond, *Spiritual Warfare: The Politics of the Christian Right*, Boston,
    MA, South End Press, 1989; D. Herman, *The Antigay Agenda: Orthodox Vision
    and the Christian Right*, Chicago, University of Chicago Press, 1997.

30 See F. Naylor, *Dewsbury: The School above the Pub*, op.cit. See also C. Dyer,
    'Constructions of Muslim Identity and the Contesting of Power: The Debate
    over Muslim Schools in the United Kingdom', in P. Jackson and J. Penrose
    (eds), *Constructions of Race, Place and Nation*, London, UCL Press, 1993.

31 See also S. Poulter, 'The Religious Education Provisions of the Education

Reform Act 1988', *Education and the Law*, vol.2, 1990, p.1; J. Tamney, 'Conservative Government and Support for the Religious Institution: Religious Education in English Schools', *The British Journal of Sociology*, vol.45, 1994, p.195; C. Hamilton, *Family, Law and Religion*, London, Sweet and Maxwell, 1995.

32 Differing provisions exist for pupils in grant-maintained, voluntary controlled, voluntary aided and special agreement schools.

33 J. Hull, 'The New Government Guidelines on Religious Education', *British Journal of Religious Education*, vol.16, 1994, p.66; G. Robson, 'Religious Education, Government Policy and Professional Practice, 1985–1995', *British Journal of Religious Education*, vol.19, 1996.

34 QBD, 26 February 1993, lexis.

35 Emphasis added.

36 C. Hamilton, *Family, Law and Religion*, op.cit., p.244.

37 See B. Steinberg, 'Anglo-Jewry and the 1944 Education Act', *Jewish Journal of Sociology*, vol.30, 1988.

38 Baroness Macleod of Borve, *Lords*, 26 February 1988, col.1475.

39 For instance, see Jack Straw, MP, *Commons*, 18 July 1988, col.819.

40 Emphasis added.

41 Baroness Cox, Lords, 3 May 1988, col.504. See also J. Haldane, 'Religious Education in a Pluralist Society', *British Journal of Educational Studies*, vol.34, 1986; for a useful critique, see R. Jackson, 'Religious Education's Representation of "Religions" and "Cultures"', *British Journal of Educational Studies*, vol.43, 1995.

42 In this chapter, I talk about England rather than Britain to reflect the Christian Right's focus; for discussion of the confusion between England and Britain, see L. Andrews, 'New Labour, New England?' in M. Perryman (ed.), *The Blair Agenda*, London, Lawrence and Wishart, 1996, p.128.

43 See also S. Ball, 'Education, Majorism and "the Curriculum of the Dead"', op.cit.

44 *Lords*, 26 February 1988, col.1469.

45 Lord Bishop of Truro, *Lords*, 26 February 1988, col.1463.

46 Anthony Coombs, MP, *Commons*, 23 March 1988, col.404.

47 See generally, F. Anthias and N. Yuval-Davis, *Racialized Boundaries*, London, Routledge, 1992, p.55.

48 See also J. Hull, *Mishmash. Religious Education in Multi-cultural Britain - A Study in Metaphor*, op.cit., p.17; R. Cohen, *Frontiers of Identity*, Harlow, Longman, 1994, p.202.

49 See for instance, A. Stoler, 'Sexual Affronts and Racial Frontiers: National Identity, "Mixed Bloods" and the Cultural Genealogies of Europeans in Colonial Southeast Asia', *Comparative Studies in Society and History*, vol.34, 1992. See also A.M. Smith, 'The Imaginary Inclusion of the Assimilable "Good Homosexual": The British New Right's Representations of Sexuality and Race', *Diacritics*, vol.24, 1994; D. Herman, *The Antigay Agenda: Orthodox*

Vision and the Christian Right, Chicago, Chicago University Press, 1996.

50 See C. Hamilton, *Family, Law and Religion*, op.cit., p.300.

51 For use of 'host' discourse in relation to religious education, see also J. Haldane, 'Religious Education in a Pluralist Society', *British Journal of Educational Studies*, vol.34, 1986, p.164.

52 Peter Emery, MP, *Commons*, 18 July 1988, col.836.

53 C. Hamilton, *Family, Law and Religion*, op.cit., p.282.

54 M. Foucault, *The History of Sexuality*, London, Penguin, 1981.

55 M. Foucault, *The History of Sexuality*, op.cit.

56 See for instance, M. Durham, *Sex and Politics*, op.cit.

57 Justice O'Connor, *Wallace* v. *Jaffree* 472 US 38, 86 LEd 2d 29, 105 Ct 2479 (1985) p.59.

58 See generally I. Hunter, 'Assembling the School', in A. Barry et al. (eds), *Foucault and Political Reason*, London, UCL Press, 1996.

59 See generally J. Simons, *Foucault and the Political*, London, Routledge, 1995, p.39; T. Osborne, 'Security and Vitality: Drains, Liberalism and Power in the Nineteenth Century', in A. Barry et al. (eds), *Foucault and Political Reason*, op.cit., p.100.

60 Lord Ashbourne, *Lords*, 26 February 1988, col.1467.

61 J. Butler, *Gender Trouble*, New York, Routledge, 1990, p.25.

62 Baroness Cox, *Lords*, 26 February 1988, col.1453; Mr Alison, MP, *Commons*, 18 July 1988, col.831; Mr Gregory, MP, ibid., 18 July 1988, col.833.

63 Lord Swinfen, *Lords*, 26 February 1988, col.1473.

64 For a useful critique of the concept of tolerance, see J. Weeks, 'Rediscovering Values', in J. Squires (ed.), *Principled Positions*, London, Lawrence and Wishart, 1993.

65 Baroness Blatch, *Lords*, 26 February 1988, col.1466; see also Lady Maitland, ibid., 10 November 1992, col.818.

66 J. Burn and C. Hart, *The Crisis in Religious Education*, op.cit., p.29.

67 See D. Cooper, 'Defiance and Non-compliance: Religious Education and the Implementation Problem', *Current Legal Problems*, vol.48, 1995; D. Cooper, 'Strategies of Power: Legislating Worship and Religious Education', in M. Lloyd and A. Thacker (eds), *The Impact of Michel Foucault on the Social Sciences and Humanities*, Basingstoke, Macmillan, 1996.

68 F. Abrams, *Independent on Sunday*, 18 September 1994. The 1992–3 HMI inspection revealed that at least twenty per cent of primary schools had no religious education, see R. Klein, *Times Education Supplement*, 9 September 1994.

69 C. Hamilton, *Family, Law and Religion*, op.cit., p.293.

70 33 U.S. 203 (1948).

71 See *Daily Telegraph* 6 January 1998, 7 January 1998.

Chapter 4

1 Whether council decisions were within their statutory discretion was a contested point. Judicial techniques were deployed not just to structure discretion but also to identify its limits, for instance, by finding the decision to have been made for a purpose outside the basis on which the statutory power was granted or was fundamentally unreasonable or irrational, see G. Peiris, 'Wednesbury Unreasonableness: The Expanding Canvass', *Cambridge Law Journal*, vol.46, 1987.

2 See J. Locke, *Two Treatises of Government*, P. Laslett (ed.), Cambridge, Cambridge University Press, 1988.

3 I use the term class in the legal rather than socio-economic sense to identify a legally-identified category of people.

4 For discussion of local government's fiduciary duty, see C. Crawford, 'Auditors, Local Government and the Fiduciary Duty', *Public Law*, 1983, p.248; J. Dignan, 'Policy-making, Local Authorities, and the Courts: The "GLC Fares" Case', *Law Quarterly Review*, vol.99, 1983, p.605; P. Fennell, '*Roberts* v. *Hopwood*: The Rule against Socialism', *Journal of Law and Society*, vol.13, 1986, p.401; W. Wade, *Administrative Law*, Oxford, Clarendon Press, 1988, pp.424–7; J. Goudie, 'Local Authorities and Fiduciary Duty', in M. Supperstone and J. Goudie (eds), *Judicial Review*, London, Butterworths, 1992; I. McLeod, 'The Local Ombudsman and the Fiduciary Duty of Local Authorities', *Local Government Review*, vol.156, 1992, p.361; M. Loughlin, *Legality and Locality: The Role of Law in Central-Local Government Relations*, Oxford, Clarendon, ch.4.

5 G. Moffat, *Trusts Law*, (second edition), London, Butterworths, 1994, p.547.

6 See discussion in L. Rotman, *Parallel Paths: Fiduciary Doctrine and the Crown-Native Relationship in Canada*, Toronto, University of Toronto Press, 1996, ch.9.

7 See B. Dickens, 'Medical Records—Patient's Right to Receive Copies—Physician's Fiduciary Duty of Disclosure: *McInerney* v. *MacDonald*', *The Canadian Bar Review*, vol.73, 1994; A. Grubb, 'The Doctor as Fiduciary', *Current Legal Problems*, vol.47, 1994; H. Kutchins, 'The Fiduciary Relationship: The Legal Basis for Social Workers', *Social Work*, vol.36, 1991.

8 T. Frankel, 'Fiduciary Law', *California Law Review*, vol.71, 1983.

9 The United States and Canadian literature on trust and fiduciary responsibilities to indigenous peoples is extensive. The references here identify a cross-section of what is available. N. Newton, 'Enforcing the Federal-Indian Trust Relationship after *Mitchell*', *Catholic University Law Review*, vol.31, 1982; J. Hurley, 'The Crown's Fiduciary Duty and Indian Title: *Guerin* v. *The Queen*', *McGill Law Journal*, vol.30, 1985; L. Leventhal, 'American Indians—The Trust Responsibility: An Overview', *Hamline Law Review*, vol.8, 1985, p.625; S. Young, 'Indian Tribal Responsibility and American Fiduciary

Undertakings', *Whittier Law Review*, vol.8, 1987; R. Bartlett, 'The Fiduciary Obligation of the Crown to the Indians', *Saskatchewan Law Review*, vol.53, 1989; A. Pratt, 'Aboriginal Self-Government and the Crown's Fiduciary Duty: Squaring the Circle or Completing the Circle', *National Journal of Constitutional Law* vol.2, 1992; R. Blowes, 'Governments: Can you Trust them with your Traditional Title: Mabo and Fiduciary Obligations of Governments', *Sydney Law Review*, vol.15, 1993; L. Rotman, *Parallel Paths*, op.cit.

10 D. Lawrence, 'Local Government Officials as Fiduciaries: The Appropriate Standard', *University of Detroit Mercy Law Review*, vol.71, 1993.

11 One case where it was raised, although barely discussed, is *West Wiltshire District Council* v. *Garland and Others* [1995] 2 All ER 17.

12 For a useful discussion of the history of LGFD, see P. Fennell, '*Roberts* v. *Hopwood*: The Rule Against Socialism', *Journal of Law and Society*, vol.13, 1986; M. Loughlin, *Legality and Locality: The Role of Law in Central-Local Government Relations*, Oxford, Clarendon, 1996, pp.206–10.

13 See generally J. Shepherd, 'Towards a Unified Concept of Fiduciary Relationships', *Law Quarterly Review*, vol.97, 1981, pp.64–8; W. Bratton, 'Self-Regulation, Normative Choice, and the Structure of Corporate Fiduciary Law', *The George Washington Law Review*, vol.61, 1993, p.1100.

14 See generally D. Prentice, 'Directors, Creditors, and Shareholders', in E. McKendrick (ed.), *Commercial Aspects of Trusts and Fiduciary Obligations*, Oxford, Clarendon, 1992; P. Davies, 'Directors' Fiduciary Duties and Individual Shareholders', in E. McKendrick (ed.), *Commercial Aspects of Trusts and Fiduciary Obligations*, op.cit., 1992.

15 See C. Brown, 'The Fiduciary Duty of Government: An Alternate Accountability Mechanism or Wishful Thinking', *Griffith Law Review*, vol.2, 1993.

16 [1954] 3 All ER 698.

17 Jenkins LJ, *Prescott* v. *Birmingham Corporation* [1954] 3 All ER 698 at p.706.

18 However, this commercial model is modified by the requirement for a higher level of prudence than would be expected from a company director. This is the result of two distinctions. First, taxpayers do not have the same degree of choice as private investors regarding whether they enter into a relationship. Second, local government's service, rather than profit, orientation means it is not expected to engage in commercial risk-taking.

19 N. Rose and P. Miller, 'Political Power Beyond the State: Problematics of Government', *British Journal of Sociology*, vol.43, 1992, p.174.

20 For one view, see Diplock LJ, *Luby* v. *Newcastle-Under-Lyme* [1964] 1 All ER 84 at p.91.

21 *Roberts* v. *Hopwood* [1925] All ER 24.

22 *Prescott* v. *Birmingham Corporation* [1954] 3 All ER 698.

23 *Cumings and Others* v. *Birkenhead Corporation* [1970] 3 All ER 308.

24 *Pickwell* v. *Camden LBC* [1983] 1 All ER 602.

25 *St. Albans City and District Council* v. *International Computers Ltd, The Times*, 11 November 1994, lexis.

26 See for instance, S*t Albans C & DC* v. *International Computers Ltd., The Times*, 11 November 1994, lexis.

27 Trust has also been described as one end of the fiduciary spectrum with agency at the other, eg, see A. Pratt, 'Aboriginal Self-Government and the Crown's Fiduciary Duty: Squaring the Circle or Completing the Circle', op.cit.

28 See generally A. Ogus, 'The Trust as Governance Structure', *University of Toronto Law Journal*, vol.36, 1986. This is less true with more recent corporate trusts, where the trust simply functions as a legal device for individual investment.

29 See for instance, *R.* v. *Secretary of State for Education and Science, ex p. ILEA* 84 LGR (1985) 454 at p.467.

30 In certain circumstances, fiduciary duty involves conventional notions of property belonging to the principal; more commonly it involves interests on the boundary of property, such as opportunity and information. In Canadian doctor-patient cases, there is precedent for the express protection of non-property based interests, see generally A. Grubb, 'The Doctor as Fiduciary', *Current Legal Problems* vol.47, 1994; P. Bartlett, 'Doctors as Fiduciaries: Possibilities and Threats for Patient Advocates', paper presented at the *American Law and Society Association*, annual conference, Toronto, June 1995.

31 Although property analysis does arise in the case of doctor-patient relationships, see A. Grubb, 'The Doctor as Fiduciary', op.cit., and in the government's duty towards indigenous peoples, see R. Blowes, 'Governments: Can you Trust them with your Traditional Title: *Mabo* and Fiduciary Obligations of Governments', op.cit.

32 See R. Flannigan, 'The Fiduciary Obligation', *Oxford Journal of Legal Studies*, vol.9, 1989, p.309.

33 D. Cooper, 'Fiduciary Government: Decentring Property and Taxpayers' Interests', *Social and Legal Studies*, vol.6, 1997.

34 Department of the Environment, *Paying for Local Government*, London, HMSO, 1986; R. Barnett et al., 'Representation without Taxation: An Empirical Assessment of the Validity of the Accountability Argument Underlying the Reform of Local Government Finance in England', *Fiscal Studies*, vol.12, 1991; R. Barnett and C. Knox, 'Accountability and Local Budgetary Policy: Unitary Principles?' *Policy and Politics*, vol.4, 1992; I. Sanderson, *Current Issues in Local Government Finance*, London, Commission for Local Democracy, 1995.

35 [1970] 3 All ER 308.

36 Ungoed-Thomas J, *Cumings and Others* v. *Birkenhead Corporation* [1970] 3 All ER 308 at p.312.

37 In a way, the question of ownership is a circular argument; identifying local

government as a fiduciary suggests it is deploying property belonging to another. Yet, whether this property 'belongs' to taxpayers *depends* on how the relationship between council and taxation is defined. Thus, while the notion of fiduciary duty and taxpayer ownership are mutually constitutive, both rely on the other as being already there.

38 Neo-liberal discourse has attempted to emphasise, at least discursively, the importance of public sector consumers, who have traditionally been seen as being of little importance. I have discussed this further in D. Cooper, 'The Citizen's Charter and Radical Democracy: Empowerment and Exclusion within Citizenship Discourse', *Social and Legal Studies*, vol.2, 1993.

39 See for instance, Scott Baker J, *St. Albans City and District Council* v. *International Computers Ltd*, *The Times*, 11 November 1994, lexis.

40 See for instance, *R.* v. *Newcastle-upon-Tyne City Council, ex p. Dixon* 92 LGR (1993) lexis.

41 See for instance, Ormrod J, *Pickwell* v. *Camden LBC* [1983] 1 All ER 602 at p.629. However, the interest may simply be in ensuring that the money is used in a lawful way 'much as trustees hold the trust fund, to apply it for the purposes authorised by the trust instrument' (Ormrod J, p.629).

42 *R.* v. *Secretary of State for the Environment, ex p. Knowsley MBC*, 31 July 1991, lexis. A different approach was adopted in the subsequent case of *R.* v. *Portsmouth City Council, ex p. Bonaco Builders Ltd and Ors*, 6 June 1995, lexis.

43 I. McLeod, 'The Local Ombudsman and the Fiduciary Duty of the Local Authority', *Local Government Review*, vol.156, 1992, p.361.

44 See *Prescott* v. *Birmingham Corporation* [1954] 3 All ER 698.

45 *Roberts* v. *Hopwood* [1925] All ER Rep 24.

46 See W. Wade, *Administrative Law*, (sixth edition) Oxford, Clarendon Press, 1988, pp.424–8. There is, perhaps, a tension here with the idea fiduciary duty imposes a high moral standard of behaviour on the fiduciary, see Frankel, 'Fiduciary Law', op.cit., p.830.

47 *Prescott* v. *Birmingham Corporation* [1954] 3 All ER 698.

48 *R.* v. *Roberts, ex p. Scurr* [1924] 2 KB 695.

49 *St. Albans C and DC* v. *International Computers Ltd*, *The Times*, 11 November 1994, lexis.

50 See also Department of the Environment, *Paying for Local Government*, op.cit., pp.6–7.

51 Although the introduction of the Uniform Business Rate means they are not included as payers of the community charge or council tax.

52 *R.* v. *Secretary of State for the Environment, ex p. Knowsley MBC*, 31 July 1991, lexis.

53 S. Leach, 'The Dimensions of Analysis: Governance, Markets and Community', in S. Leach et al. (eds), *Enabling or Disabling Local Government*, Buckingham, Open University Press, 1996, p.28.

54 [1965] 1 QB 214.

55 D. Cooper, 'Fiduciary Government: Decentring Property and Taxpayers'

Interests', op.cit.

56 Lord Greene MR, *Re Decision of Hurle Hobbs* [1944] 2 All ER 261 at p.263.

57 For earlier discussion of the balancing approach between tenants and ratepayers, see *Belcher* v. *Reading Corporation* [1949] 2 All ER 969 at p.983; *Summerfield* v. *Hampstead BC* [1957] 1 All ER 221 at p. 224; *Luby* v. *Newcastle-Under-Lyme Corporation* [1964] 1 All ER 84 at p.90.

58 *Pickwell* v. *Camden LBC* [1983] 1 All ER 602.

59 *R.* v. *Newcastle-upon-Tyne City Council, ex p. Dixon* (1993) 92 LGR 168.

60 QBD, 6 June 1995, lexis.

61 [1925] All ER Rep 24.

62 *R.* v. *Roberts, ex p. Scurr* [1924] 2 KB 695 at p.725.

63 See *R.* v. *Waltham Forest LBC, ex p. Baxter* [1988] 2 WLR 257. Although Stocker LJ, in his judgment emphasised the importance of ratepayers' interests—arguing that political unanimity among the leading party was of greater value to ratepayers than minority Labour councillors' insistence on voting in accordance with their own privately held views. This case is thus interesting in equating taxpayers' interests with the facilitation of political decision-making.

64 Jenkins LJ, *Prescott* v. *Birmingham Corporation* [1954] 3 All ER 698 at p.706.

65 *R.* v. *Secretary of State for Education and Science, ex p. ILEA* 84 LGR, QBD, 1985.

66 (*St. Albans City and District Council* v. *International Computers Ltd.*) The issue of balance between taxpayers was also raised in the Auditor's report for Haringey council; there the District Auditor declared that the council had a duty to strike a fair balance between the interests of present and future ratepayers. See Statutory Report of the District Auditor on 1985/86 Accounts of Haringey LBC, 14 April 1987, para 22, discussed in M. Loughlin, *Legality and Locality*, op.cit., p.254.

67 Cf Earl of Halsbury, *Board of Education* v. *Rice* [1911] AC 179.

68 [1944] 1 KB 644.

69 [1925] All ER Rep 24.

70 Du Parcq LJ, *In re Decision of Walker* [1944] 1 K.B. 644 at p.651.

71 See *R.* v. *GLC, ex p. Royal Borough of Kensington and Chelsea*, *The Times*, 7 April 1982; *R.* v. *Greenwich LBC, ex p. Cedar Transport Group Ltd* [1983] RA 173; see also discussion in M. Loughlin, *Legality and Locality*, op.cit., pp.251–5.

72 This was made apparent in *R.* v. *Ealing LBC, ex p. Times Newspapers Ltd* 85 LGR (1986) 316 at p.329. The case concerned a boycott of newspapers owned by the publishers who were engaged in an industrial dispute. There Watkins LJ, declared, 'no rational local authority would for a moment have thought that such a ban was open to it to impose in discharge of its duty to service libraries'.

73 See also K. Walsh, *Public Services and Market Mechanisms: Competition, Contracting and the New Public Management*, Basingstoke, Macmillan, 1995; J. Clarke and J. Newman, *The Managerial State*, London, Sage, 1997, pp.90-1.

74 For a critique of this approach, see R. Rhodes, 'The New Governance:

Governing without Government', *Political Studies*, vol.44, 1996, p.663; J. Clarke and J. Newman, *The Managerial State*, op. cit.

75 [1944] 1 KB 644.

76 [1925] All ER Rep 24.

77 Du Parcq LJ, *In re Decision of Walker* [1944] 1 KB 644 at p.650. Italics added.

78 See also *Taylor* v. *Munrow* [1960] 1 WLR 151 at pp.159–60.

79 Eg, Lord Russell of Killowen, *Kruse* v. *Johnson* (1898) 2 QB 91 at p.99; *Pickwell* v. *Camden* [1983] 1 All ER 602; McNeill J, *R.* v. *GLC, ex p. Kensington and Chelsea*, *The Times*, 7 April 1982.

80 Neo-liberalism is first and foremost a critique of the public sector rather than an attempt to re-form its identity, see J. Clarke and J. Newman, *The Managerial State*, op.cit., p.14.

81 K. Walsh, 'The Role of the Market and the Growth of Competition', in S. Leach et al. (eds), *Enabling or Disabling Local Government*, Buckingham, Open University Press, 1996.

82 See *R.* v. *Hertfordshire County Council, ex p. NALGO,* 14 February 1991, lexis. This case involved an application by NALGO for leave to judicially review a decision to grant a catering contract to a private company, inter alia, on the grounds of the cost to charge-payers. Lord Donaldson, deciding against the Union, held that financial considerations were not the only factor and that the value or quality of the service received also needed to be taken into account.

83 *Hazell* v. *Hammersmith and Fulham LBC* [1991] 1 All ER 545; see also M. Loughlin, 'Innovative Financing in Local Government: The Limits of Legal Instrumentalism—Part II', *Public Law*, 1991.

84 *R.* v. *Manchester City Council, ex p. Ling,* 89 LGR (1991) 696.

85 See for example the contributions in A. Barry et al. (eds), *Foucault and Political*, London, UCL Press, 1996.

86 See for instance *R.* v. *Portsmouth City Council, ex p. Bonaco Builders Ltd and Ors*, 6 June 1995, lexis.

87 See for instance, *R.* v. *Manchester City Council, ex p. Ling* 89 LGR (1991) 696.

88 That is, the rates were not properly taxes because of the residual interest held by contributors.

Chapter 5

1 See discussion in M. David 'The Family-education Couple: Towards an Analysis of the William Tyndale Dispute', in G. Littlejohn et al. (eds), *Power and the State*, London, Croom Helm, 1978; R. Dale, *The State and Education Policy*, Milton Keynes, Open University Press, 1989, ch.8.

2 See generally K. Foreman, 'Local Management of Schools: What Role for the Local Education Authority?', *School Organisation*, vol.9, 1989; R. Deem and M. Davies, 'Opting Out of Local Authority Control Using the Education Reform Act to Defend the Comprehensive Ideal: A Case Study in

Educational Policy Implementation', *International Studies in Sociology of Education*, vol.1, 1991; H. Kean, 'Managing Education—The Local Authority Dimension', *Journal of Education Policy*, vol.6, 1991; R. Deem and K. Brehony, 'Governing Bodies and Local Education Authorities: Who Shall Inherit the Earth?', *Local Government Studies*, vol.19, 1993.

3 See also H. Weiler, 'Education and Power: The Politics of Educational Decentralization in Comparative Perspective', *Educational Policy*, vol.3, 1989; K. Brehony and R. Deem, 'Charging for Free Education: An Exploration of a Debate in School Governing Bodies', *Journal of Education Policy*, vol.5, 1990.

4 She had been acting head since November 1991, and deputy head since 1989.

5 The *Guardian*, 27 January 1994.

6 Different versions of this statement exist.

7 Letter on file with author.

8 See the *Guardian*, 21 January 1994.

9 Hackney News Release, 'Council chiefs slam cultural philistinism', 19 January 1994.

10 The *Guardian*, 20 January 1994.

11 Statement on file with author.

12 The *Guardian*, 21 January 1994.

13 See *Evening Standard*, 21 January 1994.

14 B. Campbell, 'Hard lessons', *Diva*, (August 1995).

15 Quoted in *The Times*, 22 January 1994.

16 See the *Guardian*, 27 January 1994.

17 *The Times*, 22 January 1994.

18 Statement on file with author.

19 *The Times*, 26 January 1994.

20 See The *Guardian*, 25 January 1994.

21 J. Radford, 'Twin Leakings and Hackney Outings: The Kingsmead School Affair', *Trouble and Strife*, vol.32, 1995/6.

22 The *Guardian*, 25 January 1994.

23 *The Times*, 26 January 1994.

24 The *Daily Telegraph*, 27 January 1994.

25 Letter on file with author.

26 The *Guardian*, 28 January 1994.

27 *Kingsmead School Governors Inquiry Panel Investigating Report*, 8 June 1995.

28 Local Management of Schools—this refers to the devolvement of budgets and management from LEAs to schools under the terms of the Education Reform Act 1988.

29 T. Popkewitz, 'Rethinking Decentralization and State/Civil Society Distinctions: The State as a Problematic of Governing', *Journal of Education Policy*, vol.11, 1996; N. Rose, 'Governing "Advanced" Liberal Democracies', in A. Barry et al. (eds), *Foucault and Political Reason*, London,

UCL Press, 1996, p.45. For a discussion on the relationship between management and governing (or 'steering') at a distance, see S. Ball, 'Education Policy, Power Relations and Teachers' Work', *British Journal of Educational Studies*, vol.41, 1993.

30 See also comment of Industrial Tribunal, *Otobo* v. *Board of Governors of Kingsmead Primary School and Others*, [1996] case no. 52118/94/S.

31 See statement on file with author.

32 Letter from Gus John to Richard Reiser, Hackney Teachers Association, 24 January 1994, distributed to all Hackney teachers.

33 Hackney Council, News Release, 19 January 1994.

34 See also the interview with Gus John in the *Independent on Sunday*, 21 July 1996.

35 S. Harris, *Lesbian and Gay Issues in the English Classroom*, Buckingham, Open University Press, 1990; D. Cooper, *Sexing the City: Lesbian and Gay Politics within the Activist State*, London, Rivers Oram Press, 1994.

36 Notes on file with author.

37 Notes on file with author.

38 See also generally M. Wallace, 'Discourse of Derision: The Role of the Mass Media within the Education Policy Process', *Journal of Education Policy*, vol.8, 1993.

39 I give the term discipline both a common-sense and Foucauldian meaning. For discussion of the latter in relation to education, see S. Ball (ed.), *Foucault and Education: Disciplines and Knowledge*, London, Routledge, 1990; J. Ryan, 'Observing and Normalizing: Foucault, Discipline, and Inequality in Schooling', *The Journal of Educational Thought*, vol.25, 1991; D. Meadmore, 'The Production of Individuality through Examination', *British Journal of Sociology of Education*, vol.14, 1993; E. Millard and C. Hall, 'Discourses of Education: The Genealogy of a Profession's Discipline', *Renaissance and Modern Studies*, vol.37, 1994; R. Deacon and B. Parker, 'Education and Subjection and Refusal: An Elaboration on Foucault', *Curriculum Studies*, vol.3, 1995; D. Meadmore, 'Linking Goals of Governmentality with Policies of Assessment', *Assessment in Education*, vol.2, 1995.

40 See Leaders statement, Full Council meeting, 26 January 1994.

41 See Hackney Council News Release, 19 January 1994.

42 Hackney's proposal was for governors to request that the LEA complete the investigation and then present their findings to a broadly composed disciplinary panel (rather than just to Kingsmead governors); see Leader's statement, Full Council meeting, 26 January 1994. This approach had the merit of both extending Hackney's role and making a hearing sympathetic to Brown less likely.

43 See letters on file with author.

44 See letters on file with author.

45 See letter on file with author.

46 See letters on file with author.

47 See M. Loughlin, 'Law, Ideologies, and the Political-administrative System', *Journal of Law and Society*, vol.16, 1989; D. Cooper, 'Local Government Legal Consciousness in the Shadow of Juridification', *Journal of Law and Society*, vol.22, 1995.

48 Minutes, Kingsmead School, 25 January 1994.

49 See letters on file with author.

50 See letters on file with author.

51 Hackney Teachers Association (HTA) Newsletter, Spring 1994; HTA motion of support for Jane Brown, 7 February 1994.

52 My analysis of parental discourse and techniques is based on documentation, press coverage, and interviews with a self-selected group of approximately eight parents. Other parents were less supportive; however they remained marginal within media and other prevailing narratives of the conflict.

53 H. Kean, 'Managing Education—The Local Authority Dimension', *Journal of Education Policy*, vol.6, 1991, p.148.

54 See M. David, *Parents, Gender and Education Reform*, Cambridge, Polity, 1993, ch.7; R. Bowe et al., 'Captured by the Discourse? Issues and Concerns in Researching "Parental Choice"', *British Journal of Sociology of Education*, vol.15, 1994, p.63; P. Boulton and J. Coldron, 'Does the Rhetoric Work? Parental Responses to New Right Policy Assumptions', *British Journal of Educational Studies*, vol.44, 1996.

55 F. Naylor, *Dewsbury: The School Above the Pub*, London, Claridge Press, 1989; P. Brown, 'The "Third Wave": Education and the Ideology of Parentocracy', *British Journal of Sociology of Education*, vol.11, 1990; T. Edwards and G. Whitty, 'Parental Choice and Educational Reform in Britain and the U.S.', *British Journal of Educational Studies*, vol.40, 1992; C. Vincent, 'Tolerating Intolerance? Parental Choice and Race Relations—The Cleveland Case', *Journal of Education Policy*, vol.7, 1992 p.432.

56 D. Cooper, *Sexing the City: Lesbian and Gay Politics within the Activist State*, op.cit., 1994.

57 L. Johnston, and G. Valentine, 'Wherever I Lay My Girlfriend, That's My Home: The Performance and Surveillance of Lesbian Identities in Domestic Environments', in D. Bell and G. Valentine (eds), *Mapping Desire*, London, Routledge, 1995.

58 This contrasts with the approach of lesbian and gay Hackney employees who criticised the LEA for acting as if Jane Brown's sexuality was irrelevant, see Hackney Teachers Association Newsletter, Spring 1994, p.4.

59 See Kingsmead Support Group Newsletter, no. 1, February 1994.

60 J. Radford, 'Twin Leakings and Hackney Outings: The Kingsmead School Affair', op.cit.

61 See T. Rothenberg, '"And She Told Two Friends": Lesbians Creating Urban Social Space', in D. Bell and G. Valentine (eds), *Mapping Desire*, London, Routledge, 1995.

62 M. Castells, *The City and the Grassroots*, Berkeley, University of California Press, 1983 p.140; cf S. Adler and J. Brenner, 'Gender and Space: Lesbians and Gay Men in the City', *International Journal of Urban and Regional Research*, vol.16, 1992.

63 See D. Bell and G. Valentine, 'Introduction', in D. Bell and G. Valentine (eds), *Mapping Desire*, London, Routledge, 1995, p.6.

64 See J. Raford, op.cit.; see also generally S. Adler and J. Brenner, op.cit.; G. Valentine, 'Out and About: Geographies of Lesbian Landscapes', *International Journal of Urban and Regional Research*, vol.19, 1992.

65 See letters on file with author.

66 On fortification, see generally, D. Newman, *Defensible Space: People and Design in the Violent City*, London, Architectural Press, 1972; S. Merry, 'Defensible Space Undefended: Social Factors in Crime Control through Environmental Design', *Urban Affairs Quarterly*, vol.16, 1981; D. Judd, 'The Rise of the New Walled Cities', in H. Liggett and D. Perry (eds), *Spatial Practices*, London, Sage, 1995.

Chapter 6

1 See I. Wollaston, 'Sharing Sacred Space? The Carmelite Controversy and the Politics of Commemoration', *Patterns of Prejudice*, vol.28, 1994.

2 See *ACLU of New Jersey* v. *City of Long Branch 670* F. Supp. 1293; 1987 U.S. Dist., lexis.

3 There is also a wider US literature regarding the relationship between government and religious symbols, see for instance, J. Zarrow, 'Of Crosses and Creches: The Establishment Clause and Publicly Sponsored Displays of Religious Symbols', *The American University Law Review*, vol.35, 1985; M. C. Connor, 'The Constitutionality of Religious Symbols on Government Property: A Suggested Approach', *Journal of Church and State*, vol.37, 1995. See also Item No.5, Development and Protection Committee, Barnet Council, 8 January 1997.

4 For further discussion of the history of the planning application and the way it was dealt with by the council, planning inquiry and central government, see D. Cooper, 'Talmudic Territory? Space, Law and Modernist Discourse', *Journal of Law and Society*, vol.23, 1996.

5 D. Cooper, 'Talmudic Territory? Space, Law and Modernist Discourse', op.cit.

6 Outline of Mr. Lush and Ms. Popper's argument (objectors), quoted from Inspector's Report, para 4.41.

7 See *Encyclopedia Judaica*, vol.6, 1971, pp.849–50.

8 In Jewish law or *halakha*, the public domain bears a particularly narrow, restrictive interpretation. The prohibition on carrying or pushing was thus extended by Rabbinic law to a *carmelit*, a domain that is neither public nor private. Most public areas outside of Central London are probably

carmelits. However, since they were identified as 'public' within the Barnet eruv debate, I will do likewise, although strictly speaking within Jewish law they are not public; indeed, if they were it is doubtful whether they could become part of a private domain by means of an eruv, see J. Metzger, 'The Eruv: Can Government Constitutionally Permit Jews to Build a Fictional Wall without Breaking the Wall between Church and State', *National Jewish Law Review*, vol.4, 1989, p.68.

9 This only applies to articles that can already be carried within the home. It does not for instance allow cars to be driven.

10 See *Phoenix New Times*, 9 May 1996; insurance difficulties have also been a problem; see the *Washington Post*, 14 January 1980.

11 Problems arose in Miami Beach regarding the golf course and waterways. These were treated as recreational and therefore as residential; see *The Record*, 20 September 1994.

12 In relation to disputes over Manhattan's eruv, see letter by Ira Kellman, The *New York Times*, 19 June 1994.

13 See discussion in S. Sharot, 'Judaism and the Secularization Debate', *Sociological Analysis*, vol.52, 1991.

14 There is a growing literature on the changing and often contradictory approach of Jewish orthodoxy to women, see for instance, L. Davidman, 'Accommodation and Resistance to Modernity: A Comparison of Two Contemporary Orthodox Groups', *Sociological Analysis*, vol.51, 1990, p.43.

15 See C. Pateman, *The Sexual Contract*, Cambridge, Polity, 1988. There are also similarities with the idea of a covenant which Ebazar argues forms the basis of the Jewish political tradition. He argues covenant is more than a formal, legal contract because it involves a pledge of loyalty and ongoing commitment. These elements are apparent in the cultural contract discussed here. See D. Ebazar, 'Covenant as the Basis of the Jewish Political Tradition', *Jewish Journal of Sociology*, vol.20, 1978.

16 Most of the opponents I interviewed identified themselves as Jewish. One woman refused to disclose her identity, and two identified themselves as non-Jewish.

    Many non-Jews opposed the eruv, including high profile figures such as Lord McGregor and Lord Soper; however some non-Jews expressed ambivalence about becoming publicly active in the campaign, in case they appeared anti-semitic. According to one leading Barnet councillor, 'Jewish objectors were needed by non-Jews, so it would be legitimate to criticise' (interview). For a further analysis of Barnet's Jewish Community, see S. Waterman, *Jews in an Outer London Borough, Barnet*, Department of Geography, Queen Mary and Westfield College, London, 1989.

17 See also M. Bunting, the *Guardian*, 14 December 1993.

18 See for instance, G. Mosse, *Confronting the Nation: Jewish and Western Nationalism*, Hanover, Brandeis University Press, 1993; P. Birnbaum and I. Katznelson (eds), *Paths of Emancipation*, Princeton, Princeton University

Press, 1995.

19 Z. Bauman, 'Strangers: The Social Construction of Universality and Particularity', *Telos*, vol.78, 1988–9.

20 See *The Record*, 20 September 1992; *The Baltimore Sun*, 28 January 1995; *The Sun* (Baltimore), 25 September 1994, 5 March 1995; *St. Louis Post-Dispatch*, 20 November 1994. On the importance of names and boundaries for (re)defining communities, see A. Hunter, *Symbolic Communities:The Persistence and Change of Chicago's Local Communities*, Chicago, Chicago University Press, 1974; A. Hunter, 'The Symbolic Ecology of Suburbia', in I. Altman and A. Wandersman (eds), *Neighbourhood and Community Environments*, London, Plenum Press, 1987.

21 Outline of Mr. Thomas's argument, Inspector's Report, para 4.67.

22 See outline of Mr. Max's objections, Inspector's Report, para 4.52.

23 M. Walzer, 'Liberalism and the Art of Separation', *Political Theory*, vol.12, 1984; see also M. Shapiro and D. Neubauer, 'Spatiality and Policy Discourse: Reading the Global City', *Alternatives,* vol.14, 1989, p.307.

24 See D. MacFadyen, *Sir Ebenezer Howard and the Town Planning Movement*, Manchester, Manchester University Press, 1933; E. Howard, *Garden Cities of Tomorrow*, London, Faber and Faber, 1945; M. Miller and A. Gray, *Hampstead Garden Suburb*, Chichester, Phillimore, 1992.

25 670 F. Supp. 1293; 1987 US Dist., lexis 8572.

26 A similar argument is made by Barnet Eruv Objectors Group, Inspector's Report, para 4.12, regarding parishioners who have to pass under the eruv wires to attend church.

27 See Inspector's Report, para 5.36. For judicial rejection of the argument that an eruv imposes religious beliefs on non-participants within it, see *ACLU of New Jersey* v. *City of Long Branch et al.* 670 F. Supp. 1293 (D.N.J. 1987).

28 For a useful discussion of Jewish sacred space, see S. Kunin, 'Judaism', in J. Holm with J. Bowker (eds), *Sacred Place*, London, Pinter Publishers, 1994.

29 Collective letter sent to councillors from opponents, 2 October 1992.

30 In relation to New York's Upper West Side, see *New York Times*, 29 May 1994.

31 Cllr Frank Davis, letter, *Hampstead and Highgate Express*, 4 December 1992.

32 These fears are expressed by A. Etzioni in *The Spirit of Community: The Reinvention of American Society*, New York, Touchstone, 1993, pp.147, 156.

33 A similar communitarian perspective is expressed by A. Etzioni, *The Spirit of Community*, op.cit.

34 Thanks to Carl Stychin for this point. Areas defined as lesbian and gay ghettos provide a similar example as the division between public and private expression of homosexuality is redrawn rather than rejected.

35 *Independent Magazine*, 16 January 1993. For two studies of US ghettoes, see L. Wirth, *The Ghetto*, Chicago, Chicago University Press, 1928; V. Hannerz, *Soulside Inquiries into Ghetto Culture and Community*, New York, Columbia University Press, 1969.

36 Formally, the tree is in the private sphere of the home; however, its public visibility highlights some of the limitations of a simple public/private divide. Do passersby who find sight of the tree offensive have any right/ legitimate basis for complaint?

37 D. White, letter, *Hampstead and Highgate Express*, 16 October 1992.

38 B. Turner, *Religion and Social Theory*, London, Sage, 1991, p.9.

39 See R. Audi, 'The Separation of Church and State and the Obligations of Citizenship', *Philosophy and Public Affairs*, vol.18, 1989. This opposition, paradoxically, enables religion to retain its importance as a rationalisation for opposing religious-based, political developments.

40 See A. Bradney, *Religions, Rights and Laws*, Leicester, Leicester University Press, 1993.

41 Ibid.

42 H. Lefebvre, 'Reflections on the Politics of Space', *Antipode,* vol.8, 1976.

43 See D. Cooper, 'Defiance and Non-compliance: Religious Education and the Implementation Problem', *Current Legal Problems*, vol.48, 1995.

44 For a rich ethnographic study of the relationship between orthodox Jews and diverse legal meanings, see S. Van Praagh, 'The Chutzpah of Chasidism', *Canadian Journal of Law and Society*, vol.11, 1996. For discussion of the relationship between Jewish law and Western legal systems, see L. Pfeffer and A. Pfeffer, 'The Agunah in American Secular Law', *Journal of Church and State*, vol.31, 1989; S. Stone, 'In Pursuit of the Counter-text: The Turn to the Jewish Legal Model in Contemporary American Legal Theory', *Harvard Law Review*, vol.106, 1993; D. Ashburn, 'Appealing to a Higher Authority', *Detroit Mercy Law Review*, vol.71, 1994.

45 For critique of this approach, see J. Sachs, *Crisis and Covenant: Jewish Thought after the Holocaust*, Manchester, Manchester University Press, 1992.

46 An alternative approach would be that refusing to carry or push prams is no longer necessary to fulfil the underlying injunction to rest/ not work on the Sabbath. Thanks to Bernard Jackson for this suggestion.

47 See *Hampstead and Highgate Express*, 5 February 1993.

48 See generally J. Sachs, *Crisis and Covenant: Jewish Thought after the Holocaust*, op.cit., pp.117–18; H. Diner, 'Jewish Self-Governance, American Style', *American Jewish History*, vol.81, 1994; G. Alderman, 'English Jews or Jews of the English Persuasion', in P. Birnbaum and I. Katznelson (eds), *Paths of Emancipation,* Princeton, Princeton University Press, 1995, p.131.

49 Jacobs, Witness Statement, p.2.

50 See generally W. Connolly, 'Democracy and Territoriality', in M. Ringrose and A. Lerner (eds), *Reimagining the Nation*, Buckingham, Open University Press, 1993; J. Agnew and S. Corbridge, *Mastering Space: Hegemony, Territory and International Political Economy*, London, Routledge, 1995.

51 For a useful discussion on the current development of walled or fortified communities, see D. Judd, 'The Rise of the New Walled Cities', in H. Liggett and D.C. Perry (eds), *Spatial Practices*, London, Sage, 1995.

52 E. Balibar, *Race, Nation, Class*, London, Verso, 1991, p.95; see also M. Billig, *Banal Nationalism*, London, Sage, 1995, p.74.

53 'Jewish Zealots: We'll Patrol Eruv', *Hampstead and Highgate Express*, 15 January 1993.

54 See letters in the *Hampstead and Highgate Express*, 22 January 1993.

55 The eruv was not simply portrayed as a form of religious communalism, but also as constructing a consumerist relationship to space in which symbols could be arbitrarily installed regardless of preexisting meanings and identifications.

Chapter 7

1 For instance, see R. Epstein, *Takings: Private Property and the Power of Eminent Domain*, Cambridge, MA, Harvard University Press, 1985; M. Radin, *Reinterpreting Property*, Chicago, Chicago University Press, 1993.

2 M. Shoard, *This Land is Our Land*, London, Paladin, 1987.

3 G. Cox, '"Shooting a Line"?: Field Sports and Access Struggles in Britain', *Journal of Rural Studies*, vol.9, 1993.

4 P. Donnelly, 'The Paradox of Parks: Politics of Recreational Land Use Before and After the Mass Trespass', *Leisure Studies*, vol.5, 1986, pp.219–22; M. Shoard, *This Land is Our Land*, op.cit., p.292.

5 See R. Carr, *English Foxhunting: A History*, London, Weidenfeld and Nicolson, 1976, p.215. The leading precedent at the time of this dispute was *League Against Cruel Sports* v. *Scott and Others* [1985] 2 All ER 489 which held Hunt Masters liable when their hounds entered other people's land, providing knowledge of the risk or negligence could be proven.

6 D. Itzkowitz, *Peculiar Privilege: A Social History of English Foxhunting, 1753–1885*, Hassocks, Sussex, Harvester Press, 1977, pp.69–123.

7 See R. Thomas, *The Politics of Hunting*, Aldershot, Gower, 1983, p.99; see also *Western Daily Press*, 16 February 1994.

8 In 1997, the National Trust, after years of debate, and with much publicity, decided to ban deer hunting on its land. See the *Guardian,* 11 April 1997; the *Observer,* 13 April 1997; *The Times*, 22 August 1997; the *Guardian*, 3 October 1997; the *Independent*, 25 November 1997.

9 V. Bonham Carter, *The Essence of Exmoor*, Somerset, Exmoor Press, 1991, p.118.

10 The right to hunt does not necessary go with ownership of the land. It is a separate property right that today can be freely alienated. Other council owned land in the Quantocks was leased to the Forestry Commission which enjoyed, under the terms of the lease, the right to permit or prohibit hunting. The council also leased farmland to tenant farmers. Although hunting rights were reserved to the council, in practice the council left the decision to tenant farmers.

11 For summary of debate, see *West Somerset Morning News*, 6 August 1993.

12 T. Marsden et al., *Constructing the Countryside*, London, UCL Press, 1993.

13 See *Western Daily Press*, 20 May 1993 re: Wiltshire; *Western Daily Press*, 18 February 1994 re: Dorset.

14 See *Western Daily Press*, 8 February 1994, and *West Somerset Free Press*, 11 February 1994.

15 [1995] 1 All ER 513.

16 'For the purposes of ... the benefit, improvement or development of their area, a principal council may acquire by agreement any land...' See *R. v. Somerset County Council, ex p. Fewings* [1995] 3 All ER 20 at p.25.

17 Laws J. [1995] 3 All ER 513 at p.529.

18 *R. v. Somerset County Council, ex p. Fewings* [1995] 3 All ER 20.

19 Bingham MR [1995] 1 All ER 20 at p.28.

20 [1995] 3 All ER 20 at p.28.

21 [1995] 3 All ER 20, at p.31. My emphasis.

22 [1995] 3 All ER 20 at p.36.

23 Cf. M. Foucault, 'The Subject and Power', in H. Dreyfus and P. Rabinow (eds), *Michel Foucault: Beyond Structuralism and Hermeneutics*, Chicago, University of Chicago Press, 1982, p.224.

24 M. Foucault, 'The Subject and Power', op.cit. pp.223–4.

25 *Daily Telegraph* interview, 16 August 1993.

26 28 February 1931. Italics added.

27 *Shooting Times*, 3 March 1931. There is some evidence this occurred in the Quantocks as a result of the National Trust ban in 1997.

28 See generally, H. Dreyfus, and P. Rabinow, *Michel Foucault: Beyond Structuralism and Hermeneutics*, op.cit., p.134; J. Simons, *Foucault and the Political*, London, Routledge, 1995, pp.33–4; T. Osborne, 'Security and Vitality: Drains, Liberalism and Power in the Nineteenth Century', in A. Barry et al. (eds), *Foucault and Political Reason*, London, UCL Press, 1996.

29 See spokesperson, Council for Country Sports, consultative meeting organised by Somerset County Council, 4 March 1986; see also interview with Chief Executive of British Field Sports Society, *Country Life*, 1 June 1995.

30 The harbourer's role is to maintain a detailed knowledge of the deer in order to identify the appropriate stag to be culled. This is usually done the morning of the hunt. For an evocative account of the harbourer's work, see C. Aldin, *Exmoor: The Riding Playground of England*, London, H.F. & G. Witherby, 1935, pp.72–5.

31 Despite criticism of town and city sentimentalisation, the hunt also engaged in their own form of anthropormorphisation, see also C. Aldin, *Exmoor: The Riding Playground of England*, op.cit., pp.52–3.

32 J. Dizard, *Going Wild: Hunting, Animal Rights and the Contested Meaning of Nature*, Amherst, University of Massachusetts Press, 1994, pp.12, 103.

33 This representation of deer hunting as primordial is misleading in relation to Britain, since at least from Medieval times, deer have been kept in parks for this purpose, see J. Birrell, 'Deer and Deer Farming in Medieval

England', *Agricultural History Review*, vol.40, 1992. Deer in royal forests were, arguably, wilder, but their existence was still heavily managed.

34 According to one interviewee, the hunt will let a deer escape if they have chased it for several hours and proved unable to force it to stand at bay. For being a 'good sport' (in both senses of the word), it is rewarded with its life.

35 See J. Dizard, *Going Wild: Hunting, Animal Rights and the Contested Meaning of Nature*, op.cit., pp.118–19.

36 See *Western Morning News*, 5 August 1993; see generally Cobham Resource Consultants, *Country Sports: Their Economic and Conservation Significance*, Reading, Standing Conference on Countryside Sports, 1992.

37 G. Cox et al., 'Hunting the Wild Red Deer: The Social Organization and Ritual of a "Rural" Institution', *Sociologia Ruralis*, vol.34, 1994.

38 See also *Daily Telegraph*, 16 August 1993.

39 See also R. Thomas, 'Hunting as a Political Issue', *Parliamentary Affairs*, vol.39, 1986.

40 In conflicts over deer hunting, two outsider groups are explicitly identified. The first are poachers on whom hunt supporters project all the cruelty and irresponsibility with which they themselves are tarred. The second, demonised in Somerset for their support for hunting bans, are the new-comers: middle class migrants who see hunting as undermining their ideal of rural retreat, and with sufficient social and economic independence to challenge the hunt, see *West Somerset Free Press*, 6 August 1993.

41 See generally on this last point, C. Greenhouse et al., *Law and Community in 3 American Towns*, Ithaca, Cornell University Press, 1994, ch.6.

42 Where a novice hunter is marked by the blood of the just killed prey. See R. Manning, *Hunters and Poachers: A Social and Cultural History of Unlawful Hunting in England, 1485–1640*, Oxford, Clarendon, 1993, p.40.

43 D. Itzkowitz, *Peculiar Privilege: A Social History of English Foxhunting, 1753–1885*, Hassocks, Sussex, Harvester Press, 1977, p.20; R. Manning, *Hunters and Poachers: A Social and Cultural History of Unlawful Hunting in England 1485–1640*, op.cit., p.4.

44 J. Dizard, *Going Wild: Hunting, Animal Rights and the Contested Meaning of Nature*, op.cit., p.98. See also H. Salt, *Animals' Rights*, London, Centaur Press, 1980, p.73. The gendered character of this governance of self transcends the fact that many active hunters are women. Thus, women hunters, when acknowledged, are placed in a contradictory position. On the one hand, they are expected to aspire to a masculine sporting ideal; on the other, they are constituted according to notions of the feminised hunter, largely derived from Greek mythology.

45 I use the term land rights to refer to control, access, use, or alienation of land. My choice of language is intended to highlight the legal 'truth' that land does not generate a single, indivisible right of absolute ownership. I want to emphasise, as will become increasingly clear, the contingency, precariousness, and uncertainty that exists in allocating land rights.

46 R. Carr, *English Foxhunting: A History*, London, Weidenfeld and Nicolson, 1976.

47 However, hunting has also been a provocative symbol of power, particularly in relation to enclosure of the deer parks, see M. Shoard, *This Land is Our Land*, London, Paladin, 1987, p.52; and later enclosure, see E.P. Thompson, *Whigs and Hunters: The Origin of the Black Act*, London, Allen Lane, 1975, ch.10.

48 S. Daniels and C. Watkins, 'Friends of the Earth?' *Geographical*, 1993, pp. 19–20.

49 See K. Gray, 'Equitable Property', *Current Legal Problems, vol.47,* 1994.

50 405 US 727, 31 L Ed 2d 636 (1972).

51 Op.cit., p.651.

52 See J. Gyford, *The Politics of Local Socialism*, London, Allen and Unwin, 1985; S. Lansley et al., *Councils in Conflict: The Rise and Fall of the Municipal Left*, Basingstoke, Macmillan, 1989; D. Cooper, *Sexing the City: Lesbian and Gay Politics within the Activist State*, London, Rivers Oram, 1994.

53 For instance, Islington banned circuses in the 1970s, and subsequently in the 1980s introduced an animals charter, P. Windeatt, '"They Clearly Now See the Link": Militant Voices', in P. Singer (ed.) *In Defence of Animals*, London, Blackwell, 1985, pp.183–4; S. Carter, and I. Kinloch, 'Local Authorities and Moral Judgments', *New Law Journal,* vol.144, 1994; 1994; see also on hunt bans, R. Thomas, *The Politics of Hunting*, Aldershot, Gower, 1983, pp.99–102.

54 This was quashed in *R. v. Coventry City Council, ex p. Phoenix Aviation and Others* [1995] 3 All ER 37.

55 S. Ward, 'Thinking Global, Acting Local? British Local Authorities and their Environmental Plans', *Environmental Politics*, vol.2, 1993.

56 K. Bishop and A. Phillips, 'Seven Steps to Market—The Development of the Market-led Approach to Countryside Conservation and Recreation', *Journal of Rural Studies*, vol.9, 1993; P. Lowe et al., 'Regulating the New Rural Spaces: The Uneven Development of Land', *Journal of Rural Studies*, vol.9, 1993.

57 Both court and opponents tended to turn the question of use rights into one of exclusion from access through an equation of practice (hunting) with identity (hunters). For a useful discussion on the complex relationship between acts and identity, see C. Stychin, 'To Take Him "At his Word": Theorizing Law, Sexuality, and the US Military Exclusion Policy', *Social and Legal Studies*, vol.5, 1996. Swinton Thomas LJ (CA), makes a related point: '…[T]he debate was in fact fuelled to a substantial extent by antipathy to the hunters as opposed to a perceived cruelty to the deer', [1995] 3 All ER 20 at p.35.

58 See generally E.P. Thompson, *Customs in Common*, London, Penguin, 1993, p.134.

59 See generally A. Weale, 'Nature Versus the State? Markets, States, and

Environmental Protection', *Critical Review*, vol.6, 1993, pp.159–60.

60 Quoted in *Western Gazette*, 20 May 1993; see also *Western Gazette*, 12 August 1993.

61 See discussion in D. Oliver, 'State Property and Individual Rights', *Coexistence*, vol.25, 1988.

62 See B. Bracewell-Milnes, *Caring for the Countryside: Public Dependence on Private Interests*, London, Social Affairs Unit, no date. However, rural land ownership is far more complex than this division between state and private ownership might suggest, see for instance, S. Whatmore et al., 'The Rural Restructuring Process: Emerging Divisions of Agricultural Property Rights', *Regional Studies*, vol.24, 1990.

63 See for example, reference by Thomas Bingham MR, [1995] 3 All ER 20 at p.28.

64 See also letter to the Quantock Deer Management and Conservation Group, 7 October 1993, in which the chair of the Environment Committee stated, '[I]t is for every landholder to decide … what activities he or she wishes to allow on his [sic] land.'

65 G. Nardell, 'The Quantock Hounds and the Trojan Horse', *Public Law*, vol.95, 1995, p.31.

66 This was further complicated by the fact Over Stowey was common land which had traditionally recognised the rights, albeit not necessarily sporting rights, of its commoners.

67 Laws J, *R. v. Somerset County Council, ex p. Fewings* [1995] 1 All ER 513, at pp.524, 530.

68 Thomas Bingham MR, [1995] 3 All ER 20 at p.28.

69 J. Harris, 'Private and Non-private Property: What is the Difference', *Law Quarterly Review*, vol.111, 1995, p.435, develops the notion of public bodies as quasi-owners drawing on the case of *British Airports Authority v. Ashton* (1983) 1 WLR 1079. There the court held that the BAA's ownership was subject to the public's right of access to use facilities provided by the Authority in pursuit of its statutory duty, but not subject to the 'right' to picket.

70 [1995] 1 All ER 513 at p.524, cf. to *Costello v. Dacorum District Council* (1982) 81 LGR 1 at p.10.

71 See J.S. Barkin, and B. Cronin, 'The State and the Nation: Changing Norms and the Rules of Sovereignty in International Relations, *International Organization*, vol.48, 1994, p.111; I. Hont, 'The Permanent Crisis of a Divided Mankind: "Contemporary Crisis of the Nation State" in Historical Perspective', *Political Studies*, vol.42, 1994.

72 Interesting work on the extent of governmental authority over property has been developed in the US constitutional literature on 'public forum' doctrine, see R. Post, *Constitutional Domains*, Cambridge, Harvard University Press, 1995.

73 The question was raised whether Somerset could sell their hunting rights to

a body such as the League against Cruel Sports knowing or intending for the League to prohibit hunting, see *West Morning News*, 16 February 1994; *West Somerset Free Press*, 18 February 1994.

74 (1982) 81 LGR 1.

75 *Wheeler* v. *Leicester City Council* [1985] 1 AC 1054.

76 J. Harris, 'Private and Non-private Property: What is the Difference', *Law Quarterly Review*, vol.111, 1995, p.433.

77 See D. Cooper, *Sexing the City: Lesbian and Gay Politics within the Activist State*, op.cit.

78 D. Oliver, 'State Property and Individual Rights', *Coexistence*, op.cit. See also M. Loughlin, *Legality and Locality: The Role of Law in Central-Local Government Relations*, Oxford, Clarendon, 1996, pp.170–80.

79 G. Clark et al., *Leisure Landscapes: Leisure, Culture and the English Countryside: Challenges and Conflicts*, Lancaster, Lancaster University, 1994, p.14.

80 For instance, a spokesperson for the League Against Cruel Sports at Somerset's consultative meeting on 4 March 1986 claimed that the right to hunt was applied discriminately since it was questionable whether the council would let Hells Angels chase deer on their land. Given there was no reason why only one small elite should be allowed to hunt, the council should proscribe deer killing by all parties except themselves.

81 See for instance T. Creswell, *In Place/Out of Place: Geography, Ideology, and Transgression*, Minneapolis, University of Minnesota Press, 1996, p.134.

82 See P. Cloke and C. Park, *Rural Resource Management*, Beckenham, Croom Helm, 1985, p.3.

83 G. Clark et al., *Leisure Landscapes: Leisure, Culture and the English Countryside: Challenges and Conflicts*, op.cit., p.32.

84 Laws J, [1995] 1 All ER 513 at p.516.

85 [1995] 3 All ER 20 at p.33.

86 The *Star*, 2 July 1993.

87 [1995] 1 All ER 513 at p.516.

88 See Thomas Bingham MR, in discussion of the *Costello* case, [1995] 3 All ER 20 at p.26.

89 [1995] 3 All ER 20 at p.26.

90 See also C. Harrison, *Countryside Recreation in a Changing Society*, Bristol, TMS Partnership, 1991, p.88.

91 The court's reading of management here parallels other decisions where courts have read into a broad statutory discretion the need to act according to market or business-like principles.

92 See spokesperson for British Field Sports Society, *West Morning News*, 27 January 1994; for wider discussion of this point, see M. Kheel, 'License to Kill: An Ecofeminist Critique of Hunters' Discourse', in C. Adams and J. Donovan (eds), *Animals and Women: Feminist Theoretical Explorations*, Durham, Duke University Press, 1995.

93 See spokesperson for League against Cruel Sports, Somerset consultative

meeting, 4 March 1986. This point is also substantiated by the pro-hunting *Report of the Committee on Cruelty to Wild Animals*, HMSO, June 1951, which suggested that where fallow deer were hunted, only the buck was involved, does being unsatisfactory since they did not travel far.

94 A competing image was the portrayal of the hunt as lacking skill and courage. 'They have a tame herd chasing around a small piece of land'. (Councillor, interview)

95 See references to Full Council meeting where the ban resolution was discussed, [1995] 1 All ER 513 at p.521.

96 See spokesperson for the British Field Sports Society, Somerset consultative meeting, 4 March 1986.

97 See for example Scottish Home Department, *Report of the Committee on Cruelty to Wild Animals*, HMSO, June 1951, pp.55–6.

98 For instance, see D. Cronin, *A View From the Wild Side: A Review of the NT Position on Deer Hunting with Hounds*, which critiques the NT Report produced by the Savage Working Party in spring 1993.

99 See for instance, L Metcalfe, 'Public Management: From Imitation to Innovation', in J. Kooiman (ed.), *Modern Governance*, London, Sage, 1993.

100 See also S. Clegg and G. Palmer, 'Introduction: Producing Management Knowledge', in S. Clegg and G. Palmer (eds), *The Politics of Management Knowledge*, London, Sage, 1996.

101 D. Riches, 'Animal Rightists and Northern Native Hunters', *Anthropos*, vol.90, 1995. See also K.P. Huntingdon, *Wildlife Management and Subsistence Hunting in Alaska*, London, Belhaven, 1992.

102 See J. Clarke and J. Newman, *The Managerial State*, London, Sage, 1997, p.159.

Chapter 8

1 W. Connolly discussing Ricoeur in 'Democracy and Territoriality', in M. Ringrose and A. Lerner (eds), *Reimagining the Nation*, Buckingham, Open University Press, 1993, p.52.

2 See for instance, J. Gyford, *The Politics of Local Socialism*, London, George Allen and Unwin, 1985; H. Hobbs, *City Hall goes Abroad: The Foreign Policy of Local Politics*, Thousand Oaks, Ca, Sage, 1994; W. Magnusson, *The Search for Political Space*, Toronto, University of Toronto Press, 1996.

3 See also *Sexing the City: Lesbian and Gay Politics within the Activist State*, London, Rivers Oram Press, 1994.

4 *East York v. Ontario* [1997] O.J. No. 3064.

5 This is particularly true for institutional power based on minority religious commitment (see chapter six).

6 J. Clarke and J. Newman, *The Managerial State*, London, Sage, 1997, p.25; see also for a more limited view of governmental power, R. Rhodes, *Understanding Governance: Policy Networks, Governance, Reflexivity and*

Accountability, Buckingham, Open University Press, 1997, pp.132–3.

7 See K. Foreman, 'Local Management of Schools: What Role for the Local Education Authority', *School Organisation*, vol.9, 1989; H. Kean, 'Managing Education—The Local Authority Dimension', *Journal of Education Policy*, vol.6, 1991; R. Deem and K. Brehony, 'Governing Bodies and Local Education Authorities: Who Shall Inherit the Earth?', *Local Government Studies*, vol.19, 1993.

8 For further discussion of institutional disobedience, see D. Cooper, 'Institutional Illegality and Disobedience: Local Government Narratives', *Oxford Journal of Legal Studies*, vol.16, 1996.

9 W. Magnusson, *The Search for Political Space*, op.cit., pp.174–7, 217–40; M. Loughlin, *Legality and Locality: The Role of Law in Central-Local Government Relations*, Oxford, Clarendon, 1996, pp.185–99.

10 See for instance, D. Skinner and J. Langdon, *The Story of Clay Cross*, Nottingham, Spokesman Books, 1974, about a local authority that refused to raise housing rents in defiance of government legislation.

11 See D. Skinner and J. Langdon, *The Story of Clay Cross*, op.cit.; see also N. Branson, *Poplarism 1919–1925*, London, Lawrence and Wishart, 1979; M. Parkinson, *Liverpool on the Brink*, Hermitage Policy Journals, 1985.

12 For further development of this argument, see D. Cooper, 'Institutional Illegality and Disobedience: Local Government Narratives', op.cit.

13 *R. v. Ealing LBC, ex p. Times Newspapers Ltd* (1987) 85 LGR 316.

14 I have critiqued transgression in more detail in D. Cooper, *Power in Struggle*, Buckingham, Open University Press, 1995, pp.48–50.

15 For further elaboration on the ways in which ideological politics is organised out, see D. Cooper, *Sexing the City: Lesbian and Gay Politics within the Activist State*, op.cit.

16 *R. v. Somerset County Council, ex p. Fewings* [1995] 1 ALL ER 513.

17 For further discussion of my understanding of ideology, see D. Cooper, *Sexing the City: Lesbian and Gay Politics within the Activist State*, London, op.cit., pp.7–8, 151–5.

18 This emphasis on 'underlying' may seem to some problematic. First, ideological discourses, for instance, of race, may in some instances be used to obscure other reasons. Second, it suggests that technocratic or managerial reasons are somehow more superficial, not ideological, or not the real reasons for a decision.

  My stress on underlying concerns applies to those contexts where technocratic or managerial reasons are *strategically* deployed to obscure less acceptable motives or objectives (see chapters three and seven). It also applies to circumstances where the positivist grounds may *seem* the bases for decisions, but where closer examination reveals a range of other, rudimentary anxieties (as I discuss, for instance, in chapter six).

19 Albeit with the support of (male) trade unionists and experienced legal counsel.

20 The Quantock Staghounds did argue that deer enjoyed the hunt and did not suffer particular stress. However, this argument did not prove particularly successful. In 1997, research findings demonstrating the extreme stress suffered by hunted deer provided the impetus for a ban by the National Trust, see P. Bateson, *The Behavioural and Physiological Effects of Culling Red Deer*, Report to the Council of the National Trust, 1997; see also the *Guardian*, 11 April 1997.

21 For one analysis of how this works, see R. Rhodes, 'The New Governance: Governing Without Government', *Political Studies*, vol.44, 1996.

22 See for instance S. Lansley et al., *Councils in Conflict: The Rise and Fall of the Municipal Left*, Basingstoke, Macmillan, 1989; M. Mandel, *The Charter of Rights and the Legalization of Politics in Canada*, Toronto, Wall and Thompson, 1989; D. Cooper, *Sexing the City: Lesbian and Gay Politics within the Activist State*, op.cit.; D. Herman, *Rights of Passage: Struggles for Lesbian and Gay Legal Equality*, Toronto, University of Toronto Press, 1994; J. Bakan, *Just Words: Constitutional Rights and Social Wrongs*, Toronto, University of Toronto Press, 1997.

23 For a good discussion of a number of these issues, see J. Weeks, *Invented Moralities: Sexual Values in an Age of Uncertainty*, Cambridge, Polity, 1995, ch.4.

24 An example of this is the mobilisation around S.28 Local Government Act 1988 prohibiting local authorities from promoting homosexuality; see generally T. Kaufmann and P. Lincoln (eds), *High Risk Lives: Lesbian and Gay Politics After the Clause*, Bridport, Prism, 1991; V. Carter, 'Abseil Makes the Heart Grow Fonder: Lesbian and Gay Campaigning Tactics and S.28', in K. Plummer (ed.), *Modern Homosexualities*, London, Routledge, 1992.

Bibliography

Abrams, S. 'European Economic Community: Entry of Spain and Portugal', *Harvard International Law Journal*, vol.27, 1986.

Adler, S. and J. Brenner, 'Gender and Space: Lesbians and Gay Men in the City', *International Journal of Urban and Regional Research*, vol.16, 1992.

Agnew, J. et al. (eds), *The Power of Place*, London, Unwin Hyman, 1989.

Agnew, J. and S. Corbridge, *Mastering Space: Hegemony, Territory and International Political Economy*, London, Routledge, 1995.

Alderman, G. 'English Jews or Jews of the English Persuasion', in P. Birnbaum and I. Katznelson (eds), *Paths of Emancipation* Princeton, Princeton University Press, 1995.

Aldin, C. *Exmoor: The Riding Playground of England,* London, H.F. & G. Witherby, 1935.

Althusser, L. *Lenin and Philosophy and Other Essays*, London, New Left Books, 1971.

Anderson, J. 'The Shifting Stage of Politics: New Medieval and Postmodern Territories?', *Environment and Planning D: Society and Space*, vol.14, 1996.

Andrews, J. 'Don't Pass Us By: Keeping Lesbian and Gay Issues on the Agenda', *Gender and Education*, vol.2, 1990.

Andrews, L. 'New Labour, New England?', in M. Perryman (ed.), *The Blair Agenda*, London, Lawrence and Wishart, 1996.

Anthias, F. and N. Yuval-Davis, *Racialized Boundaries*, London, Routledge, 1992.

Arnot, M. 'Equality and Democracy: A Decade of Struggle Over Education', *British Journal of Sociology of Education*, vol.12, 1991.

Asad, T. 'Multiculturalism and British Identity in the Wake of the Rushdie Affair', *Politics and Society*, vol.18, 1990.

Ashburn, D. 'Appealing to a Higher Authority', *Detroit Mercy Law Review*, vol.71, 1994.

Audi, R. 'The Separation of Church and State and the Obligations of Citizenship', *Philosophy and Public Affairs*, vol.18, 1989.

Aulich, J. (ed.), *Framing the Falklands War: Nationhood, Culture and Identity,* Milton Keynes, Open University Press, 1992.

Aurrecoechea, I. 'Some Problems Concerning the Constitutional Basis for

Spain's Accession to the European Community', *International and Comparative Law Quartery*, vol.36, 1987.

Aurrecoechea, I. 'The Role of the Autonomous Communities in the Implementation of European Community Law in Spain', *International and Comparative Law Quarterly*, vol. 38, 1989.

Bakan, J. *Just Words: Constitutional Rights and Social Wrongs*, Toronto, University of Toronto Press, 1997.

Balibar, E. and I. Wallerstein, *Race, Nation, Class*, London, Verso, 1991.

Ball, S. (ed.), *Foucault and Education: Disciplines and Knowledge*, London, Routledge, 1990.

Ball, S. 'Education Policy, Power Relations and Teachers' Work', *British Journal of Educational Studies*, vol.41, 1993.

Ball, S. 'Education, Majorism and "the Curriculum of the Dead"', *Curriculum Studies*, vol.1, 1993.

Barkin, J.S. and B. Cronin, 'The State and the Nation: Changing Norms and the Rules of Sovereignty in International Relations, *International Organization*, vol.48, 1994.

Barlow, J. 'Landowners, Property Ownership and the Rural Locality', *International Journal of Urban and Regional Research*, vol. 10, 1986.

Barnett, R. and C. Knox, 'Accountability and Local Budgetary Policy: Unitary Principles?' *Policy and Politics*, vol.4, 1992.

Barnett, R. et al., 'Representation without Taxation: An Empirical Assessment of the Validity of the Accountability Argument Underlying the Reform of Local Government Finance in England', *Fiscal Studies*, vol.12, 1991.

Barrett, M. and A. Phillips (eds), *Destabilising Theory: Contemporary Feminist Debates*, Cambridge, Polity, 1992.

Barry, A. et al., 'The European Community and European Government. Harmonization, Mobility and Space', *Economy and Society Review*, vol.22, 1993.

Bartlett, P. 'Doctors as Fiduciaries: Possibilities and Threats for Patient Advocates', paper presented at the American Law and Society Association, annual conference, Toronto, June 1995.

Bartlett, R. 'The Fiduciary Obligation of the Crown to the Indians', *Saskatchewan Law Review*, vol.53, 1989.

Bauman, Z. 'Strangers: The Social Construction of Universality and Particularity', *Telos*, vol.78, 1988–89.

Bauman, Z. 'Soil, Blood, Identity', *Sociological Review*, vol. 1992.

Beck, J. 'Nation, Curriculum and Identity in Conservative Cultural Analysis', *Cambridge Journal of Education*, vol.26, 1996.

Bell, D. and G. Valentine (eds), *Mapping Desire*, London, Routledge, 1995.

Bell, D. and G. Valentine, 'Introduction', in D. Bell and G. Valentine (eds), *Mapping Desire*, London, Routledge, 1995.

Benyon, H. and R. Hudson, 'Place and Space in Contemporary Europe: Some Lessons and Reflections', *Antipode*, vol.25, 1993.

Bhabha, H. (ed.), *Nation and Nationalism*, London, Routledge, 1990.

Billig, M. *Banal Nationalism*, London, Sage, 1995.

Birnbaum, P. and I. Katznelson (eds), *Paths of Emancipation,* Princeton, Princeton University Press, 1995.

Birrell, J. 'Deer and Deer Farming in Medieval England', *Agricultural History Review*, vol.40, 1992.

Bishop, K. and A. Phillips, 'Seven Steps to Market—The Development of the Market-led Approach to Countryside Conservation and Recreation', *Journal of Rural Studies*, vol.9, 1993.

Blomley, N. *Law, Space and the Geographies of Power*, New York, Guilford Press, 1994.

Blomley N. and J. Bakan, 'Spacing Out: Towards a Critical Geography of Law', *Osgoode Hall Law Journal*, vol.30, 1992.

Blowes, R. 'Governments: Can you Trust them with your Traditional Title: Mabo and Fiduciary Obligations of Governments', *Sydney Law Review*, vol.15, 1993.

Bondi, L. 'Feminism, Postmodernism, and Geography: Space for Women?' *Antipode*, vol.22, 1990.

Bonham Carter, V. *The Essence of Exmoor,* Somerset, Exmoor Press, 1991.

Boulton, P. and J. Coldron, 'Does the Rhetoric Work? Parental Responses to New Right Policy Assumptions', *British Journal of Educational Studies*, vol.44, 1996.

Bowe, R. et al., 'Captured by the Discourse? Issues and Concerns in Researching "Parental Choice"', *British Journal of Sociology of Eduction*, vol.15, 1994.

Bracewell-Milnes, B. *Caring for the Countryside: Public Dependence on Private Interests*, London, Social Affairs Unit, no date.

Bradney, A. 'The Dewsbury Affair and the Education Reform Act', *Education and the Law*, vol.1, 1989.

Bradney, A. *Religions, Rights and Laws*, Leicester, Leicester University Press, 1993.

Brah, A. 'Reframing Europe: En-gendered Racisms, Ethnicities and Nationalisms in Contemporary Europe', *Feminist Review*, vol.45, 1993.

Branson, N. *Poplarism 1919–1925*, London, Lawrence and Wishart, 1979.

Bratton, W. 'Self-Regulation, Normative Choice, and the Structure of Corporate Fiduciary Law', *The George Washington Law Review*, vol.61, 1993.

Brehony, K. and R. Deem, 'School Governing Bodies: Reshaping Education in their Own Image', *Sociological Review*, vol.43, 1995.

Brehony, K. and R. Deem, 'Charging for Free Education: An Exploration of a Debate in School Governing Bodies', *Journal of Education Policy*, vol.5, 1990.

Briffault, R. 'Who Rules at Home?: One Person/One Vote and Local Governments', *The University of Chicago Law Review*, vol. 60, 1993.

Brown, C. 'The Fiduciary Duty of Government: An Alternate Accountability Mechanism or Wishful Thinking', *Griffith Law Review*, vol.2, 1993.

Brown, P. 'The "Third Wave": Education and the Ideology of Parentocracy', *British Journal of Sociology of Education*, vol.11, 1990.

Brown, W. 'Finding the Man in the State', *Feminist Studies*, vol.18, 1992.

Bruce, S. (ed.), *Religion and Modernization*, Oxford, Clarendon, 1992.

Burchell, G. et al. (eds), *The Foucault Effect*, Chicago, University of Chicago Press, 1991.

Burg, B.R. *Sodomy and the Pirate Tradition*, New York, New York University Press, 1983.

Burn, J. and C. Hart, *The Crisis in Religious Education*, London, The Educational Research Trust, 1988.

Butler, J. *Gender Trouble*, New York, Routledge, 1990.

Carr, R. *English Foxhunting: A History*, London, Weidenfeld and Nicolson, 1976.

Carter, S. and I. Kinloch, 'Local Authorities and Moral Judgments', *New Law Journal*, vol.144, 1994.

Carter, V. 'Abseil Makes the Heart Grow Fonder: Lesbian and Gay Campaigning Tactics and S. 28', in K. Plummer (ed.), *Modern Homosexualities*, London, Routledge, 1992.

Castells, M. *The City and the Grassroots*, Berkeley, University of California, 1983.

Chandhoke, N. *State and Civil Society*, New Delhi, Sage, 1995.

Charlesworth, A. 'Contesting Places of Memory: The Case of Auschwitz', *Environment and Planning D: Society and Space*, vol.12, 1994.

Churchill, R.R. *EC Fisheries Law*, Dordecht, ND, Martinus Nijoff, 1987.

Clark, G.L. *Judges and the Cities*, Chicago, University of Chicago Press, 1985.

Clark, G. et al., *Leisure Landscapes: Leisure, Culture and the English Countryside: Challenges and Conflicts*, Lancaster, Lancaster University, 1994.

Clarke, J. and J. Newman, *The Managerial State*, London, Sage, 1997.

Clarke, M. and J. Stewart, 'The Local Authority and the New Community Governance', *Regional Studies*, vol.28, 1993.

Clegg, S. and G. Palmer (eds), *The Politics of Management Knowledge*, London, Sage, 1996.

Cloke, P. and C. Park, *Rural Resource Management*, Beckenham, Croom Helm, 1985.

Cobham Resource Consultants, *Country Sports: Their Economic and Conservation Significance*, Reading, Standing Conference on Countryside Sports, 1992.

Cohen, A. (ed.), *Belonging. Identity and Social Organisation in British Rural Cultures*, Manchester, Manchester University Press, 1982.

Cohen, R. *Frontiers of Identity*, Harlow, Longman, 1994.

Connolly, W. 'Democracy and Territoriality', in M. Ringrose and A. Lerner (eds), *Reimagining the Nation*, Buckingham, Open University Press, 1993.

Connor, M.C. 'The Constitutionality of Religious Symbols on Government Property: A Suggested Approach', *Journal of Church and State*, vol.37, 1995.

Cook, P.J. 'Reservations about Deer and the Law', *Solicitors Journal*, vol.133, 1989.

Cooper, D. 'The Citizen's Charter and Radical Democracy: Empowerment and

Exclusion within Citizenship Discourse', *Social and Legal Studies*, vol.2, 1993.

Cooper, D. *Sexing the City: Lesbian and Gay Politics within the Activist State*, London, Rivers Oram, 1994.

Cooper, D. *Power in Struggle: Feminism, Sexuality and the State*, Buckingham, Open University Press, 1995.

Cooper, D. 'Defiance and Non-compliance: Religious Education and the Implementation Problem', *Current Legal Problems*, vol. 48, 1995.

Cooper, D. 'Local Government Legal Consciousness in the Shadow of Juridification', *Journal of Law and Society*, vol.22, 1995.

Cooper, D. 'Talmudic Territory? Space, Law and Modernist Discourse', *Journal of Law and Society*, vol.23, 1996.

Cooper, D. 'Institutional Illegality and Disobedience: Local Government Narratives', *Oxford Journal of Legal Studies*, vol.16, 1996.

Cooper, D. 'Strategies of Power: Legislating Worship and Religious Education', in M. Lloyd and A. Thacker (eds), *The Impact of Michel Foucault on the Social Sciences and Humanities*, Basingstoke, Macmillan, 1996.

Cooper, D. 'Fiduciary Government: Decentring Property and Taxpayers' Interests', *Social and Legal Studies*, vol.6, 1997.

Corbridge, S. et al. (eds), *Money, Power and Space*, Oxford, Blackwell, 1994.

Cotterrell, R. 'Judicial Review and Legal Theory', in G. Richardson and H. Genn (eds), *Administrative Law and Government Action*, Oxford, Clarendon Press, 1994.

Cox, G. '"Shooting a Line"?: Field Sports and Access Struggles in Britain', *Journal of Rural Studies*, vol.9, 1993.

Cox, G. et al., 'Hunting the Wild Red Deer: The Social Organization and Ritual of a "Rural" Institution', *Sociologia Ruralis*, vol.34, 1994.

Crawford, C. 'Auditors, Local Government and the Fiduciary Duty', *Public Law*, 1983.

Crawford, M. 'Contesting the Public Realm: Struggles over Public Space in Los Angeles', *Journal of Architectural Education*, vol.49, 1995.

Cream, J. 'Child Sexual Abuse and the Symbolic Geographies of Cleveland', *Environment and Planning D: Society and Space*, vol.11, 1993.

Creswell, T. *In Place / Out of Place: Geography, Ideology, and Transgression*, Minneapolis, University of Minnesota Press, 1996.

Cuba, L.J. *Identity and Community on the Alaskan Frontier*, Philadelphia, Temple University Press, 1987.

Curtis, B. 'Taking the State back Out: Rose and Miller on Political Power', *British Journal of Sociology*, vol.46, 1995.

Dale, R. *The State and Education Policy*, Milton Keynes, Open University Press, 1989.

Daniels, S. and C. Watkins, 'Friends of the Earth?' *Geographical*, 1993.

Darian-Smith, E. 'Law in Place: Legal Mediations of National Identity and State Territory in Europe', in P. Fitzpatrick (ed.), *Nationalism, Racism and the Rule of Law*, Aldershot, Dartmouth, 1995.

David, M. The Family-education Couple: Towards an Analysis of the William Tyndale Dispute, in G. Littlejohn et al. (eds), *Power and the State*, London, Croom Helm, 1978.

David, M. *Parents, Gender and Education Reform*, Cambridge, Polity, 1993.

Davidman, L. 'Accommodation and Resistance to Modernity: A Comparison of Two Contemporary Orthodox Groups', *Sociological Analysis*, vol.51, 1990.

Davies, P. 'Directors' Fiduciary Duties and Individual Shareholders', in E. McKendrick (ed.), *Commercial Aspects of Trusts and Fiduciary Obligations*, Oxford, Clarendon, 1992.

Davies, P. and C. Redgwell, The International Legal Regulation of Straddling Fish Stocks', *British Yearbook of International Law*, vol.67, 1998.

Deacon, R. and B. Parker, 'Education and Subjection and Refusal: An Elaboration on Foucault', *Curriculum Studies*, vol.3, 1995.

Dean, M. *Critical and Effective Histories. Foucault's Methods and Historical Sociology*, London, Routledge, 1994.

Deem, R. and M. Davies, 'Opting Out of Local Authority Control—Using the Education Reform Act to Defend the Comprehensive Ideal: A Case Study in Educational Policy Implementation', *International Studies in Sociology of Education*, vol.1, 1991.

Deem, R. and K. Brehony, 'Governing Bodies and Local Education Authorities: Who shall Inherit the Earth?' *Local Government Studies*, vol.19, 1993.

Delanty, G. *Inventing Europe*, Basingstoke, Macmillan, 1995.

Delhi, K. 'Creating a Dense and Intelligent Community: Local State Formation in Early 19th Century Upper Canada', *Journal of Historical Sociology*, vol.3, 1990.

Department of the Environment, *Paying for Local Government*, London, HMSO, 1986.

Diamond, S. *Spiritual Warfare: The Politics of the Christian Right*, Boston, MA, South End Press, 1989.

Dickens, B. 'Medical Records—Patient's Right to Receive Copies—Physician's Fiduciary Duty of Disclosure: *McInerney* v. *MacDonald*', *The Canadian Bar Review*, vol.73, 1994.

Dignan, J. 'Policy-making, Local Authorities, and the Courts: The "GLC Fares" Case', *Law Quarterly Review*, vol.99, 1983.

Diner, H.R. 'Jewish Self-governance, American Style', *American Jewish History*, vol.81, 1994.

Dizard, J. *Going Wild: Hunting, Animal Rights and the Contested Meaning of Nature*, Amherst, University of Massachusetts Press, 1994.

Donnelly, P. 'The Paradox of Parks: Politics of Recreational Land Use Before and After the Mass Trespass', *Leisure Studies*, vol.5, 1986.

Doty, R.L. 'Sovereignty and the Nation: Constructing the Boundaries of National Identity', in T. Biersteker and C. Weber (eds), *State Sovereignty as Social Construct*, Melbourne, Cambridge University Press, 1996.

Dreyfus, H. and P. Rabinow, *Michel Foucault*, Chicago, University of Chicago Press, 1982.

Dumm, T. *Michel Foucault and the Politics of Freedom*, London, Sage, 1996.

Duncan, J. and D. Ley (eds), *Place, Culture and Representation*, London, Routledge, 1993.

Duncan, N. (ed.), *BodySpace: Destabilizing Geographies of Gender and Sexuality*, London, Routledge, 1996.

Durham, M. *Sex and Politics*, London, Macmillan, 1991.

Dwyer, C. 'Constructions of Muslim Identity and the Contesting of Power; The Debate over Muslim Schools in the United Kingdon', in P. Jackson and J. Penrose (eds), *Constructions of Race, Place and Nation*, London UCL Press, 1993.

Edwards, T. and G. Whitty, 'Parental Choice and Educational Reform in Britain and the U.S.', *British Journal of Educational Studies*, vol.40, 1992.

Eisen, A.M. 'Rethinking Jewish Modernity', *Jewish Social Studies*, vol.1, 1994.

Eisenstein, Z. *The Female Body and the Law*, Berkeley, California, University of California Press, 1988.

Elmore, R. 'Backward Mapping: Implementation Research and Policy Decisions', *Political Science Quarterly*, vol.94, 1979–80.

Elazar, D. 'Covenant as the Basis of the Jewish Political Tradition', *Jewish Journal of Sociology*, vol.20, 1978.

Encyclopaedia Judaica, Jerusalem, Keter Publishing House, 1971.

Engel, D. 'Litigation Across Space and Time: Courts, Conflict, and Social Change', *Law and Society Review*, vol. 24, 1990.

Enloe, C. *The Morning After*, Berkeley, University of California Press, 1993.

Entrikin, J.E. *The Betweenness of Place. Towards a Geography of Modernity*, Baltimore, John Hopkins University Press, 1991.

Epstein, R. *Takings: Private Property and the Power of Eminent Domain*, Cambridge, MA, Harvard University Press, 1985.

Etzioni, A. *The Spirit of Community: The Reinvention of American Society*, New York, Touchstone, 1993.

Farnell, J. and J. Elles, *In Search of a Common Fisheries Policy*, Aldershot, Gower, 1984.

Fennell, P. '*Roberts v. Hopwood*: The Rule Against Socialism', *Journal of Law and Society*, vol.13, 1986.

Fishman, A. 'Modern Orthodox Judaism: A Study in Ambivalence', *Social Compass*, vol.42, 1995.

Fitzpatrick, P. *The Mythology of Modern Law*, London, Routledge, 1992.

Fitzpatrick, P. (ed.), *Nationalism, Racism and the Rule of Law*, Aldershot, Dartmouth, 1995.

Flannigan, R. 'The Fiduciary Obligation', *Oxford Journal of Legal Studies*, vol.9, 1989.

Foreman, K. 'Local Management of Schools: What Role for the Local Education Authority?', *School Organisation*, vol.9, 1989.

Foucault, M. *The History of Sexuality*, London, Penguin, 1981.

Foucault, M. 'Afterword—The Subject and Power', in H. Dreyfus and P. Rabinow, *Michel Foucault: Beyond Structuralism and Hermeneutics* (second edition), Chicago, University of Chicago Press, 1982.

Foucault, M. 'Of Other Spaces', *Diacritics*, vol.22, 1986.

Francis, M. 'Race and the Education Reform Act', *Urban Review*, vol.22, 1990.

Frankel, T. 'Fiduciary Law', *California Law Review*, vol.71, 1983.

Franzway, S. et al., *Staking a Claim: Feminism, Bureaucracy and the State*, Cambridge, Polity, 1989.

Fraser, N. 'Rethinking the Public Sphere: A Contribution to the Critique of Actually Existing Democracy', *Social Text*, vol.25/26, 1990.

Freeman, E. 'The Morality of Field Sports', *The Fortnightly Review*, vol.14, 1869.

Gadea, F. S. and S. M. Lage, 'Spanish Accession to the European Communities: Legal and Constitutional Implications', *Common Market Law Review*, vol.23, 1986.

Gamberale, C. 'European Citizenship and Political Identity', *Space and Polity*, vol.1, 1997.

Geisler, C. 'Ownership: An Overview', *Rural Sociology*, vol.58, 1993.

Gilroy, P. *There Ain't No Black in the Union Jack*, London, Routledge, 1991.

Goodson, I. '"Nations at Risk" and "National Curriculum": Ideology and Identity', *Cultural Diversity and the School*, vol.1, 1992.

Gordon, C. 'Governmental Rationality: An Introduction', in G. Burchell et al. (eds), *The Foucault Effect: Studies in Governmentality*, Chicago, University of Chicago Press, 1991.

Gottdiener, M. *The Social Production of Urban Space*, Austin, Teaxs, University of Texas Press, 1985.

Goudie, J. 'Local Authorities and Fiduciary Duty', in M. Supperstone and J. Goudie (eds), *Judicial Review*, London, Butterworths, 1992.

Graves, C. 'Social Space in the English Medieval Parish Church', *Economy and Society*, vol.18, 1989.

Gray, K. 'Equitable Property', *Current Legal Problems*, vol.47, 1994.

Greenhouse, C. et al. *Law and Community in Three American Towns*, Ithaca, Cornell University Press, 1994.

Grubb, A. 'The Doctor as Fiduciary', *Current Legal Problems*, vol.47, 1994.

Gyford, J. *The Politics of Local Socialism*, London, George Allen and Unwin, 1985.

Habermas, J. *The Structural Transformation of the Public Sphere: An Inquiry into a Category of Bourgeois Society*, Cambridge, Mass, MIT Press, 1989.

Habermas, J. 'Citizenship and National Identity: Some Reflections on the Future of Europe', *Praxis International*, vol.12, 1992.

Habermas, J. 'European Citizenship and National Identities', in B. Van Steenbergen (ed.), *The Conditions of Citizenship*, London, Sage, 1994.

Hadjimichalis, C. and D. Sadler (eds), *Europe at the Margins: New Mosaics of Inequality*, London, Wiley, 1993.

Hagendoorn, L. 'Ethnic Categorization and Outgroup Exclusion: Cultural Values and Social Stereotypes in the Construction of Ethnic Hierarchies', *Ethnic and Racial Studies*, vol.16, 1993.

Haldane, J. 'Religious Education in a Pluralist Society', *British Journal of Educational Studies*, vol. 34, 1986.

Halfacree, K. 'Out of Place in the Country: Travellers and the "Rural Idyll"', *Antipode*, vol.28, 1996.

Hall, S. *The Hard Road to Renewal*, London, Verso, 1988.

Hamilton, C. *Family, Law and Religion*, London, Sweet and Maxwell, 1995.

Hannerz, V. *Soulside. Inquiries into Ghetto Culture and Community*, New York, Columbia University Press, 1969.

Harding, S. 'Representing Fundamentalism: The Problem of the Repugnant Cultural Other', *Social Research*, vol.58, 1991.

Harris, S. *Lesbian and Gay Issues in the English Classroom*, Buckingham, Open University Press, 1990.

Harris, J. 'Private and Non-private Property: What is the Difference?', *Law Quarterly Review*, vol.111, 1995.

Harrison, C. *Countryside Recreation in a Changing Society*, Bristol, TMS Partnership, 1991.

Hart, C. 'Legislation and Religious Education', *Education and the Law*, vol.5, 1993.

Harvey, D. *The Condition of Postmodernity*, Oxford, Blackwell, 1989.

Hatcher, R. 'Market Relationships and the Management of Teachers', *British Journal of Sociology of Education*, vol.15, 1994.

Hay, C. *Re-Stating Social and Political Change*, Buckingham, Open University Press, 1996.

Haywood, C. and M. Mac An Ghaill, 'The Sexual Politics of the Curriculum: Contesting Values', *International Studies in Sociology of Education*, vol.5, 1995.

Held, *Political Theory and the Modern State*, Cambridge, Polity, 1989.

Herman, D. *Rights of Passage: Struggles for Lesbian and Gay Legal Equality*, Toronto, University of Toronto Press, 1994.

Herman, D. *The Antigay Agenda: Orthodox Vision and the Christian Right*, Chicago, University of Chicago Press, 1997.

Herman, D. and D. Cooper, 'Anarchic Armadas, Brussels Bureaucrats, and the Valiant Maple Leaf: Constructing British Nationhood through the Canada-Spain Fish War', *Legal Studies*, vol.17, 1997.

Hervieu-Leger, D. 'Religion and Modernity in the French Context: for a New Approach to Secularization', *Sociological Analysis*, vol.51, 1990.

Hetherington, K. *The Badlands of Modernity: Heterotopia and Social Ordering*, London, Routledge, 1997.

Hobbs, H. *City Hall goes Abroad: The Foreign Policy of Local Politics*, Thousand Oaks, Ca, Sage, 1994.

Holm, J. with J. Bowker, *Sacred Place*, London, Pinter Publishers, 1994.

Hont, I. 'The Permanent Crisis of a Divided Mankind: "Contemporary Crisis of the Nation State" in Historical Perspective', *Political Studies*, vol.42, 1994.

Howard, J. 'The Library, The Park, and the Pervert: Public Space and Homosexual Encounter in Post-world War II Atlanta', *Radical History Review*, vol.62, 1995.

Howard, E. *Garden Cities of Tomorrow*, London, Faber and Faber, 1945.

Hull, J. *Mishmash: Religious Education in Multi-cultural Britain—A Study in Metaphor*, Birmingham, University of Birmingham and the Christian Education Movement, 1991.

Hull, J. 'The New Government Guidelines on Religious Education', *British Journal of Religious Education*, vol.16, 1994.

Humphrey, M. 'Community, Mosque and Ethnic Politics', *Australian and New Zealand Journal of Sociology*, vol.23, 1987.

Hunt, A. and G. Wickham, *Foucault and Law: Towards a Sociology of Law as Governance*, London, Pluto Press, 1994.

Hunter, A. 'The Symbolic Ecology of Suburbia', in I. Altman and A. Wandersman (eds), *Neighbourhood and Community Environments*, London, Plenum Press, 1987.

Hunter, I. 'Assembling the School', in A. Barry et al. (eds), *Foucault and Political Reason*, London, UCL Press, 1996.

Huntingdon, K.P. *Wildlife Management and Subsistence Hunting in Alaska*, London, Belhaven, 1992.

Hurley, J. 'The Crown's Fiduciary Duty and Indian Title: *Guerin v. The Queen*', *McGill Law Journal*, vol.30, 1985.

Itzkowitz, D. *Peculiar Privilege: A Social History of English Foxhunting, 1753–1885*, Hassocks, Sussex, Harvester Press, 1977.

Jackson, P. *Maps of Meaning*, London, Routledge, 1992.

Jackson, R. 'Religious Education's Representation of "Religions" and "Cultures"', *British Journal of Educational Studies*, vol. 43, 1995.

Jackson, R. *Religious Education. An Interpretive Approach*, London, Hodder and Stoughton, 1997.

Jenson, J. 'What's in a Name? Nationalist Movements and Public Discourse', in H. Johnstone and B. Klandermans (ed.), *Social Movements and Culture*, London, UCL Press, 1993.

Jessop, B. *State Theory*, Cambridge, Polity, 1990.

Johnson, G.R. 'In the Name of the Fatherland: An Analysis of Kin Term Usage in Patriotic Speech and Literature', *International Political Science Review*, vol.8, 1987.

Johnston, L. and G. Valentine, 'Wherever I Lay My Girlfriend, That's My Home: The Performance and Surveillance of Lesbian Identities in Domestic Environments', in D. Bell and G. Valentine (eds), *Mapping Desire*, London, Routledge, 1995.

Jowell, J. and A. Lester, 'Beyond Wednesbury: Substantive Principles of Administrative Law', *Public Law*, 1987.

Judd, D. 'The Rise of the New Walled Cities', in H. Liggett and D. Perry (eds),

Spatial Practices, London, Sage, 1995.

Kaplan, W. *Belonging: The Meaning and Future of Canadian Citizenship*, Montreal and Kingston, McGill–Queen's University Press, 1993.

Karagiannakos, A. *Fisheries Management in the European Union*, Aldershot, Avebury, 1995.

Kaufmann, T. and P. Lincoln (eds), *High Risk Lives: Lesbian and Gay Politics After the Clause*, Bridport, Prism, 1991.

Kean, H. 'Managing Education—The Local Authority Dimension', *Journal of Education Policy*, vol.6, 1991.

Keane, J. *Democracy and Civil Society*, London, Verso, 1988.

Kickert, W. 'Complexity, Governance and Dynamics: Conceptual Explorations of Public Network Management', in J. Kooiman (ed.), *Modern Governance*, London, Sage, 1993.

Kooiman, J. (ed.), *Modern Governance*, London, Sage, 1993.

Kuehls, T. 'The Nature of the State: An Ecological (Re)reading of Sovereignty and Territory', in M. Ringrose and A. J. Lerner (eds), *Reimagining the Nation*, Milton Keynes, Open University Press, 1993.

Kunin, S. 'Judaism', in J. Holm with J. Bowker (eds), *Sacred Place*, London, Pinter Publishers, 1994.

Kutchins, H. 'The Fiduciary Relationship: The Legal Basis for Social Workers', *Social Work*, vol.36, 1991.

Lacey, N. 'Theory into Practice? Pornography and the Public/ Private Divide', *Journal of Law and Society*, vol.20, 1993.

Lansley, S. et al., *Councils in Conflict: The Rise and Fall of the Municipal Left*, Basingstoke, Macmillan, 1989.

Lash, S. and J. Urry, *Economies of Signs and Space*, London, Sage, 1994.

Lawrence, D. 'Local Government Officials as Fiduciaries: The Appropriate Standard', *University of Detroit Mercy Law Review*, vol.71, 1993.

Leach, S. 'The Dimensions of Analysis: Governance, Markets and Community', in S. Leach et al. (eds), *Enabling or Disabling Local Government*, Buckingham, Open University, 1996.

Lees, S. 'Talking about Sex in Education', *Gender and Education*, vol.6, 1994.

Lefebvre, H. 'Reflections on the Politics of Space', *Antipode*, vol.8, 1976.

Leonetti, I. T. 'From Multicultural to Intercultural: Is it Necessary to Move from One to the Other', *Cultural Diversity and the School*, vol.1, 1992.

Leventhal, L. 'American Indians—The Trust Responsibility: An Overview', *Hamline Law Review*, vol. 8, 1985.

Lindsay, A. 'Blood Sports and Public Law', *New Law Journal*, vol.145, 1995.

Locke, J. *Two Treatises of Government* (ed. P. Laslett), Cambridge, Cambridge University Press, 1988.

Loughlin, M. 'Law, Ideologies, and the Political-administrative System', *Journal of Law and Society*, vol.16, 1989.

Loughlin, M. 'Innovative Financing in Local Government: The Limits of Legal Instrumentalism—Part II', *Public Law*, 1991.

Loughlin, M. *Legality and Locality: The Role of Law in Central-Local Government Relations*, Oxford, Clarendon, 1996.

Low, S. 'Spatializing Culture: The Social Production and Social Construction of Public Space in Costa Rica', *American Ethnologist*, vol.23, 1996.

Lowe, P. et al., 'Regulating the New Rural Spaces: The Uneven Development of Land', *Journal of Rural Studies*, vol.9, 1993.

Lowndes, V. 'Change in Public Service Management: New Institutions and New Management Regimes', *Local Government Studies*, vol.23, 1997.

Mac An Ghaill, M. 'Schooling, Sexuality and Male Power: Towards an Emancipatory Curriculum', *Gender and Education*, vol.3, 1991.

MacFadyen, D. *Sir Ebenezer Howard and the Town Planning Movement*, Manchester, Manchester University Press, 1933.

Magnusson, W. *The Search for Political Space*, Toronto, University of Toronto Press, 1996.

Mandel, M. *The Charter of Rights and the Legalization of Politics in Canada*, Toronto, Wall and Thompson, 1989.

Manning, R. *Hunters and Poachers: A Social and Cultural History of Unlawful Hunting in England 1485–1640*, Oxford, Clarendon, 1993.

Marks, G. et al., 'European Integration from the 1980s: State-Centric v. Multi-Level Governance', *Journal of Common Market Studies*, vol.34, 1996.

Marsden, T. et al., *Constructing the Countryside*, London, UCL Press, 1993.

Massey, D. 'A Place called Home?', *New Formations*, vol.17, 1992.

Massey, D. *Space, Place and Gender*, Cambridge, Polity, 1994.

Masson, J. 'Implementing Change for Children: Action at the Centre and Local Reaction', *Journal of Law and Society*, vol.19, 1992.

May, J. 'Globalization and the Politics of Place: Place and Identity in an Inner London Neighbourhood', *Transactions of the Institute of British Geographers*, vol.21, 1996.

Mayntz, R. 'Governing Failures and the Problem of Governability: Some Comments on a Theoretical Paradigm', in J. Kooiman (ed.), *Modern Governance*, London, Sage, 1993.

McCarthy, M. 'People of Faith as Political Activists in Public Schools', *Education and Urban Society*, vol.28, 1996.

McClintock, A. '"No Longer in a Future Heaven": Nationalism, Gender, and Race', in G. Eley and R. Suny (eds), *Becoming National*, New York, Oxford University Press, 1996.

McLeod, I. 'The Local Ombudsman and the Fiduciary Duty of the Local Authority', *Local Government Review*, vol.156, 1992.

Meadmore, D. 'The Production of Individuality through Examination', *British Journal of Sociology of Education*, vol.14, 1993.

Meadmore, D. 'Linking Goals of Governmentality with Policies of Assessment', *Assessment in Education*, vol.2, 1995.

Mellor, P. and C. Shilling, 'Reflexive Modernity and the Religious Body', *Religion*, vol.24, 1994.

Merry, S.E. 'Defensible Space Undefended: Social Factors in Crime Control through Environmental Design', *Urban Affairs Quarterly*, Vol.16, 1981.

Merry, S.E. 'Legal Pluralism', *Law and Society Review*, vol.22, 1988.

Metcalfe, L. 'Public Management: From Imitation to Innovation', in J. Kooiman (ed.), *Modern Governance*, London, Sage, 1993.

Metzger, J. 'The Eruv: Can Government Constitutionally Permit Jews to Build a Fictional Wall without Breaking the Wall between Church and State', *National Jewish Law Review*, vol.4, 1989.

Miliband, R. *Marxism and Politics*, Oxford, Oxford University Press, 1977.

Miliband, R. *Capitalist Democracy in Britain*, Oxford, Oxford University Press, 1982.

Millard, E. and C. Hall, 'Discourses of Education: The Genealogy of a Profession's Discipline', *Renaissance and Modern Studies*, vol.37, 1994.

Miller, M. and A. Gray, *Hampstead Garden Suburb*, Chichester, Phillimore, 1992.

Mitchell, T. 'The Limits of the State: Beyond Statist Approaches and their Critics', *American Political Science Review*, vol.85, 1991.

Moffat, G. *Trusts Law* (second edition), London, Butterworth, 1994.

Morley, D. and K. Robins, 'No Place like Heimat: Images of Home(land) in European Culture', *New Formations*, vol.12, 1990.

Mosse, G. *Nationalism and Sexuality*, New York, Howard Fertig, 1985.

Mosse, G. *Confronting the Nation: Jewish and Western Nationalism*, Hanover, Brandeis University Press, 1993.

Munch, R. 'Between Nation-State, Regionalism and World Society: The European Integration Process', *Journal of Common Market Studies,* vol.34, 1996.

Murphy, A. ' The Sovereign State System as Political-Territorial Ideal: Historical and Contemporary Considerations', in T. Biersteker and C. Weber (eds), *State Sovereignty as Social Construct*, Melbourne, Cambridge University Press, 1996.

Nardell, G. 'The Quantock Hounds and the Trojan Horse', *Public Law*, 1995.

Naylor, F. *The School Above the Pub*, London, The Claridge Press, 1989.

Newman, D. *Defensible Space: People and Design in the Violent City*, London, Architectural Press, 1972.

Newton, N. 'Enforcing the Federal-Indian Trust Relationship after *Mitchell*', *Catholic University Law Review*, vol.31, 1982.

Nørgaard, A.S. 'Institutions and Post-modernity in IR. The "New" EC', *Cooperation and Conflict*, vol.24, 1994.

Norman, E.R. 'The Threat to Religion', in C. Cox and R. Boyson (eds), *Black Paper 1977*, London, Maurice Temple Smith, 1977.

O'Donovan, K. *Sexual Divisions in Law*, London, Weidenfeld and Nicolson, 1985.

O'Keeffe, D. 'The Emergence of a European Immigration Policy', *European Law Review*, vol.20, 1995.

Ogus, A. 'The Trust as Governance Structure', *University of Toronto Law Journal*, vol.36, 1986.

Oliver, D. 'State Property and Individual Rights', *Coexistence*, vol.25, 1988.

Osborne, T. 'Security and Vitality: Drains, Liberalism and Power in the Nineteenth Century', in A. Barry et al. (eds), *Foucault and Political Reason* London, UCL Press, 1996.

Owers, A. 'The Age of Internal Controls?' in S. Spencer (ed.), *Strangers and Citizens*, London, Rivers Oram, 1994.

Paliwala, A. 'Law and the Constitution of the "Immigrant" in Europe: A UK Policy Perspective', in P. Fitzpatrick (ed.), *Nationalism, Racism and the Rule of Law*, Aldershot, Dartmouth, 1995.

Parker, A. *Nationalisms and Sexualities*, London, Routledge, 1992.

Parkinson, M. *Liverpool on the Brink*, Hermitage, Policy Journals, 1985.

Parr, H. 'Mental Health, Public Space, and the City: Questions of Individual and Collective Access', *Environment and Planning D: Society and Space*, vol.15, 1997.

Pateman, C. *The Sexual Contract*, Cambridge, Polity, 1988.

Pateman, C. *The Disorder of Women*, Cambridge, Polity, 1989.

Peake, L. '"Race" and Sexuality: Challenging the Patriarchal Structuring of Urban Social Space', *Environment and Planning D: Society and Space*, vol.11, 1993.

Peiris, G. 'Wednesbury Unreasonableness: The Expanding Canvass', *Cambridge Law Journal*, vol.46, 1987.

Pfeffer, L. and A. Pfeffer, 'The Agunah in American Secular Law', *Journal of Church and State*, vol.31, 1989.

Popkewitz, T. 'Rethinking Decentralization and State/ Civil Society Distinctions: The State as a Problematic of Governing', *Journal of Education Policy*, vol.11, 1996.

Post, R. *Constitutional Domains*, Cambridge, Harvard University Press, 1995.

Poulantzas, N. *State, Power, Socialism*, London, New Left Books, 1978.

Poulter, S. 'The Religious Education Provisions of the Eduction Reform Act 1988', *Education and the Law*, vol.2, 1990.

Pratt, A. 'Aboriginal Self-Government and the Crown's Fiduciary Duty: Squaring the Circle or Completing the Circle', *National Journal of Constitutional Law*, vol.2, 1992.

Prentice, D. 'Directors, Creditors, and Shareholders', in E. McKendrick (ed.), *Commercial Aspects of Trusts and Fiduciary Obligations*, Oxford, Clarendon, 1992.

Preuß, U. 'Two Challenges to European Citizenship', *Political Studies*, vol.44, 1996.

Pringle R. and S. Watson, 'Women's Interests and the Post-structuralist State', in M. Barrett and A. Phillips (eds), *Destabilising Theory: Contemporary Feminist Debates*, Cambridge, Polity, 1992.

Probyn, E. *Outside Belongings*, New York, Routledge, 1996.

Radford, J. 'Twin Leakings and Hackney Outings: The Kingsmead School

Affair', *Trouble and Strife*, vol.32, 1995/6.

Radin, M. *Reinterpreting Property*, Chicago, Chicago University Press, 1993.

Rayside, D. 'Homophobia, Class and Party in England', *Canadian Journal of Political Science*, vol.25, 1992.

Reif, K. 'Cultural Convergence and Cultural Diversity as Factors in European Identity', in S. Garcia (ed.), *European Identity and the Search for Legitimacy*, London, Pinter, 1993.

Renan, E. 'What is a Nation?', in H.K. Bhabha (ed.), *Nation and Narration*, London, Routledge, 1990.

Rhodes, R. 'The New Governance: Governing Without Government', *Political Studies*, vol.44, 1996.

Rhodes, R. *Understanding Governance: Policy Networks, Governance, Reflexivity and Accountability*, Buckingham, Open University Press, 1997.

Riches, D. 'Animal Rightists and Northern Native Hunters', *Anthropos*, vol.90, 1995.

Roberts R. and J. Emel, 'Uneven Development and the Tragedy of the Commons: Competing Images for Nature-Society Analysis', *Economic Geography*, vol.68, 1992.

Robertson, D. 'Program Implementation versus Program Design: Which Accounts for Policy "Failure"?', *Policy Studies Review*, vol.3, 1984.

Robson, G. 'Religious Education, Government Policy and Professional Practice, 1985-1995', *British Journal of Religious Education*, vol.19, 1996.

Rose, N. 'The Death of the Social? Re-figuring the Territory of Government', *Economy and Society*, vol. 25, 1996.

Rose, N. 'Governing "Advanced" Liberal Democracies', in A. Barry et al. (eds), *Foucault and Political Reason*, London, UCL, 1996.

Rose, N. and P. Miller, 'Political Power Beyond the State: Problematics of Government', *British Journal of Sociology*, vol.43, 1992.

Rothenberg, T. '"And She Told Two Friends": Lesbians Creating Urban Social Space', in D. Bell and G. Valentine (eds), *Mapping Desire*, London, Routledge, 1995.

Rotman, L. *Parallel Paths: Fiduciary Doctrine and the Crown-Native Relationship in Canada*, Toronto, University of Toronto Press, 1996.

Ryan, J. 'Observing and Normalizing: Foucault, Discipline, and Inequality in Schooling', *The Journal of Educational Thought*, vol.25, 1991.

Sachs, J. *Crisis and Covenant: Jewish Thought after the Holocaust*, Manchester, Manchester University Press, 1992.

Salamon, S. and J. Tornatore, 'Territory Contested Through Property in a Midwestern Post-agricultural Community', *Rural Sociology*, vol.59, 1994.

Salt, H. *Animals' Rights*, London, Centaur Press, 1980.

Sanderson, I. *Current Issues in Local Government Finance*, London, Commission for Local Democracy, 1995.

Schlager, E. and E. Ostrom, 'Property-Rights Regimes and Natural Resources: A Conceptual Analysis', *Land Economics*, vol.68, 1992.

Seidel, G. and R. Gunther, '"Nation" and "Family" in the British Media Reporting of the "Falklands conflict"', in G. Seidel (ed.), *The Nature of the Right*, Amsterdam, John Benjamins, 1988.

Shapiro, M. and D. Neubauer, 'Spatiality and Policy Discourse: Reading the Global City', *Alternatives*, vol.14, 1989.

Sharot, S. 'Judaism and the Secularization Debate', *Sociological Analysis*, vol.52, 1991.

Shearn, D. et al., 'The Changing Face of School Governor Responsibilities: A Mismatch Between Government Intention and Actuality?', *School Organisation*, vol.15, 1995.

Shepherd, J. 'Towards a Unified Concept of Fiduciary Relationships', *Law Quarterly Review*, vol.97, 1981.

Shields, R. *Places on the Margin. Alternative Geographies of Modernity*, London, Routledge, 1991.

Shilhav, Y. 'Spatial Strategies of the "Haredi" Population in Jerusalem', *Socio-Economic Planning Sciences*, vol.18, 1984.

Shilhav, Y. 'The Haredi Ghetto: The Theology Behind the Ghetto', *Contemporary Jewry*, vol.10, 1989.

Shoard, M. *This Land is Our Land*, London, Paladin, 1987.

Simons, J. *Foucault and the Political*, London, Routledge, 1995.

Skinner, D and J. Langdon, *The Story of Clay Cross*, Nottingham, Spokesman Books, 1974.

Smith, A.M. 'The Imaginary Inclusion of the Assimilable "Good Homosexual": The British New Right's Representation of Sexuality and Race', *Diacritics*, vol.24, 1994.

Soja, E. *Postmodern Geographies: The Reassertion of Space in Critical Social Theory*, London, Verso, 1989.

Solomon, N. 'Judaism and Modernity: The Whole Agenda', *The Jewish Journal of Sociology*, vol.36, 1994.

Sorenson, G. 'Religion and American Public Education', *Education and Urban Society*, vol.28, 1996.

Sorg, J. 'A Typology of Implementation Behaviors of Street-Level Bureaucrats', *Policy Studies Review*, vol.2, 1983.

Squirrell, G. 'Teachers and Issues of Sexual Orientation', *Gender and Education*, vol.1, 1989.

Staeheli, L. 'Publicity, Privacy, and Women's Political Action', *Environment and Planning D: Society and Space*, vol. 14, 1996.

Steinberg, B. 'Anglo-Jewry and the 1944 Education Act', *Jewish Journal of Sociology*, vol.30, 1988.

Stoler, A. 'Sexual Affronts and Racial Frontiers: National Identity, "Mixed Bloods" and the Cultural Genealogies of Europeans in Colonial Southeast Asia', *Comparative Studies in Society and History*, vol.34, 1992.

Stone, S. 'In Pursuit of the Counter-text: The Turn to the Jewish Legal Model in Contemporary American Legal Theory', *Harvard Law Review*, vol.106, 1993.

Stychin, C. 'A Postmodern Constitutionalism: Equality Rights, Identity Politics, and the Canadian National Imagination', *Dalhousie Law Journal*, vol.17, 1994.

Stychin, C. 'To Take Him "At his Word": Theorizing Law, Sexuality, and the US Military Exclusion Policy', *Social and Legal Studies*, vol.5, 1996.

Stychin, C. 'Queer Nations: Nationalism, Sexuality and the Discourse of Rights in Quebec', *Feminist Legal Studies*, vol.5, 1997.

Stychin, C. *A Nation by Rights: National Cultures, Sexual Identity Politics, and the Discourse of Rights*, Philadelphia, Temple University Press, 1998.

Tamney, J. 'Conservative Government and Support for the Religious Institution: Religious Education in English Schools', *The British Journal of Sociology*, vol.45, 1994.

Tannenbaum, J. 'Animals and the Law: Property, Cruelty, Rights', *Social Research*, vol.62, 1995.

Teubner, G. 'After Legal Instrumentalism?', in G. Teubner (ed.), *Dilemmas of Law in the Welfare State*, Berlin, de Gruyter, 1986.

Teubner, G. (ed.), *Dilemmas of Law in the Welfare State*, Berlin, de Gruyter, 1996.

Teubner, G. (ed.), *Juridification of Social Spheres*, Berlin, de Gruyter, 1987.

Teubner, G. (ed.), *Autopoietic Law: A New Approach to Law and Society*, Berlin, de Gruyter, 1988.

The Hillgate Group, *The Reform of British Education*, London, The Claridge Press, 1987.

Thomas, R. *The Politics of Hunting*, Aldershot, Gower, 1983.

Thomas, R. 'Hunting as a Political Issue', *Parliamentary Affairs*, vol.39, 1986.

Thompson, E.P. *Whigs and Hunters: The Origin of the Black Act*, London, Allen Lane, 1975.

Thompson, E.P. *Customs in Common*, London, Penguin, 1993.

Thornton, M. (ed.), *Public and Private: Feminist Legal Debates*, Melbourne, Oxford University Press, 1995.

Valentine, G. 'Out and About: Geographies of Lesbian Landscapes', *International Journal of Urban and Regional Research*, vol.19, 1992.

Valentine, G. 'Desperately Seeking Susan: A Geography of Lesbian Friendships', *Area*, vol. 25, 1993.

Valverde, M. '"Despotism" and Ethical Liberal Governance', *Economy and Society*, vol.25, 1996.

Van Praagh, S. 'The Chutzpah of Chasidism', *Canadian Journal of Law and Society*, vol.11, 1996.

Vincent, C. 'Tolerating Intolerance? Parental Choice and Race Relations—The Cleveland Case', *Journal of Education Policy*, vol.7, 1992.

Wade, W. *Administrative Law* (sixth edition), Oxford, Clarendon Press, 1988.

Wallace, M. 'Discourse of Derision: The Role of the Mass Media within the Education Policy Process', *Journal of Education Policy*, vol.8, 1993.

Walsh, K. *Public Services and Market Mechanisms: Competition, Contracting and the New Public Management*, Basingstoke, Macmillan, 1995.

Walsh, K. 'The Role of the Market and the Growth of Competition', in S. Leach et al. (eds), *Enabling or Disabling Local Government*, Buckingham, Open University Press, 1996.

Walzer, M. 'Liberalism and the Art of Separation', *Political Theory*, vol.12, 1984.

Ward, S. 'Thinking Global, Acting Local? British Local Authorities and their Environmental Plans', *Environmental Politics*, vol.2, 1993.

Waterman, S. *Jews in an Outer London Borough, Barnet*, London, Queen Mary and Westfield College, 1989.

Watson, S. and K. Gibson (eds), *Postmodern Cities and Spaces*, Oxford, Blackwell, 1995.

Weale, A. 'Nature versus the State? Markets, States, and Environmental Protection', *Critical Review*, vol.6, 1993.

Weber, C. 'Reconsidering Statehood: Examining the Sovereignty/ Intervention Boundary', *Review of International Studies*, vol.18, 1992.

Weber, M. *From Max Weber*, H. Gerth and C. Wright Mills (eds), Oxford, Oxford University Press, 1946.

Weeks, J. 'Rediscovering Values', in J. Squires (ed.), *Principled Positions*, London, Lawrence and Wishart, 1993.

Weeks, J. *Invented Moralities: Sexual Values in an Age of Uncertainty*, Cambridge, Polity, 1995.

Weiler, H. 'Education and Power: The Politics of Educational Decentralization in Comparative Perspective', *Educational Policy*, vol.3, 1989.

Whittle, S. (ed.), *The Margins of the City: Gay Men's Urban Lives*, Aldershot, Arena, 1994.

Wilson, K. and J. Van der Dussen (eds), *The History of the Idea of Europe*, Milton Keynes, Open University, 1995.

Windeatt, P. '"They Clearly now See the Link": Militant Voices', in P. Singer (ed.), *In Defence of Animals*, London, Blackwell, 1985.

Wirth, L. *The Ghetto*, Chicago, University of Chicago Press, 1992.

Wollaston, I. 'Sharing Sacred Space? The Carmelite Controversy and the Politics of Commemoration', *Patterns of Prejudice*, vol.28, 1994.

Young, I.M. 'The Ideal of Community and the Politics of Difference', in L. Nicholson (ed.), *Feminism/Postmodernism*, London, Routledge, 1990.

Young, S. 'Indian Tribal Responsibility and American Fiduciary Undertakings', *Whittier Law Review*, vol.8, 1987.

Yuval-Davis, N. 'Gender and Nation', *Ethnic and Racial Studies*, vol.16, 1993.

Yuval-Davis, N. *Gender and Nation*, London, Sage, 1997.

Zarrow, J. 'Of Crosses and Creches: The Establishment Clause and Publicly Sponsored Displays of Religious Symbols', *The American University Law Review*, vol.35, 1985.

Index